DEVOTIONS

Peace I leave
with you; my
peace I give
you.

—John 14:27

JANUARY

Photo © Eyewire

Gary Allen, Editor

O9-BHI-460

WYSIWYG

This was John's testimony when the Jews of Jerusalem sent priests and Levites to ask him who he was. He . . . confessed freely, "I am not the Christ" (John 1:19, 20).

Scripture: John 1:19-28
Song: "Just As I Am"

The youngest of four children, I struggled with my identity and desperately wanted to be like my older sister. I would dress up in her clothing, right down to her high heels, and pretend to be her. But I'd usually get caught in the act and hear the inevitable question, "Just who do you think you *are*, young lady?"

I wonder how I'd answer that question today. Can I be as forthright as John when questioned by the priests and Levites about who he was?

I suppose we're all guilty of some sort of role-playing occasionally. Whatever may compel us at times to put on appearances, perhaps it's best to follow the computer-age WYSIWYG principle: What you see is what you get. John was sure of his purpose and his position with regard to the Christ. The priests were looking at a humble, courageous preacher of Christ's coming. There was no hiding it.

Dear Heavenly Father, You love me just as I am—while calling me to grow in holiness day by day. Thank You so much for not basing salvation on my potential but on my need! In the name of the Father, the Son, and the Holy Spirit, I pray. Amen.

January 1–7. **Michelle Starkey,** brain aneurysm survivor, thanks God for a second chance at life. She lives life to the fullest with her husband, Keith, in New York.

Final Rinse Cycle

The next day John saw Jesus coming toward him and said, "Look, the Lamb of God, who takes away the sin of the world!" (John 1:29).

Scripture: **John 1:29-34**
Song: **"Behold, the Lamb of God"**

A late-night infomercial blared from the TV set. I'd fallen asleep on the couch and woke up just in time to catch the announcer's concluding sales pitch: "Just add a capful to your final rinse cycle, and it will miraculously wash the garment clean. Whatever you've spilled on it, dripped on it, or dragged it through . . . will be wiped clean."

This is exactly what the Lamb of God has done for our hearts. The sin stains within us are miraculously washed away (see Titus 3:5, 6). The Son of God was sent to earth to rinse away our sins through the washing of rebirth and baptism. I like the way King David put it in Psalm 51:1—"Have mercy on me, O God, according to your unfailing love; according to your great compassion blot out my transgressions. Wash away all my iniquity and cleanse me from my sin."

Here we have the greatest truth about the gospel and also the most formidable obstacle for its critics: that we are saved by pure grace alone. This wonderful washing is a gracious gift.

*Thank You, **Father,** that Your Son, who led a blameless life, took the burden of the world upon His shoulders and bore the entire load of my sins. Praise to Him for washing me clean! Through Christ I pray. Amen.*

Softening a Hardened Heart

This people's heart has become calloused; they hardly hear with their ears, and they have closed their eyes (Matthew 13:15).

Scripture: **Matthew 13:10-17**
Song: **"Hearken to the Solemn Voice"**

The Holy Spirit works in us to soften the calluses on our hardened hearts. No doubt it was He who opened my heart to the distressed woman I encountered downtown last week.

The shoppers rushed past her as she stopped by the curb. She had paused to fasten the only button on the tattered coat hanging loosely on her thin frame. No one paid attention to the old woman. Even I watched her from a safe distance as she nervously glanced at the busyness surrounding her. It was a bitter cold morning, and her only gloved hand held tight to her shopping cart full of worldly possessions. We don't seem to notice such folks until they "get in our way." But this time I smiled and offered her some help.

Matthew tells us that our hearts can be closed not only to people but to God's message of salvation as well. It was true in his day, and we must beware of it in our own lives. Can you tell when your heart is soft to God's Word? Or are certain calluses, even now, making the message seem less than crucial to your spiritual life?

*Open my heart to Your Word, **Lord**, and keep me ever willing to practice what I learn. In Jesus' name I pray. Amen.*

It Is Well

Peace I leave with you; my peace I give you. I do not give to you as the world gives. Do not let your hearts be troubled and do not be afraid (John 14:27).

Scripture: **John 14:23-31**
Song: **"Peace, Troubled Soul"**

My husband seems to exude the essence of peace, even under the most stressful situations. He is the most peaceful person I know, especially when it comes to raising our teenage daughters.

Have you noticed that teenagers can easily stretch the limits of parental endurance? On one occasion this involved our eldest daughter slamming a door after she left the dinner table abruptly. My husband calmly approached her closed bedroom door, opened it, and offered this observation in his most peaceful tones, "This should come off these hinges easily." I heard her gasp, even though I was a room away. "No, Daddy, please don't take my door away!"

He calmly replied, "If you slam it, you lose it." No one (even me) ever slammed a door in this home again.

It is well with my husband's soul. I know he has the peace only Jesus can offer us in this world of slamming doors. When I asked him, "How did you manage to maintain your composure?" he replied, "I prayed for calm, strength, and peace. I wouldn't let my heart be troubled."

Lord, *I accept Your gift of peace. Help me package up my fears and anxieties today and lean on You. In Christ's name, amen.*

Show Your ID, Please!

Are you the one who was to come, or should we expect someone else? (Matthew 11:3).

Scripture: **Matthew 11:2-6**
Song: **"Messiah, Prince of Peace"**

Anticipation. We all experience it. We happily anticipate the holidays. We anxiously await the birth of a child. We nervously predict the verdict in a courtroom. Our anticipation applies to both good and bad events.

John the Baptist spent his life anticipating the arrival of the Son of God, for this would surely be a time for happy celebration. Yet John harbored some doubts about the identity of Jesus. He needed some assurance that Jesus was truly the prophesied Messiah.

So, locked in his prison cell, awaiting an uncertain fate, John sent his disciples to question this Jesus. Did He have a heavenly ID? We can imagine John's anxious moments.

The reply Jesus delivered was more of a status report than an actual identity check: just observe the miracles abounding in my ministry!

Who else could this young man be? Or, as Jesus later put it: "Even though you do not believe me, believe the miracles, that you may know and understand that the Father is in me, and I in the Father" (John 10:38). The person and his works go hand in hand as perfect IDs.

Lord, amid my anxious moments of doubt and uncertainty, fill me with Your blessed assurance. In all that You have revealed of Your Son, it's clear He is worthy of all my worship. In His holy name I pray. Amen.

Pathway to Freedom

You will know the truth, and the truth will set you free (John 8:32).

Scripture: **John 8:31-38**
Song: **"Victory All the Time"**

A bumper sticker proclaims, "Freedom isn't free." In other words, someone is always paying the cost of freedom whether it's warriors who battle for democracy or missionaries who fight against injustice. Jesus taught us "the truth will set you free," and He himself *is* the truth (John 14:6). Thankfully, He has paid the price for our freedom from sin.

As a little girl, I heard my own father often saying, "If you just tell me the truth. . . ." I learned early on that it was better to tell the truth than to try lying my way out of things. And we've passed along this principle to our own children. Admitting wrongdoing is the right way; if we choose to lie, we become a slave to our sin.

When the children of Abraham asked Jesus how He could tell them that they'd be set free, He replied that "if the Son sets you free, you will be free indeed" (John 8:36). In other words, we have found a pathway to freedom by following Jesus.

Almighty Father, I am "free at last"—but not without cost. Thank You for sending Jesus to pay the price for redemption that I could never pay on my own. Please let Your mercy and grace fill me with Your joy today. And keep Your truth ever in my heart and upon my lips. In the holy name of Jesus, my Lord and Savior, I pray. Amen.

Eternal Existence

"I tell you the truth," Jesus answered, "before Abraham was born, I am!" (John 8:58).

Scripture: **John 8:48-59**
Song: **"Eternal Son, Eternal Love"**

One evening I went outside and marveled at the infinite number of stars in the sky. Millions upon millions of tiny lights sparkled above my head. Yet infinity is a difficult concept for the human mind to grasp. Even mathematicians struggle to conceive it and represent it. And, of course, the actual number of stars is finite.

Jesus spent much time justifying His eternal nature to others—an existence that extends into infinity, beyond time, looking in all directions. Naturally, His statements baffled the religious critics. "You are not yet fifty years old," the Jews said to Him, "and you have seen Abraham!" (John 8:57). These folks just couldn't fathom the idea that Jesus knew their ancient forefathers.

Today I'm reminded that "Jesus Christ is the same yesterday and today and forever" (Hebrews 13:8). And it is a blessed thing to know. Anyone who has ever stood below the expanse of an evening sky glistening with stars knows the awesomeness of the created cosmos. Just how awesome, then, is the eternal, uncreated being who is as close to me as my next breath?

Eternal One, I stand in awe of Your presence. You are everywhere—in the farthest reaches of the universe and in the deepest recesses of my soul. In this quiet moment, I lift my heart in grateful praise. Through Christ, amen.

Excess Baggage

Get up! Pick up your mat and walk (John 5:8).

Scripture: **John 5:1-9**
Song: **"Walking in the King's Highway"**

In India I slept on a straw mat, which just doesn't compare in comfort to the Western sleeping bag. I know the discomfort of that thin layer next to hard ground. So the very idea of a person with a disability sleeping on a mat makes me cringe in empathy.

The words of Jesus presented a challenge to this man who hadn't been able to walk for 38 years. It was a three-part command: get up, pick up that mat, and walk. A marvelous healing then took place.

The story causes me to consider: What is the "mat" in my life? It's not necessarily a place of discomfort, but it could represent a situation in which I am stuck, seemingly unable to help myself. For instance, when am I paralyzed with fear? When do past failures discourage me? And what questionable thought patterns are immobilizing me at the moment?

Yes, the man picked up his mat. But I'm quite sure that, once he began walking, he let go of that shabby excess baggage forever.

Father, Your hand lifts me out of my unworthy preoccupations and into Your plans for me. Help me rise above past mistakes and present difficulties to affirm Your sovereignty over all things. In Jesus' name, amen.

January 8–14. **Penny Smith,** of Harrisburg, Pennsylvania, wrote *Gateways to Growth,* based upon the book of Esther. Penny has five grandchildren.

Cloudy Vision?

He who comes from above is above all, he who is of the earth is from the earth and speaks of the earth. He who comes from heaven is above all (John 3:31, *New American Standard Bible*).

Scripture: **John 3:31-36**
Song: **"Hail to the Lord Who Comes"**

Flying is my favorite mode of travel. How exhilarating to break through the clouds and cruise above them, where blue skies seem brighter and even bluer! The songwriters who penned the words and music to "Above All" have captured the truth that John the Baptist proclaimed before he was imprisoned. John, the forerunner, spoke of the heavenly bridegroom as being above all.

The apostle Paul witnessed to this same truth in Ephesians 4:10, "He who descended is Himself also He who ascended far above all the heavens, that He might fill all things" *(NASB)*. And in Philippians 2:9 we read, "God highly exalted Him, and bestowed on Him the name which is above every name"*(NASB)*.

No wonder Paul admonished the Colossian believers to set their thoughts on the things of Heaven rather than keeping their eyes glued to the earth (see Colossians 3:2). Ironic, isn't it, that if we're thoroughly entangled in things down here, our spiritual vision will be . . . clouded?

*Thank You, **God,** for enabling me, through the power of Your Spirit and the finished work of Christ, to break through the clouds of despondency and live above the many pressures of life. In the name of the Father, the Son, and the Holy Spirit, I pray. Amen.*

Identity Crisis Solution

Jesus declared, "I who speak to you am he" (John 4:26).

Scripture: **John 4:19-26**
Song: **"Speak, O Lord, Thy Servant Heareth"**

When my younger son would call me on the telephone, he had the habit of saying, "Mom, this is Blain." I thought it was cute. I have only two sons, and I sure do know their voices.

But Blain doesn't do that anymore. Perhaps he thinks he has identified himself on the phone often enough through the years that my ears are now thoroughly trained to his unique tones. Or is it because he has children of his own and realizes how *individual* each one is? I am certain he recognizes their voices, even when they're out of his sight.

As we develop the pattern of daily prayer, Bible reading, and worship, we learn to recognize the voice of our brother Jesus. I am more sensitive to His nudging today than I was when my Christian pilgrimage began years ago, and I expect that sensitivity to increase with time. Furthermore, the greater my spiritual capacity, the greater is my desire to worship Him. For though He is "family," He is also my Lord—the *royal* brother, Savior, and God.

The woman at the well was waiting for Messiah to "call" someday. Jesus told her clearly: just listen; recognize this voice. I'm already here.

Dear Lord, keep me attentive to Your voice this day, especially when You speak in the times of stillness. In Jesus' name I pray. Amen.

Listen . . . Listen . . . Listen

The result was that when Jesus had finished these words, the multitudes were amazed at His teaching (Matthew 7:28, *New American Standard Bible*).

Scripture: **Matthew 7:24-29**
Song: **"Alleluia! Sing to Jesus!"**

In the stillness of the early dawn, I sat with my Bible in my lap. The only sound was the crackling of the fire in the potbellied stove. As I meditated upon the words of Scripture, I became aware of another sound, gradually increasing in volume as I focused upon it. It was the sound of water, like a rushing river. As it became louder, I looked to see what could be causing it.

I found nothing. Then I glanced at the Bible text again. I had been reading the words of Jesus, "He who believes in Me, as the Scripture said, 'From his innermost being shall flow rivers of living water'" (John 7:38, *NASB*). Had I heard the sound of this river of God?

Just as the crowds were amazed with Jesus' teaching centuries ago, so I am often amazed in His presence today. Whether we experience some glorious revelation or the simple humdrum of daily life, the living waters are flowing within. When the only sound seems to be the drip of a faucet or the crackling of a fireplace, we can listen . . . listen . . . listen a bit more closely.

O God, let me hide Your amazing Word in my heart, and give me boldness to share it with others who need the revelation of Your eternal life. In the name of Jesus, my Savior, I pray. Amen.

Seasoned Prayers

Preach the Word; be prepared in season and out of season; correct, rebuke and encourage—with great patience and careful instruction (2 Timothy 4:2).

Scripture: 2 Timothy 4:1-5
Song: "How Good Is the God We Adore"

After teaching our adult Bible class, I greeted one of the ladies—only to face a cold stare and: "Why did you say that to me last week?" I didn't have a clue as to what she meant. She explained that when she'd shared a problem with me, I'd walked away saying, "Pity, pity, pity."

But this seemed so foreign to my nature! I asked whether she might have misheard my response. But when she insisted she'd gotten it right, I asked her to forgive me. Her response was less than satisfying though: "I forgive you, but I *know* what I heard." Sadly, this scenario was replayed for weeks, after every Bible class that I taught.

In this instance, I believe I learned what Paul meant by those words, "with great patience and careful instruction." The problem would not go away, and it was difficult to teach with this lady staring me down.

Sometimes the "out of season" seems longer than the "in season," doesn't it? However, I not only learned to prepare a lesson but also to prepare myself to meet whatever offense might come. Thanks be to God!

Lord, *I forgive in advance any who might offend me today, and I ask You to bless them. In Jesus' name, amen.*

Trinitarian Honor

In order that all may honor the Son, even as they honor the Father. He who does not honor the Son does not honor the Father who sent Him (John 5:23, *New American Standard Bible*).

Scripture: John 5:19-23
Song: "Blessing and Honor and Glory and Power"

My Uncle Ike celebrated his 95th birthday without any fanfare. Referring to his longevity, he says with a chuckle, "Had I known I was going to live this long, I'd have taken better care of myself!" As far as his health is concerned, he doesn't have any life-threatening illnesses, but sometimes he feels quite weak. After he naps for a while, his physical strength returns along with his sense of humor. He does realize that God is the source of his strength.

Let us all honor our three-in-one strengthener. The Holy Spirit is a life-giving Spirit. His quickening affects not only our spirits but our physical beings also. And Jesus—who healed the sick, opened blind eyes, unstopped deaf ears, and raised the dead—testified that He only did that which He saw His Father do.

With each renewal, whether physical or spiritual, we can remind ourselves that our Father is initiating a quickening force within us that we may bring honor to Him. It delights the Father's heart when His children, in the power of the Spirit, praise and glorify His Son.

Father, even as Your Son has glorified You, work by Your Spirit within me that I may faithfully give glory to Your Son for His sacrifice on Calvary's cross. In His precious name I pray. Amen.

Love Drew a Circle

Truly, truly, I say to you, he who hears My word, and believes Him who sent Me, has eternal life, and does not come into judgment, but has passed out of death into life (John 5:24, *New American Standard Bible*).

Scripture: **John 5:24-30**
Song: **"Bring Them In"**

The Kenyan minister escorted us through his village, which was largely comprised of his extended family members. His parents lived in their own hut, then the siblings with their families in mud huts that formed a circle around the village floor.

As we approached one of the huts, a small elderly lady ran down the path to welcome us into her "house." Although there was a language barrier, her pleasure was obvious to us. Two days later, she showed up at the church building—for the first time—and after hearing my message, she responded to the invitation to trust in Christ and be baptized. She told the minister that she had come because my friend and I were the only white people from America ever to enter her home.

We never know what it will take for a particular person to listen—to truly *hear*—the message of Christ. In this case, "Mama" had her own criteria, and our gracious Savior met it. It is His desire to bring us all to himself.

*Your ways are so much higher than ours, **Lord.** Help me to see through Your eyes so that I won't miss any opportunity to declare Your life-giving Word to open ears. In the name of Christ I pray. Amen.*

Exaggerated Report

I pray that out of his glorious riches he may strengthen you with power through his Spirit in your inner being (Ephesians 3:16).

Scripture: **Ephesians 3:14-21**
Song: **"Prayer Is the Soul's Sincere Desire"**

"It was 1983. I came home from college to find a street full of emergency vehicles," said our minister, Jeff. "I pushed through and saw Mom stretched out on the floor. On the way to the hospital, I prayed the only verse I knew, 'God so loved the world . . . that none should perish' (see John 3:16). Please, God, don't let her die."

Jeff rushed into the hospital to find his mother unattended. He ran into the hall for help and was informed she'd been reported DOA (dead on arrival).

"Mom, are you dead?" Jeff called out.

"I don't think so, Jeff," answered his mom.

Medical personnel rushed into the room. One heart ventricle wasn't pumping blood. They didn't expect her to survive, but Jeff kept praying. Until then, Jeff's faith had been in medical science. Since then, his faith is in God's Word. For, I'm happy to say, Jeff's mother visited our church recently. Her heart is still going strong.

Lord God, *thank You for answering my prayers and doing immeasurably more than I could ask or imagine through Your power at work within me. Through Christ I pray. Amen.*

January 15–21. **SanDee Hardwig** writes material for her church and does prison ministry near Milwaukee. Her cats are Mr. Miagi, Paddywhacker, and Angel.

In Any Weather

They saw Jesus approaching the boat, walking on the water; and they were terrified. But he said to them, "It is I; don't be afraid" (John 6:19, 20).

Scripture: **John 6:16-21**
Song: **"The Storm Is Passing Over"**

Three storms collided off the coast of Nova Scotia on October 28, 1991. "She's comin' on, boys, and she's comin' on strong," radioed Captain Billy Tyne. Minutes later, the *Andrea Gail*, a swordfishing boat from Gloucester, Massachusetts, and her six-man crew disappeared. Waves rising 30 to 99 feet were reported. Imagine the terror in those men.

Jesus' disciples were experienced fishermen, so they'd encountered plenty of other storms, though this one was apparently also comin' on strong. But no doubt the most frightening thing for them was to see a man actually *walking* on those rough waters. Jesus calmed their fears, though, and when they took Him into the boat, they immediately reached shore. Two marvelous miracles!

We might wonder how to apply this unusual event to our own daily lives. One thing that strikes me is this: Christ is always present with me, but how often during the day do I stop to look, to simply *recognize* Him? What a blessing to do so in any kind of weather!

Father God, when I look, let me see. Help me recognize Your presence with me amid every difficulty and stormy trial. And in moments of peace, too, keep my focus on You. Through Christ I pray. Amen.

Who's Holy?

Jesus answered, "The work of God is this: to believe in the one he has sent" (John 6:29).

Scripture: **John 6:25-34**
Song: **"Believe Not Those Who Say"**

Three-year-old Uriah and I sang, "Open the eyes of my heart, Lord. I want to see You. Pour out Your power and love. . . ." We repeated the last verse, "Holy, holy, holy" three times before it was time for him to go to sleep.

"Who's holy?" asked Uriah. "God is holy," I said.

"Why is God holy?"

"Because God is perfect."

"Why is God perfect?"

I had to think for a moment. Then I said, "God never has to sleep. Everyone else has to sleep—even your mom and dad. But they trust God to watch over you while you're sleeping because He *never sleeps.*" The next day, Uriah told his mother, "You know what? God is perfect and God is holy."

A crowd questioned Jesus the day after He fed 5,000 of them with a little boy's lunch. They wanted to know what works God required of them. So Jesus told them the perfect work they could perform: simply believe in Him. In this case—regarding our own "perfection"—it can be nothing less than to rely on the truly perfect one from Heaven. Every other work falls short of salvation.

Heavenly Father, *I desire to be holy. Help me to do good works motivated by Your Spirit through heart-deep belief. In the holy name of Jesus, amen.*

Have a Taste!

I am the bread of life. He who comes to me will never go hungry (John 6:35).

Scripture: **John 6:35-40**
Song: **"My Life, Dear Lord, I Give to Thee"**

I just love the smell of freshly baked bread. The first time I helped Grandma bake bread, we rolled dough into fat strips and laid them on cookie sheets. Then we waited patiently for them to bake. I still remember how great that finger bread tasted. I ate until I couldn't eat anymore. . . . But in a few hours, I was hungry again.

The people knew their ancestors were fed manna, a kind of bread that dropped from Heaven, for 40 years. That's why they weren't overly impressed with just one meal. Yet Jesus said they were seeking bread that wouldn't last—though one "meal" of faith in Him would satisfy them forever. No wonder He is the bread of life!

The Greek word *artos* ("bread") appears 13 times in the book of John, and six times Jesus says He comes from Heaven (see John 6:33-58) and that God sent Him so all might have eternal life (v. 40).

You see, before Adam and Eve sinned, God created humans to live forever with Him in complete fulfillment and peace. But the sin caused hunger—a burning desire for more, more, more. Only the living bread can satisfy that spiritual yearning. Taste and see!

Father, *You gave me the bread of life in Jesus. Make me willing to share this soul-nourishment with others who need Him. In Christ's name, amen.*

He Wants . . . Me

No one can come to me unless the Father who sent me draws him, and I will raise him up at the last day (John 6:44).

Scripture: John 6:41-51
Song: "Come Believing!"

A cat meowed forlornly outside my building. I walked into the dark and kneeled on the damp earth. I held out my arms and called, "Come, kitty, kitty." A skinny, black cat ran straight into my arms. She wrapped her paws around my neck and licked my face enthusiastically. No one answered my ads seeking her owner, so I named her Tatsinda and raised her as my own.

I loved, fed, and cared for Tatsinda. But nothing I did prevented her from contracting feline leukemia. I had her put to sleep when she was 6.

Jesus holds out His arms. He loves and cares for us. But He offers us much more than I could offer Tatsinda. He offers more than food for our physical bodies and love for our souls. He offers eternal life with Him in Heaven.

The most wonderful thing about all of this is that we can come to Him because the Father draws us. The Lord of the universe *wants* us—wants us to be with Him, to know His love and care, to fellowship with Him now and throughout eternity.

Lord God of Heaven, *thank You for loving me completely and unconditionally. Thank You for never giving up on me. And thank You for guiding and protecting me during my days on earth. I pray that I never will be found resisting Your call. In Jesus' name, amen.*

Be Free

Say to the captives, "Come out," and to those in darkness, "Be free!" (Isaiah 49:9).

Scripture: **Isaiah 49:7-13**
Song: **"Where He Leads Me"**

Captain Stottlemeyer consults Monk when investigating a difficult crime. The annoying yet endearing Monk (played on TV by actor Tony Shaloub) isn't allowed to carry a weapon because of his many phobias and obsessive compulsions. But with the help of his nurse-assistant, this significantly flawed human being fights through his irrational fears and solves criminal cases.

Messiah, who was completely without flaws, did what was impossible for any other person. He reconciled flawed humans with God.

The prophet Isaiah describes the majesty of this awesome work of God through His servant, a work of freeing the captives. This was especially crucial for the captive nation of Israel, but it applies to each of us today as well. You see, we all struggle as captives to some form of flaw. We may not be OCD like Monk, but many of us do have neuroses, physical ailments, destructive habits, addictions, and besetting sins.

The good news is that a better day looms ahead. We await our complete freedom, a full redemption that will surely come to pass (see Romans 8:17-25).

How I long for that day of complete freedom, **Dear Father!** *Come, Lord Jesus, in whom I pray. Amen.*

A Real Advantage

Others said, "He is the Christ." Still others asked, "How can the Christ come from Galilee?" (John 7:41)

Scripture: **John 7:37-41**
Song: **"The Comforter Has Come"**

When I was young I use to think how wonderful it would have been to live on earth when Jesus Christ, the Son of God, was born in a manger in Bethlehem. Yet we have an advantage over those who lived in Jesus' day. They knew His family was from Galilee, but Messiah was prophesied to be born in Bethlehem of David. So many doubted that Jesus was who He said He was. But we today have the New Testament, which clearly tells us that Jesus was born in Bethlehem, though His family later moved to Galilee, where Jesus began His earthly ministry.

We have another advantage over those folks. After Jesus ascended back to Heaven, He sent the Holy Spirit to be our comforter and to guide us into truth. No longer is God's holy presence out of reach: He's chosen to live within us. Lori Wilke sings, "But nothing can exceed the view of seeing Jesus born in you." So we know where He was born, but we also know *why* He was born—that we might be born again. What a privilege to know this Christ!

O God, how awesome that You have chosen to live in me through Your indwelling Spirit, the Spirit of Christ! Holy Trinity, please reveal anything in my heart that may displease You today. In the name of the Father, Son, and Holy Spirit, amen.

Joy to Come

Then will the lame leap like a deer, and the mute tongue shout for joy (Isaiah 35:6).

Scripture: **Isaiah 35:3-10**
Song: **"Joy Unspeakable"**

I hate to admit this, but on some days my body feels the wear and tear of the decades and of the four children, some of whom are now adults. Nothing too serious, just the normal aging process we're promised this side of Heaven. It may take me just a bit longer to rise from a low couch, or I may find an unexpected stiffness after sitting for a while. Gone are the days when I leaped up gracefully without a moment's thought.

I accept this process—and am resoundingly thankful to be getting up at all. But this reality also makes the promise of our verse today all the sweeter to anticipate. What joy we will experience when we leave behind the frailties of our human bodies! I envision unrestrained joy and wholeness, with crutches tossed to the side in excitement.

The hand of God has planted this future within our hearts, whether we're young or old. Brothers and sisters, let faith rise up as you dream of the glorious days to come.

*Thank You so much, **Lord,** for promising and preparing such a magnificent future for Your children. And thank You for the joy you've placed within my heart already, my delight in knowing You and being Yours. May my life reflect that gratitude and delight daily. I pray in Jesus' name. Amen.*

January 22–28. **Kevan Breitinger** lives with her family of six in Ocean City, New Jersey, where she writes and pursues other adventures with the Lord.

Worship the Son!

The people living in darkness have seen a great light; on those living in the land of the shadow of death a light has dawned (Matthew 4:16).

Scripture: **Matthew 4:12-17**
Song: **"Dark Is the Night"**

Living in a seaside resort, I watch thousands of out-of-towners pour into town each Friday night during the summers. They endure long, hot drives on congested highways to reach the beach, to follow the sun. Sun worshipers, they're called. The light they love is physical, but I see their connection with today's verse, especially when I observe their enthusiastic chasing after the sun's rays.

God has sent us another light, far greater than the brilliant one in the sky so adored by these eventually well-tanned travelers. He sent it to a people who lived in great darkness, whether they recognized the gloom or not. He sent it to fulfill His eternal promises and to express His great love. Truly a light worth worshiping.

My sun-starved tourists bear myriad inconveniences and discomforts to attain their skin-deep goal. The Son we worship—who has saved us to the depths of our being by His radiant grace—deserves a similar desire and commitment, and so much more. Yes, may our lives display even greater passion as we long for the light of the world to light up our pathway each day.

Father, Your love lights my world with the intensity of a thousand suns. All thanks for leading me out of the darkness of sin. Through the Son, amen.

Forever Changed

He himself insisted, "I am the man" (John 9:9).

Scripture: **John 9:1-11**
Song: **"I'm Happy in Jesus Today"**

What a drastic change in the man born blind! After Jesus healed him, his neighbors wondered, "Is this the same guy we know?" With no driver's license or social security card to offer as proof of identity, he could only keep insisting: "Yes, it really is *me!*"

The Gospel writer shows us Jesus, light of the world, often invading the dark existences of human beings in wonderful, surprising ways—but always for the purpose of glorifying God. Yes, Jesus works distinctly and uniquely in each heart. How has He worked in you so far? For this blind man, He mixed mud with saliva before applying it to the man's eyes, an unusual approach to healing.

The light may have entered your life in a very unique and emotional encounter. Or maybe your initial experience with Christ was somewhat low-key by comparison. Either way, the entrance of the light was perfectly personal and transformational. We who were blind see now with new eyes, and we will never be the same. May our lives reflect this wondrous healing in a way that pleases and honors the one who is our light.

Father, I echo my brother's words today: "I am one touched by Him." I will never get over it, nor do I want to. Lord, have Your way in me today. May I glorify You with this gift of light within. I am Yours forever. I pray this prayer in the name of Jesus, my great physician. Amen.

The Rest Is Just Details

The man said, "Lord, I believe," and he worshiped him (John 9:38).

Scripture: **John 9:35-41**
Song: **"Don't Lose the Vision"**

Have you ever wakened from sleep in the pitch dark and found yourself trying to figure out the room's conditions? Maybe your spouse added an extra blanket while you were asleep, and you can't understand why you're sweating. Or you feel a draft that wasn't there before. You only know you're chilly, until you turn the light on and realize somebody opened a window. So *that's* it!

The man healed of blindness had no theological explanation, and certainly no scientific facts, with which he might enlighten his critics. All he knew was that he was once blind but now he could see. He didn't understand his own miracle . . . until Christ revealed who had produced that miracle. So *that's* it—the Son of God did it! Then everything made sense, and the man offered the most appropriate response: He worshiped Jesus.

There is much we still don't understand about light and darkness, about life and death. But we do know that the light has come to our planet and led us out of the darkness of sin by His death and resurrection; everything else is details.

Dear God, You are my light on the days when I understand and on the more confusing days as well. I thank You for rescuing me from the darkness and for leading me into Your marvelous light. Through Christ, amen.

Joy of Worship

Sing and make music in your heart to the Lord (Ephesians 5:19).

Scripture: **Ephesians 5:15-21**
Song: **"Sing Aloud with Gladness"**

The babysitter was gentle as she put the two sisters in bed for the night, but for the younger girl the combination of the dark room and her parents' absence was too much. Her quiet sobs filled the room shortly after the door closed. It was only when she took a deep breath that she heard her older sister's soft voice singing from the top bunk. The familiar hymn soothed her fears, and she found herself humming along with the old songs of devotion she knew so well.

Yes, the days are evil, and the darkness can appear overwhelming at times. But we are not left without comfort or hope, for Paul's wise instructions come to us as encouragement on our spiritual journey. Speaking and singing of the things of God can only strengthen us for the vital tasks ahead. In fact, singing to Him of our devotion is its own reward.

Will you join me today in pushing back the darkness by intentionally lifting His glorious name in worship? See if your spirits don't rise in thanksgiving. Simply put: make His praise glorious!

O God, *I'm happy to sing of Your goodness and offer my praise to You today, for You are more than worthy! Thank You for overcoming every evil day with the power of Your love. All praise to You, in Christ's name. Amen.*

Uniquely One

I stand with the Father, who sent me (John 8:16).

Scripture: **John 8:12-20**
Song: **"With One Consent Let All the Earth"**

Those who are married can testify to the extraordinary oneness found in a God-centered marriage. We don't necessarily get along perfectly with our mates at all times, but generally we do feel one another's sorrows, joys, and mistakes. If my husband is struggling in a particular area, I usually feel as if something is just a bit "off" in me, even if I don't know the specifics. We are one flesh before the Lord, whether our lives always reflect that or not.

The oneness between the Father and the Son is much the same, except for the fact that it is perfect, unmarred by the human frailties we carry. The Pharisees' own law honored the testimony of two witnesses. But the complete harmony, the total unity of these two witnesses was like no other. If they knew Jesus, they would know the Father; that's how cohesive they were.

The Father sent the light into the world to draw men and women to himself. But even as Christ traveled the rough earth, He stood with the Father, for this was a oneness that could not be diminished by distance or broken by even the sinfulness of humankind.

*I stand amazed at Your power, **Mighty God,** and the intricacies of Your ways. My finite mind cannot comprehend all the fullness of Your experience, but I know enough to bow before You in awe, in complete surrender. For You, O Lord, are wholly perfect. In Jesus' name, amen.*

God's Circle of Life

I have come into the world as a light, so that no one who believes in me should stay in darkness (John 12:46).

Scripture: **John 12:44-50**
Song: **"And Can It Be That I Should Gain?"**

One of the things I love about God's creation is the way things work together perfectly to fulfill a purpose. The sun heats the earth and the plants on it, the plants grow, purifying the air and feeding the animals, who breathe the air and provide us with food and service, under the sun. All of the creations in this circle of life, in serving their purpose, glorify God.

Jesus the Son was equally committed to fulfilling His purpose. Sent to rescue fallen sinners from the darkness of their own creation, He never wavered from His appointed mission. The Father sent His love and mercy in the person of Jesus, recognizing our great need and providing the precise sacrifice needed to accomplish His goal—the salvation of our souls. The light illuminated the darkness and enabled us to see, finally, our perilous condition. In seeing Jesus, we saw the Father and His love incarnate, and our hearts opened to believe.

No mission was ever more perfectly completed, no errand more breathtaking in its generosity. My heart melts at the lavish love in God's purposes for us.

O Lord, I can scarcely grasp the depths of Your amazing love. My understanding is so small, and Your mercies are so great. May my life show forth my gratitude for Your glory today. Through Jesus Christ I pray. Amen.

A Real Perfectionist

Whom did the LORD consult to enlighten him, and who taught him the right way? (Isaiah 40:14).

Scripture: **Isaiah 40:10-14**
Song: **"An Awe-Full Mystery Is Here"**

I remember vividly the day my husband told our 8-year-old son, Chad, to take some rotten grapes "out to the street." What he really meant was for Chad to take the grapes out and put them in the garbage cans sitting *near* the street for the garbage truck to come along. Eight-year-olds are still quite literal in their thinking, so you can probably imagine what happened next. He took those rotten globs and put them next to the curb, in the neatest little pile you've ever seen.

We have chuckled over that story for years. And for us, the moral of the story is: we all need clear instruction; we all need to be taught how to do things the right way. But this doesn't come naturally! Often we tend to do things only as we see fit.

In contrast, our creator God didn't need any help. Our Scripture verse tells us that He didn't need anyone to enlighten Him. He is the original perfectionist, perfection being a quality that fits Him. Perfectly.

Lord, You are perfectly amazing. I can't fathom how You measure the oceans or weigh the mountains. And so I trust You, Almighty God, creator of the universe, to care for me today. In Jesus' name, amen.

January 29–31. **Maralee Parker** is a wife, mother, and marketing manager of an accelerated adult degree program at a Christian college in the Chicago suburbs.

The Devoted Shepherd

Should not shepherds take care of the flock? (Ezekiel 34:2).

Scripture: **Ezekiel 34:1-6**
Song: **"Shepherd of Souls, Refresh and Bless"**

My cousin is a sheep-whisperer. Yes, she talks to sheep. She raises sheep. She loves sheep. I personally don't see the allure of hanging around with sheep, but she doesn't think it's baaaaaad at all (forgive the pun).

Actually, nothing could make her happier. She talks as if these gentle creatures are her babies, finds great joy in their every move, and paces the floor like a worried mother if any of them are sick. When the time comes for them to have babies each spring, she's out there in the barn all night long, if need be, waiting for her grandsheep to arrive.

I must say that when we were kids, I don't remember her telling me she wanted to be a shepherd someday. But that's what she is, and she lovingly tends to her beloved flock.

And aren't shepherds supposed to be like that? Her life excellently represents for me the loving relationship between a trusted shepherd and a helpless sheep as the prophet Ezekiel envisioned it. In that relationship, each lamb must rely on the shepherd for dear life. I am that lamb, and Christ is my shepherd. How I long to follow Him, moment by moment, and remain in His loving care!

*My life is in Your gentle hands, **Father.** I thank You for upholding me always in loving arms. In the name of the good shepherd, I pray. Amen.*

Stormy Day Savior

I will rescue them from all the places where they were scattered on a day of clouds and darkness (Ezekiel 34:12).

Scripture: **Ezekiel 34:11-16**
Song: **"A Shelter in the Time of Storm"**

You may have heard the old saying, "God never gives you more than you can handle." However, some of us may respond: "He has too much confidence in me!"

I do sometimes feel that way. My early life was idyllic—I grew up on a farm, graduated with honors from a small high school, then went on to graduate from college. I married, and we welcomed Child Number One at just the "right time." To our surprise, Baby Number Two didn't come three years later, as indicated in our master plan. Nor four years later, nor five. We then decided to adopt.

That was 16 years ago. We love our daughter immensely, but her "surprise" diagnoses of autism, social anxiety, and bipolar disorder make daily living challenging, to say the least. Then four years ago, I was diagnosed with kidney cancer. Those days were extremely scary, as I waited for surgery to determine the extent of the growth (stage III, but they got it all).

Though the fairy-tale life has left, I have learned, through life's challenges, to trust my Savior, as He has always provided for me. Before the storm begins, during the crisis, and after . . . He is ever faithful.

God, no matter what a day may bring, I know You will be with me. Keep me clinging to You, even in clouds and darkness. In Jesus' name, amen.

DEVOTIONS®

***N*ow then . . . listen to me; blessed are those who keep my ways.**

—(Proverbs 8:32)

FEBRUARY

Photo © Eyewire

Gary Allen, Editor

© 2006 STANDARD PUBLISHING, 8121 Hamilton Avenue, Cincinnati, Ohio, 45231, a division of STANDEX INTERNATIONAL Corporation. Topics based on the Home Daily Bible Readings, International Sunday School Lessons. © 2003 by the Committee on the Uniform Series. Printed in the U.S.A. Scripture taken from the HOLY BIBLE, NEW INTERNATIONAL VERSION®. NIV®. COPYRIGHT © 1973, 1978, 1984 by International Bible Society. Used by permission of Zondervan Publishing House. All rights reserved. Where noted, Scripture quotations are from the following, used with permission of the copyright holders, all rights reserved: *New American Standard Bible (NASB)*, © The Lockman Foundation, 1960, 1962, 1963, 1968, 1971, 1972, 1973, 1975, 1977, 1995. *King James Version (KJV)*, public domain.

More than Maslow

They will live in safety, and no one will make them afraid (Ezekiel 34:28).

Scripture: **Ezekiel 34:25-31**
Song: **"Safely Through Another Week"**

If you've ever studied psychology, you've probably heard of Maslow's Hierarchy of Needs. According to Abraham Maslow, physiological needs are our most basic requirements—air, water, food, and so on. Only after those needs are met can we move our attention to the second level: our safety needs. We need to feel safe and secure in order to function as human beings. Then come the needs for belonging, esteem, and self-actualization.

As I look around me, I realize that many people in our society just don't feel safe. Some children grow up in abusive homes, for example, and never feel secure—even years after they've endured horrific experiences. Even as adults, some have trouble developing trusting relationships; they've never felt safe within another person's love.

Through Ezekiel, God assures His people of protection. Wrapped in His love, they need not fear. So it is today. Will you thank God with me that He offers us a peace that passes all understanding? In fact, He *is* our peace.

Lord of all creation, I trust You for the very breath I breathe. You are my safe haven, Lord God, and I thank You for meeting my physical, emotional, and spiritual needs. In Jesus' name, amen.

February 1–4. **Maralee Parker** is a wife, mother, and marketing manager of an adult degree program at a Christian college in the Chicago suburbs.

Listen Up!

His sheep follow him because they know his voice (John 10:4).

Scripture: **John 10:1-5**
Song: **"Softly and Tenderly"**

I am a cat person. Cats allow me to keep my busy lifestyle and still have warm, fuzzy, loving critters around. My husband and I can go away for a long weekend, put out plenty of food, water, and clean litter boxes—and the pets will stay happy.

It's interesting though: no matter how nicely my husband treats our lovable felines, they prefer me. They can be hiding, as kitties sometimes do, and when I sit down on the couch, they come out and want to cuddle up in my lap. My husband often asks them, "Why don't you do that when *I* sit down?" (He's still waiting for a response.)

Even when I'm sitting and watching old family videos, if the cats hear my voice on a tape, they come out from hiding. I guess just the sound of my voice makes them happy.

So it is with the sheep in today's Scripture passage. The sheep implicitly trust their shepherd, so much that merely the sound of his voice beckons them. They will not come when a stranger calls, but when their beloved shepherd calls, there is no hesitation.

May it be so with us and our great shepherd!

Father, in my busy world, help me to be still and listen for Your voice. I thank You for speaking through my intuition and more clearly through the written Word—and the living Word, Your Son, in whom I pray. Amen.

Muddy Abundance

I came that they might have life, and might have it abundantly
(John 10:10, *New American Standard Bible*).

Scripture: **John 10:7-11**
Song: **"Afflictions, Though They Seem Severe"**

One day a friend of mine drove her elderly mother to the doctor's office. When they arrived, her mother quickly stepped out of the car and began sinking into some soft mud next to the sidewalk. Being a fastidious lady, she exclaimed, "Oh no, oh no, *oh no!*"

By this time my friend was running to rescue her, apologizing all the way, when she also inadvertently stepped into the mud. She stood there, wondering what she should do next, when she noticed her mom starting to totter a little. She reached out to support her, taking a step, but her shoe was stuck firmly in the mud. Her foot came out, and she ended up planting her foot, sock and all, into more mud. To make matters worse, shortly after that, her mom ended up . . . accidentally . . . *sitting* in the mud.

At that point, all sanity was lost. My friend and her mom looked at each other and started to giggle. They snickered and chortled and laughed. They didn't fall down laughing; they stood up laughing! It was a piece of life—*abundant* life—that they will treasure always.

O God, You are the source of abundant life. I couldn't make it through this crazy, stressful world with my sanity intact if I didn't know that You love me so deeply, so much that You laid down Your life for me. Thank You, in Jesus' name. Amen.

God, Your Supervisor

The man runs away because he is a hired hand and cares noth-ing for the sheep (John 10:13).

Scripture: **John 10:12-18**
Song: **"Safe in the Shepherd's Care"**

I aspired to my current management position, but on some days I wonder . . . *why?* Supervising people can be extremely challenging. I can't manufacture a desire for success in my employees; ultimately, they must find an inner motivation.

I've learned that when I assign a project and tell my folks *exactly how it must be done*—allowing little input—they are often less than enthusiastic. However, if I tell them the goal, let them have at it in their own way (and stop hovering over them), they develop ownership and a legitimate pride in their work. Simply put, they care more because it's theirs. And we all enjoy a better result.

In today's Scripture, the hired hand ran away when danger approached. He wanted to protect himself more than the sheep. After all, the sheep weren't his.

Lately I'm realizing that if I want to be like Jesus, the good shepherd, I need to put my whole heart into what-ever I'm doing. My work reflects who I am, as well as my commitment to the one who created me. As the apostle Paul put it: "Whatever you do, work at it with all your heart, as working for the Lord" (Colossians 3:23).

Father, help me to model Your model of commitment, whether it be with family, friends, or colleagues at work. In Jesus' name I pray. Amen.

Real Christians: Please Stand Up!

There will be scoffers who will follow their own ungodly desires . . . and do not have the Spirit (Jude 18, 19).

Scripture: **Jude 17-25**
Song: **"Stand Up, Stand Up for Jesus"**

Years ago, Mom enjoyed watching *To Tell the Truth*, boasting of her ability to discern the real McCoy from the impostors. You may recall that this TV show hosted three candidates, all claiming to be the same interesting person. Each looked the part and answered pointed questions with suitable ease. However, only one of them was telling the truth. Eventually that person would stand up.

In ancient days and today, our churches may harbor impostors. Jude tells us that these folks—although they will look like Christians and talk like Christians—have never received the indwelling Holy Spirit.

But what a blessing to have this Spirit, given us through baptism! His ministry is to guide us into all truth, even helping us discern those who are true brothers and sisters in the Lord. Perhaps more importantly, He gives us the ability to assess ourselves. Yes, the Spirit enables us to know who we are in Christ. Isn't it comforting to know that He abides with us forever and is the down payment on our heavenly home (see Ephesians 1:14)?

Father God, thank You for Your Spirit who gives me the power to seek Your will today. In Jesus' name I pray. Amen.

February 5–11. **Vivian Stiles** is a writer, speaker, and evangelism counselor. She lives with her husband, Larry, in Palmyra, New Jersey.

Highway Hearkening

Now therefore hearken unto me, O ye children: for blessed are they that keep my ways (Proverbs 8:32, *King James Version*).

Scripture: **Proverbs 8:22-32**
Song: **"Ye Sons of Men, Oh, Hearken"**

It was a gorgeous day, just right for traveling. Traffic was at a minimum. In fact, at times we were all alone on the road. But suddenly I felt we ought to take a different route.

I couldn't explain why. Nevertheless, my husband reluctantly honored my request and made a quick turn that took us onto a road that was under construction and heavily congested. Under my breath I prayed, "Did I really hear You right, Lord?"

When we stopped and entered a convenience store for something to drink, a truck driver came up to us and said, "I really like what's on your T-shirts: *Lift the Savior Up!* It reminds me of when I was close to the Lord." Then he confided that he'd been getting ready to do something he knew was wrong. He continued, "You know, I think maybe the Lord is warning me to change my direction."

I believe this was an instance of "hearkening" to the Lord. What do you think? In any case, I'm certainly thankful that our truck driver did, indeed, hear our T-shirt message. Will you spend this moment with me in prayer for him?

Father God, let me hear Your voice in this stillness. As I hear of Your ways, give me the will and the strength to keep them. In Jesus' name, amen.

Delayed, But . . .

When he heard that Lazarus was sick, he stayed where he was two more days (John 11:6).

Scripture: **John 11:1-6**
Song: **"Jesus! The Name High over All"**

They'd ordered several tests; I'd gotten second and third opinions. Final diagnosis: a tumor on my right kidney. I prayed night and day that God would shrink it out of existence. I studied every healing Scripture I could find.

Then, at three o'clock one morning, I lay on the floor praying and crying until I was physically weak. In my spirit I felt that God may have healed me. I thanked and praised Him for His faithfulness; however, several days later the pain returned with more intensity. The next step was surgery. And I was devastated.

As I was being prepared for the operation, the anesthesiologist told me to count backwards from 100. The next thing I knew, the doctor was waking me up. He said, "I didn't have to operate. I can't explain it, but the tumor has disappeared." This thought leaped to mind: delayed, not denied.

I know God doesn't heal all our diseases. He calls us to live by faith amid all the painful circumstances of earthly life. We won't be perfectly healthy until we're with the Lord in Heaven. But from now on, when He says "Wait," I will do it with hopeful expectation.

Lord, *You let Lazarus wait in the grave, and You still let me wait amid trying times. Strengthen my patience this day! In Jesus' name, amen.*

Will You Believe the Truth?

I am glad for your sakes that I was not there, to the intent ye may believe (John 11:15, *King James Version*).

Scripture: **John 11:7-16**
Song: **"Only Believe"**

The eagle is one of the largest and most powerful birds in the world, typically building its nest on high cliffs or in tall trees. When a baby eagle is about 12 weeks old, it is gently pushed out of its high, cozy shelter. Imagine the eaglet's trauma suddenly realizing it is all alone, falling through the air! But how else could it learn to fly?

Sometimes an eaglet will struggle to flap its wings, but the force of the wind is too strong; it starts to fall. As it rapidly descends to the ground, the mother swoops in—in the nick of time—and comes to the baby bird's rescue.

At times we face desperate situations, when no one is able to help us, and our only hope is God. However, His presence feels hidden from us. Yet it seems our Father allows these fiery trials, in His apparent absence, in order to increase our faith. We're forced to distinguish feeling from fact. We're gently pushed into a walk of faith.

No, we don't always *feel* the presence of the Lord, but the *truth* is, He never leaves us. For the disciples who arrived with Jesus at Lazarus's grave—what a blessing to have the ultimate test of faith, to think the dead could rise!

Dear God, I can relate to Lazarus. I was dead in my trespasses and sins, yet You refused to forsake me. By Your grace You raised me to new life. I praise You in the name of Jesus, my merciful Savior and Lord. Amen.

Believe and Receive

He who believes in me will live, even though he dies; and whoever lives and believes in me will never die. Do you believe this? (John 11:25, 26).

Scripture: **John 11:17-27**
Song: **"And Am I Only Born to Die?"**

It was a special Women's Day in our church assembly, and a young woman squeezed herself into the pew next to me. There was plenty of room elsewhere, but she ignored the usher. She stepped over several people, absolutely determined to sit next to me. I wondered if I'd met her previously. I usually don't forget a face.

Soon the congregation was lifting praises to God, but the young woman next to me hung her head and cried hysterically. I put my arm around her to comfort her, and before I could ask what was wrong, she ran out of the building.

I followed her. She said, "I recently lost my mother. I want to see her again, but I've done so many horrible things." I showed her from the Scriptures that it was for us—the *sinners*—that Christ died. And whoever believes in Him will never die an eternal death. Then I asked her the profound question that Christ still asks all of us: "Do you believe this?"

Heavenly Father, like all human beings, I dread the thought of having to die someday. However, I am so thankful that Your Son Jesus broke through the chains of death and prepared the way to Heaven for all who cling to Him in faith. I believe it! In His name, amen.

Tranquil Washing Away

Jesus wept. Then said the Jews, Behold how he loved him!
(John 11:35, 36, *King James Version*).

Scripture: **John 11:28-37**
Song: **"Beautiful Vale of Rest"**

The water glistened in the burning hot rays of the sun, but a breeze was blowing in across the shore. It was a perfect day to be at the beach. Watching the ocean waves gave me a feeling of tranquility. I started taking inventory of my life. I thought about the tragedies I'd been through—the bitter divorce and loss of children. My mind seemed to focus on all the mistakes.

We've all made them! We've blundered and tripped, so often looking for the loopholes to justify doing our own thing. Some of us have been in painful, desolate places merely because of our obstinate wills. And yet Jesus weeps for the human condition, our existence filled with sin and death.

The great thing is that when the king of the universe weeps for you, you've got a mighty ally indeed. He goes beyond tears, though, and offers new life. What love!

I wonder how it felt to be wrapped in grave clothes, struggling to walk out of a tomb? Of course, I must say it's a wonderful feeling to walk away from a past that is buried and forgiven. I think I'll sit here a little longer by these rippling waves as they wash . . . wash . . . wash.

God, nothing I've done, or could do, will make You love me any more or less than You already do. How good You are! Through Christ, amen.

Experience the Glory!

Jesus said, "Did I not tell you that if you believed, you would see the glory of God?" (John 11:40).

Scripture: **John 11:38-44**
Song: **"In the Cross of Christ I Glory"**

When we stopped to visit some friends who were celebrating their seventh wedding anniversary, we expected to see two people still madly in love. Instead, Karen greeted us with tears running down her face.

I asked, "What's wrong—is there anything we can do to help?" She said, "We're not celebrating tonight because Greg is working late again. I know we need the money, but this is our anniversary. It's so inconsiderate!" As she continued talking, I realized this was just the tip of the iceberg. I asked if we could pray.

Karen opened up even more. She said Greg had been gone for a few days, and she feared he was thinking about making it permanent. She admitted they both had made some mistakes, but she wanted a chance to work things out. So we held hands and prayed again—that the Lord would bring Greg home with a desire to resolve their problems.

An hour later, Greg walked in. He asked Karen to forgive him. He said, "I've been praying. I know that if we believe, we'll see the glory of God in our marriage."

God, even when it seems the life has gone out of us—or out of a relationship—You can restore it all through Your mighty power. Give me the faith to trust Your perfect will in all things, for Your glory. In Jesus' name, amen.

My Passport

Brothers, . . . we have confidence to enter the Most Holy Place by the blood of Jesus (Hebrews 10:19).

Scripture: **Hebrews 10:19-23**
Song: **"I Come, O Savior, to Thy Table"**

My passport identifies me as an American citizen, but with it I've entered Ireland, Italy, and Canada. With that little document I can go just about anywhere.

Jesus' blood is somewhat like a passport, isn't it? By it, God has identified His people. Whereas a government-issued passport gives the place and year of birth, our God-issued passport details our cleansed, new hearts. With Jesus' blood we can go with confidence to the only place that really matters: the most holy place; that is, near to God" (v. 22). We will be admitted with open arms.

Italy is nice, Canada is too, and I do long to see more of the world with my U.S. passport. However, each day I can use my other passport and find rest or invigoration in the presence of my holy Lord. Through prayer and worship—in the car or at the kitchen table—I'm so thankful I can enter in with boldness.

Holy God, thank You that I can enter into Your presence with confidence because of the sacrifice of the perfect Lamb on my behalf. As I enjoy Your company, let my faith be bolstered and my trust in You be multiplied, so I can bring You glory through my life. In the name of Jesus, Lord and Savior of all, I pray. Amen.

February 12–18. **Elizabeth Fabiani,** of New Jersey, loves to write, quilt, and collect rocks. She and her best friend run an online magazine for women.

Why Were You Born?

"You are a king, then!" said Pilate. Jesus answered, "You are right in saying I am a king. In fact, for this reason I was born, and for this I came into the world, to testify to the truth. Everyone on the side of truth listens to me" (John 18:37).

Scripture: **John 18:33-40**
Song: **"Who Are These Like Stars Appearing?"**

My little brother Louis was born with birth defects. He would never walk, do simple math, or carry on the family name, yet God had a purpose for his life. God used my brother's life to lead our parents to Jesus.

Jesus knew His own purpose was to save the world from sin and death. This didn't make sense to the people of His day, because they were more concerned with Roman occupation than freedom for the soul. Though His path was painful, Jesus was never derailed in His mission.

It's not our job to save the world from death, but we can be teachers or mothers or businessmen who financially support missionaries. In myriad ways we, too, can testify to the truth.

We are all born for a purpose, just as my brother was. Day by day our mission is to submit to the filling and guidance of the Holy Spirit. Then, as we follow His lead in our witnessing, we will surely encounter openhearted listeners.

Lord, help me to live out my purpose with passion as You did. Keep in the forefront of my mind what You've planned for me each day, whether it's big or small. Help me be the person I was born to be. In Jesus' name, amen.

Grace for Each Day

Join with me in suffering for the gospel, by the power of God, who has saved us and called us to a holy life—not because of anything we have done but because of his own purpose and grace (2 Timothy 1:8, 9).

Scripture: **2 Timothy 1:8-14**
Song: **"Grace, Enough for Me"**

Do you ever find God to be somewhat ironic? I haven't had a valentine in years, and here I am writing a devotional that falls on Valentine's Day. (It was hard to write, too, believe it or not.) Yet God knew in advance I would be assigned to write for this day. He also knew that eventually I would look to His grace to help me finish it, without a hint of bitterness or disappointment that may sometimes simmer in the soul of a single woman.

Paul asks us to join him in suffering for the gospel. I know I would rather run the other way! Just as I would rather wear black and avoid restaurants on Valentine's Day. Yet with grace we can handle each new day whether it holds suffering or joy.

Thankfully, we can face each new trial and trust that the grace to endure it has already been provided. Today, if you find yourself suffering from singleness, arthritic hands, or a coworker's persecutions, remember that before the beginning of time, God planned just the right amount of grace to get you through this day.

God, what a thrill to know the saving power of Your grace! It gets me through the best and worst of days. Praise to You, in Christ's name. Amen.

Dress with Holiness

Put on the new self, created to be like God in true righteousness and holiness (Ephesians 4:24).

Scripture: **Ephesians 4:17-24**
Song: **"Washed in the Blood"**

While working for our township one summer, I learned about wood chippers, the sewage plant, and the trash truck. One day I watched Sam, a longtime township worker, put on his grubby, greasy coveralls and climb inside the trash truck to grease the hydraulic system. This kept the truck crushing trash smoothly. When finished, he stepped out and hung up the coveralls for next time. I, on the other hand, would have used latex gloves to undress after the grease job. Then I would have boiled and bleached the clothes. But that's just me.

Grubby and greasy could describe a lot of people, but all who have chosen to follow Christ have had their "selves" laundered, no matter the state of their wardrobes. The believer's inner life now resembles a new Easter outfit more than dirty coveralls.

But even Easter clothes get soiled. Though forgiven, we're not perfect. Every day, I must consciously refuse "deceitful desires" (v. 22) and let this new life in me—the indwelling Spirit of God—guide me in the paths of righteousness. What a miracle: to be able to dress as God does!

O Lord, You cleaned me up and made me new. I pray that others may see Your gracious work and long to put on a new self as well. I praise and adore You, Father, in the name of Your Son, Jesus. Amen.

Tell It from the Lawn Chair

It gave me great joy to have some brothers come and tell about your faithfulness to the truth and how you continue to walk in the truth. I have no greater joy than to hear that my children are walking in the truth (3 John 3, 4).

Scripture: 3 John 2-8
Song: "Go, Tell It on the Mountain"

By the side of a lonely country road, she sat on her lawn chair with mobile phone in hand. She was talking and laughing with great animation. Surprised by her random location for a friendly conversation, I laughed out loud in my car as I passed her by. I figured that, with our area's poor cellular reception, she probably had to leave her house—lawn chair in hand—and walk to a spot on the road that allowed a good connection. She reminded me of how important it is to keep in touch with people, despite our busy lives.

Similarly, according to our Scripture today, it's important to keep communicating encouraging things about one another in the church. When we see good things happening in our lives, we ought to tell about them and give thanks to God. That is what gave the apostle John such great joy, and it can launch us into rejoicing as well. Our listening ear, encouraging word, or uplifting story may be just what's needed to help someone to keep walking in the truth.

Dear Heavenly Father, remind me to remind others that we need to keep believing the truth, even when it's difficult to do. In Jesus' name, amen.

Decor Debate?

Do not let your hearts be troubled. Trust in God; trust also in me. In my Father's house are many rooms; if it were not so, I would have told you. I am going there to prepare a place for you (John 14:1, 2).

Scripture: **John 14:1-7**
Song: **"I've Got a Mansion Just Over the Hilltop"**

"I'm just not sure You'd know how to decorate my heavenly mansion the way I would like it. What if You give me a Mediterranean-style dining room when I would prefer something more contemporary?"

OK, I doubt you'll ever hear a Christian debating God about celestial mansion decor. Getting bent out of shape over heavenly draperies does sound pretty ridiculous. Yet how many equally trivial things so often trouble our hearts? Once we gain a little perspective, we see them as unworthy of worry. But in the middle of worrisome circumstances, our dismal projections of the future can seem ever so real.

Can you let Christ speak His words of comfort into your heart at those times? Naturally, concerns over finances, children, finding love, or losing a loved one, are legitimate and do trouble every caring heart. At those times it helps to remember: Jesus has prepared a wonderful place for us to spend eternity with Him. In the meantime, He won't leave us to fend for ourselves down here.

Father, I know Heaven is beyond my imagining. But amid my troubles, do give me glimpses of this all-surpassing reality. Through Christ, amen.

What Have You Been Doing?

I tell you the truth, anyone who has faith in me will do what I have been doing. He will do even greater things than these, because I am going to the Father (John 14:12).

Scripture: **John 14:8-14**
Song: **"I Would Be Like Jesus"**

"What have you been doing?" A question like that makes me think of children left unattended for too long. Did they get hold of the dog's dish, Mom's makeup, or the sewing scissors?

Of course, for an adult it can be a good question to hear and answer—especially if we're proud of our work. If asked this question, Jesus might have said, "I healed the sick, lame, blind, and deaf. I comforted the lonely, the mourners, and the forgotten. I brought hope. I spoke truth. I lived out love."

It's amazing to think that we—Christ's ambassadors here on earth—could answer in similar ways as we allow Him to work through us. For with faith in Christ, we can do great things. We even have His promise that whatever we ask, if it will bring glory to the Father, He will do it. So come, brothers and sisters, with our Lord Jesus let us pray the lost into the kingdom, comfort the inconsolable, and fulfill the needs of the needy this day!

Heavenly Father, I want to be like Jesus and do great things in His name for Your glory. But teach me to take the smallest first step toward that end as I hold tightly to Your hand. Wherever I go today, may I be ready to minister with faith. I pray in the name of Jesus. Amen.

My Life: A Parable

He told them still another parable (Matthew 13:33).

Scripture: **Matthew 13:18-33**
Song: **"I Love to Tell the Story"**

"The story of my life!" That's what we say when something unpleasant happens to us. When bad things happen, we ask, "Where are You, God?" When sickness, disappointment, and personal failure come, guilt may wash over us. So I wonder: Why do we persist in the illusion that only comfort and ease betoken God's blessing?

Bad things often happen to God's people. Job had no picnic. Joseph and Daniel sometimes must have wondered. Maybe even John chafed on Patmos (what kind of retirement was that?). While we value the words these men gave us, their lives bear a powerful message.

Fanny Crosby lost her sight when she was 6 weeks old. Some blame an incompetent physician, but hear her words: "Oh, what a happy soul am I. Although I cannot see, I am resolved that in this world, contented I will be."

Fanny Crosby's poems and hymns by the thousands reveal her vibrant relationship with God. Yet while her pen blessed the world, we cannot escape the lesson of her life.

Every life is a parable. What story will I tell today?

God, remind me that more people watch my actions than hear my words. May I be a parable of Your goodness, through Christ my Lord. Amen.

February 19–25. **Lloyd Mattson** is a retired minister and author of Christian camping books. He and his wife, Elsie, live in Duluth, Minnesota.

Let It Shine!

My prayer is not that you take them out of the world but that you protect them from the evil one (John 17:15).

Scripture: **John 17:13-19**
Song: **"Stepping in the Light"**

Frenchy Lamont lived in a weathered cabin just north of town. He couldn't read or write, he'd lost an eye in a fight, and he spent most of his time in a small pub that was walking distance from his home. White-haired and bent over, Frenchy was nevertheless still quite spry after his 80 years on earth.

One evening Paul, a local minister, came upon Frenchy walking home and gave him a lift in his car. Gently, the minister told Frenchy about Jesus—and then offered him a ride to church and dinner at the parsonage the next day.

The congregation took this old man into their hearts, and he became a regular in attending worship services. He was baptized, learned God's love through the love of His people, and soon asked Paul to teach him to read (so he could immerse himself in the Bible).

But one day an anxious church member phoned Paul: "I just saw Frenchy going into that pub!" Paul went and found him there. "Frenchy," he said, "is this really where you want to be?"

The old man looked puzzled. "Didn't you say we should tell our friends about Jesus?"

Heavenly Father, *help me carry the light of the gospel to the dark corners, where so many need Your redeeming love. Through Christ I pray. Amen.*

Where? With You!

See that what you have heard from the beginning remains in you. If it does, you also will remain in the Son and in the Father (1 John 2:24).

Scripture: **1 John 2:24-29**
Song: **"Lead On, O King Eternal"**

During my Boy Scout years, our leader always said, "Trust your compass!" On a few occasions, in real wilderness, that advice came in quite handy. My mind said *go this way;* my compass said *no.* The compass was right.

Perhaps today's Scouts still carry a compass, but that venerable guide seems to have yielded to the Global Positioning System (GPS), an electronic wonder you can carry in your pocket. GPS can pinpoint your precise location anywhere on earth.

I understand fairly well how a compass works, with its deviations from true North. I haven't a clue how GPS works, apart from a vague idea of what it means for satellite signals to triangulate. But, of course, I don't have to know *how* a compass or GPS works, only *that* they work and that I must learn to trust them.

When you know your destination, these devices will keep you on track. God's Word does that too. Keep it close to your heart and consult it often. If that Word remains in you, then wherever you are, Immanuel—"God with us"—is always with . . . *you.*

*Thank You, **Lord,** for giving me Your Word to be a light to my path and a guide toward home when I stray. In Jesus' name, amen.*

Loving, with Due Care

Many deceivers, who do not acknowledge Jesus Christ as coming in the flesh, have gone out into the world. . . . If anyone comes to you and does not bring this teaching, do not take him into your house or welcome him (2 John 7, 10).

Scripture: 2 John 7-11
Song: "Jesus, Brightness of the Father"

My home is my castle, so I am told, which means I can choose my guests and set the agenda for all who visit. One afternoon, two neatly dressed women came to my door. I invited them in, and they immediately asked whether I knew God's name. "Yes," I replied, "His name is Jehovah." The women smiled.

"I know His other name too," I continued without pausing. "It's Jesus." The women frowned.

With enthusiasm I told them how I had met Jesus in my youth, how I had received the gift of eternal life that He purchased for me on the cross, and how Jesus had blessed me with a family, church, and many friends. I told them how I longed for the day when Jesus would return.

My guests grew increasingly agitated before I asked whether I might pray with them. But when I ceased praying, they were gone, without so much as a good-bye.

Perhaps that was the wrong approach. I know it wasn't quite politically correct. But, after all, they came to my castle, a place God calls me to guard with due care.

*Help me, **Father,** to make my home a loving witness to Your grace but to refuse entry to any questioning of Your Son's deity, in Him I pray. Amen.*

All It Takes Is Water

He is like a tree planted by streams of water, which yields its fruit in season (Psalm 1:3).

Scripture: **Psalm 1**
Song: **"Lo! From the Desert Homes"**

A small raspberry patch flourishes close to our back door. For three weeks each summer it provides all the fresh fruit we want—plus pints of jam for the winter. My neighbors, who often struggle with their berries, wonder why my patch never fails.

Water is the secret. Sixty years ago, a small stream flowed through a ravine where three homes now stand, ours in the middle. The developer filled the ravine with red clay, but the stream draining the hillside had to go somewhere. As a result, our backyards have a high water table that requires sump pumps to protect our basements.

All summer, my neighbor's sump issues a gentle, clear flow near my berry patch. I capture the water in a plastic vat and a meandering seep hose directs it to my thirsty raspberry plants.

Like my neighbors, I cultivate, weed, and mulch the patch. I remove spent canes in autumn and stake new growth against the coming snow. But I have a steady supply of water, and my neighbors do not.

It makes me realize a truth of the Spirit: if you want unfailing kingdom fruit, stay close to the living water.

Heavenly Father, keep me close to the living water, that my life may bear fruit in its season. Through the name of Jesus I pray. Amen.

Do Something for the Lord

If a man remains in me and I in him, he will bear much fruit (John 15:5).

Scripture: **John 15:1-8**
Song: **"Servant of God, Well Done!"**

Roger Green spent his 79 years as a farmer, cabinet maker, truck driver, logger, and Alaskan gold miner. He was a kind man and my best friend. A craftsman with wood, he sang sweetly and played the accordion (poorly). He always considered himself a man of ordinary gifts. Again and again I heard him say, "I wish I could do something for the Lord!"

Roger died of cancer at home. Among the mourners who packed the large church to say good-bye was a group of Chinese students from the nearby university. The group included a young seminarian, one of several students who learned of Christ in Roger's home. For several years, Roger and his wife, Lois, had hosted a Chinese congregation guided by a missionary from Taiwan.

Roger did far more for the Lord than he knew. His eldest daughter became a career missionary to the country of Chad. And through the integrity of his person and hospitality of his home, scores of young nationals returned home to China with the gospel impressed upon their hearts.

All his life, Roger walked with God, offering the sacrament of friendship. I live with blessed memories.

Father, I desire a legacy of fruit-bearing at the end of my life. Remind me, each new day, that I must stay connected to Jesus, in whom I pray. Amen.

Tall Order Here

My command is this: Love each other as I have loved you. Greater love has no one than this, that he lay down his life for his friends (John 15:12, 13).

Scripture: **John 15:9-17**
Song: **"O Brother Man"**

A young woman, a stranger to me, entered our small church building one Sunday morning. She carried a smiling child, but I found it hard not to stare at the woman's scarred, disfigured face. A friend explained, "Those are love scars. She ran into their burning house to rescue her baby. It nearly cost her life."

Love can be costly, but cheap love is not the love taught in the Bible. We think of love primarily as a warm feeling, a desire to be close to the person of our affections. But that kind of love can be subtly self-serving.

Bible love, though it may well be infused with emotion, ultimately transcends feelings, deferring self-interest to meet the needs of others, no matter who they are or how they respond. That love enables us to reach out to those we may not like, even our enemies. Bible love surely includes sacrifice for those dear to us, and it also calls us to treat everyone in a Christlike manner, no matter how we feel. It's a tall order. But that's how Christian love works.

I know, Lord, that warm and affectionate love is perhaps life's greatest treasure. But the love You give keeps giving even when there is no other warmth. Help me to love that way today, for Your glory. I pray this prayer in the name of Jesus, my merciful Savior and Lord. Amen.

Marital Kindness

Make every effort to add to your faith goodness; and to goodness, knowledge; and to knowledge, self-control; and to self-control, perseverance; and to perseverance, godliness; and to godliness, brotherly kindness; and to brotherly kindness love (2 Peter 1:5-7).

Scripture: **2 Peter 1:5-11**
Song: **"We All Can Do Good"**

Cheryl was born prematurely 50 years ago before we had the miracle treatments preventing blindness in preemies. She's legally blind, yet she manages to play the piano beautifully and is so sweet that everyone loves her.

One day at a church dinner she set her soda on the floor by her chair and forgot it for a few minutes. When she stood up, her heel knocked the glass over, pouring the contents onto the floor. Her husband, Dave, cleaned up the mess without saying a word—and Cheryl never knew it.

In our passage today, Peter says Christians are "nearsighted and blind" (v. 9) unless they exhibit certain godly traits. When I saw Dave's actions, I thought of brotherly kindness. Amazing! Even in a marriage we can show that special kind of selfless love (a love that's beautiful, too, among all brothers and sisters in Christ).

Father, I can only express the virtues that You grow in my life through Your indwelling Spirit. Work in me today! Through Christ, amen.

February 26–28. **Audrey Hebbert**, freelance writer, lives in Omaha, Nebraska. Her *Dirt Bike Rider,* for kids ages 9–12, is published by Tweener Press.

Surprised by Love

Do not be overcome by evil, but overcome evil with good (Romans 12:21).

Scripture: **Romans 12:9-21**
Song: **"They That Overcome"**

I moved into this house one July 28 years ago, and within a month some "surprise lilies" bloomed—pink ones, with touches of blue on 15-inch stems that rose out of the lawn without any hint they had been hiding there. These old-fashioned darlings have been my favorites for all these years, and I've divided those first bulbs and planted them in all the flower beds for a showy display. In the spring the leaves appear, dark green and about 12 inches long, narrow, with a rounded tip. They die down in May, and I anticipate the August performance.

Could the apostle Paul have known about surprise lilies when he penned today's Scripture? These pink wonders rise from the earth without fail, regardless of what is growing around them, and their perfume sweetens the air. Their matchless beauty brightens the world because of their God-given nature. Paul begins this chapter with the secret to living out verses 9-21: Sink deep into God, be buried in Him as a living sacrifice. Seek Him above all, allowing the Holy Spirit to do His work in you that you may be transformed. Then from your nature will spring a goodness from God that will surely overcome evil.

Lord, I open my heart for the transforming power of Your work in me. Give me courage to confront evil—first, within myself. In Jesus' name, amen.

She Just Adores Him!

Clothe yourselves with the Lord Jesus Christ, and do not think about how to gratify the desires of the sinful nature (Romans 13:14).

Scripture: **Romans 13:8-14**
Song: **"Put Thou Thy Trust in God"**

Gwen is a small woman with beautiful blue eyes that twinkle with love for everyone she meets. She has traveled to many foreign countries on short-term mission trips. Today she talked to a young man as he walked his dog near her apartment building and asked him whether he knew Jesus. She also lovingly prepared a marvelous beef and vegetable lunch for me, though she had cataract surgery yesterday. Little children and adults alike know they are safe with Gwen because she fulfills the apostle's reminder in verse 9: "Love your neighbor as yourself."

I suppose Gwen never even thinks about the deeds of darkness mentioned in verses 12 and 13 of our Scripture today. From all I can tell, she has clothed herself with Christ, for He shines through her eyes and behavior. Her love reaches out to the Chinese restaurant owner who needs prayer and financial advice, to the missionary on furlough from Russia needing a home, to the temporarily unemployed man who has no food. I see all of the love flowing from Gwen, and I am inspired to lift my praises to this same Lord Jesus Christ whom she so clearly adores.

Lord, clothe me in the love of Your Son this day. Let me remember that I am His ambassador to every person I meet. In His name I pray. Amen.

My Prayer Notes

My Prayer Notes

My Prayer Notes

DEVOTIONS

*G*od is the
builder of
everything.

—Hebrews 3:4b

MARCH

Photo © Díamar

Gary Allen, Editor

Devotions® is published quarterly by Standard Publishing, 8121 Hamilton Avenue, Cincinnati, Ohio, 45231. A division of Standex International Corporation. © 2006 by Standard Publishing. All rights reserved. Topics based on the Home Daily Bible Readings, International Sunday School Lessons. © 2003 by the Committee on the Uniform Series. Printed in the U.S.A. All Scripture quotations, unless otherwise indicated, are taken from the HOLY BIBLE, NEW INTERNATIONAL VERSION®. NIV®. Copyright © 1973, 1978, 1984 by International Bible Society. Used by permission of Zondervan. All rights reserved. Where noted, Scripture quotations are from the following, used with permission of the copyright holders, all rights reserved. *King James Version, (KJV),* public domain.

Cute Habit, Holy Fruit

Since we live by the Spirit, let us keep in step with the Spirit
(Galatians 5:25).

Scripture: **Galatians 5:13-26**
Song: **"Guide Me, O Thou Great Jehovah"**

Ellie, age 2, and Gracie, 11 months, suffered one respiratory infection after another for three months. Every time Ellie coughed, her parents said, "Cover your mouth, Ellie." Then she placed her hand over her mouth. One day her parents noticed Gracie placing her own tiny, dimpled hand over her mouth, coughing, and pulling her hand away. Now she covers her mouth every time before she coughs.

Gracie's cute habit developed from the influence of her family around her. We individual believers are a reflection of our heavenly family too. Ellie and Gracie's parents instructed Ellie over and over, and the apostle Paul repeated commands like "serve one another in love" (v. 13) in every book he wrote. He also revealed the secret to this life: live by the Spirit, and the result will be love, along with eight other character traits, or fruit of the Spirit. So let us keep in step with the Holy Spirit. Walking with Him this way can become a blessed habit.

Dear God, help me to know how to keep in step with You today. I want to become all You want me to be, through the power of Your Spirit working within me. Through Christ I pray. Amen.

March 1–4. **Audrey Hebbert** is a freelance writer who contributes regularly to devotional periodicals. She lives in Omaha, Nebraska.

One Hundred Percent Sellout

To him be the glory and the power for ever and ever (1 Peter 4:11).

Scripture: **1 Peter 4:1-11**
Song: **"Glory Be to the Father"**

"Why are those people crying?" an American visitor to a Chinese church service asked the minister.

"They're sad because they have not been allowed to suffer for Christ," came the reply.

"Do you mean they *want* to be persecuted and suffer?" the visitor asked, astonished.

"In a sense, yes," replied the minister. "You see, they realize, in the depths of their being, how much Christ suffered for them; they want to give Him glory by suffering too as they live their lives in gratitude."

In verse 1 of our passage, Peter assumes that we will all suffer for Christ because He suffered for us. In the next verses Peter explains the formula for reaching that state where we are allowed to suffer for Christ. Our teacher explained it to our Sunday school class this way: "We are not in this for what we get out of it."

No, it's about what God gets out of it. Therefore, Peter reminds us in verse 11 of the motive for all Christian behavior, "that in all things God may be praised." He deserves all the glory and worship we can give Him.

Dear Heavenly Father, *I can do nothing without You. As I go about my day, let me depend upon Your guidance and wisdom each moment. In all I do, may I somehow demonstrate Your greatness. Through Christ, amen.*

To See or Not to See

Whoever loves his brother lives in the light, and there is nothing in him to make him stumble (1 John 2:7-10).

Scripture: **1 John 2:7-11**
Song: **"Here, O Lord, I See Thee"**

Chance was almost 3 when he discovered his eyelids. "It's dark!" he declared at the dinner table with his eyes squinted shut. "It's dark," he said, and collided with a chair as he crossed the dining room in his self-imposed night. "It's dark," he announced, when he tumbled off the sidewalk with his eyes closed and landed in the grass.

There are indeed times when it is dark, even as the sun shines brightly. John tells us that if we hate our brother, we're swirling around in the shadows. *Forgive him? You don't know what he did!*

John reminds his readers that the command to forgive first surfaced when unforgiveness killed Abel. But forgiveness is difficult! It's like having a car splash mud all over you, the driver roaring on his way, and your choosing to clean up the mess and get over it. Or . . . you let it be dark within; you remain mud-caked and angry.

The mud splasher won't care either way. The question is: would I rather walk in the light or stumble around in the darkness?

Lord, I need Your help to forgive when my heart feels the sting of unkind words and actions. Thank You for Your mercy and gentleness as I wrestle daily with forgiving those around me. In Christ I pray. Amen.

Finite Treasures

The world and its desires pass away, but the man who does the will of God lives forever (1 John 2:17).

Scripture: **1 John 2:12-17**
Song: **"Lead Me to Calvary"**

John Wesley, great preacher of heart-deep discipleship, serves even today as an example of the Christian walk. One day his house burned down, and he was soon quietly thankful. "Now I have fewer worldly things to concern me," he said. "I can spend more time serving God."

A modern-day writer echoed John Wesley's sentiments when she said, "When I stand before the King of the Universe, He won't ask me what I owned on this earth, but how I treated His Son." And I heard a minister instruct his TV audience to "create an atmosphere within them that God can dwell in comfortably." His insight, too, seemed to echo John Wesley's desire to please God.

But they are all simply reiterating the most basic message about our relationship with God, the principle John stated so long ago: daily we are becoming a certain sort of person—one oriented primarily to the things of the world, or one whose loves and cares center in the will of the great lover of our souls.

I would be sad if my house were to burn down. But I hope, at least, I would come to see that even my home is a finite treasure, small in the light of God's eternal will.

Father, I'm often tempted to follow the culture with my choices. But may my decisions today please only You. Thank You, in Jesus' name. Amen.

The Three Tenors

These three remain: faith, hope and love. But the greatest of these is love (1 Corinthians 13:13).

Scripture: **1 Corinthians 13**
Song: **"Your Love Compels Me"**

Placido Domingo, Jose Carreras, and Luciano Pavarotti— together they're known as the three tenors. And now you know everything I know about opera. My musical ability stops with playing the radio, but somewhere I heard those three famous names, so, for me, they always go together.

I do know that music basically has three parts that work together too—melody, rhythm, and harmony. When put together artistically, the result is pleasing to the ear.

The Bible tells us of another three: faith, hope, and love. Faith, like rhythm, controls the speed in my life. Hope, like harmony, is the blend, or color. Love, like a melody, makes my life flow. When I practice all three, my life produces a concert that demonstrates just how good the Lord is to His children. Yet without love, faith and hope are nothing more than senseless clatter, an opera with no story, an orchestra with no violins.

Father in Heaven, *I give You my life as a blank sheet of music. I want to be more than noise to those around me. I pray You will compose faith, hope, and love into my spirit and make me into something pleasing to Your ears. In the name of Your Son, my Savior, I pray. Amen.*

March 5–11. Originally from Nashville, Tennessee, **Kevin Riggs** now ministers in west central Arkansas. He is married to his high school sweetheart, Misty.

New Approach to Love

A new command I give you: Love one another. As I have loved you, so you must love one another (John 13:34).

Scripture: **John 13:31-35**
Song: **"Shine, Jesus, Shine"**

I remember when the governor of Tennessee announced plans for a new car company to be located in a small town outside Nashville where I lived and ministered. I was there when Saturn Corporation set up shop.

Saturn advertised itself as being a "different kind of car company." I didn't see much *difference*, though, in the cars themselves. Was the company being dishonest? No, the difference they were trying to achieve had to do with the basic approach to organizational structure and function. Theirs was a typical car in look and design, but the company was "dedicated to finding ways for people *to work together* to design, build, and sell cars."

When Jesus told His disciples He had a "new command," it really wasn't a *different* command. After all, God had always commanded His people to live in love for one another. The newness was in the basic approach. The old way called for loving others as you wanted to be loved. The new command was to love others the way Jesus loves you—unconditionally, sacrificially. No one had been commanded to love that way before, but that is how He wants us to love. It's a brand new approach.

O Lord, thank You for loving me the way You do. And may my love for others convince them You are real. I pray these things in Jesus' name. Amen.

The Unknown Lady

They all gave out of their wealth; but she, out of her poverty, put in everything—all she had to live on (Mark 12:44).

Scripture: **Mark 12:38-44**
Song: **"We Are an Offering"**

Hundreds of people lined up outside the gates. Children with dirty faces squeezed their heads through the bars to get a closer look. Moms and dads, wearing tattered clothes, showing tired eyes, waited patiently. All, hoping against hope, stood in line to see the doctor.

The makeshift clinic had been set up within a church in Tegucigalpa, Honduras. The people waiting were the poorest of the poor, and some stood there in the hot sun for more than 10 hours.

Near the end of the day, though, something wonderful occurred.

One of the volunteer medical workers gave a piece of bread to a lady who looked like she had not eaten in days. Instead of eating, she broke the bread into smaller pieces, handing them to as many people as she could. As far as I know, she didn't save a single piece for herself. For me, witnessing the scene brought today's Scripture to life. The unknown lady gave out of her poverty. She gave everything. She gave all she had to live on.

Oh God, please forgive me for being selfish. Help me be a giver instead of a taker. May I always be sensitive to the needs around me, and may I give all that I have in service to You and to others. In Jesus' name I pray. Amen.

The Great Bimini Wall

How great is the love the Father has lavished on us, that we should be called children of God! (1 John 3:1).

Scripture: **1 John 3:1-5**
Song: **"Jesus, Lover of My Soul"**

In the Atlantic Ocean, 40 miles off the coast of Miami, Florida, south of Bimini, lies the great Bimini Wall. The Bimini Wall faces the Gulf Stream, starts in 120 feet of water, and drops 1,000 or so feet straight to the bottom of the ocean. Scuba diving along the wall is an exhilarating experience. At about 80 feet, you swim through a beautiful coral reef system, full of aquatic life. Look carefully into the distance and you might see a hammerhead shark. At the edge of the reef is the beginning of the wall. At 120 feet, you can look over the wall—into total darkness. Looking down into the pit is one of the eeriest things I have ever done.

As I was swimming along the reef, looking over into that great chasm, it hit me. My sins are buried at the bottom! God lavished His love on me by sending Jesus to die on the cross so I could be forgiven. He has taken my sins and cast them into the sea of forgetfulness. I now have a visual picture of what that sea looks like. Not only are my sins at the bottom, so are yours; and that is why we can be called the children of God.

Oh gracious Heavenly Father, words are not enough to express how thankful I am for Your love, mercy, and grace. You have forgiven me of my sins. You have adopted me into Your family, making me Your child. I am humbled and speechless. I love You. What more can I say? Amen.

Heavenly Rescue

No one who is born of God will continue to sin, because God's seed remains in him; he cannot go on sinning, because he has been born of God (1 John 3:9).

Scripture: 1 John 3:6-10
Song: "There Is a Redeemer"

As a child I loved the TV show *Gilligan's Island.* So imagine my dismay as an adult when I considered a possible connection between the characters and the traditional "seven deadly sins." Think about it: those sins shipwreck us, keeping us captive on our own little islands.

What's the connection? Gilligan's *laziness* caused the group to become castaways in the first place. Ginger used *lust* to her advantage. Mrs. Howell was often in a *rage* at anyone who didn't meet her demands. The professor knew he was the smartest, and his *pride* clearly showed. Mary Ann never measured up to the glamour of Ginger, leading her to an *envious* spirit, while the Skipper apparently never missed a chance to exercise . . . a little *gluttony.* And Mr. Howell? What better illustration of *greed* than a man who takes a trunk of money on a three-hour tour?

Through three years and 98 episodes, these seven castaways couldn't escape their tropical prison. Likewise, our sins, no matter how beautiful the scenery, can keep us captive forever. But it doesn't have to be that way. Thanks be to God, His Son came to the rescue!

Dear Father, because I am Your child, I have been rescued from continuous sinning. I seek to please You today in all things. Through Christ, amen.

No Surprise Here!

Do not be surprised, my brothers, if the world hates you (1 John 3:13).

Scripture: **1 John 3:11-15**
Song: **"Dear Lord, for All in Pain"**

Sergej Besserab grew up on the mean streets of Tajikistan in the former Soviet Union. A tough street fighter and hardened criminal, he was arrested five times, spending 18 years in prison before giving his life to Christ in 1996.

After his release, Sergej felt called to start a church in the city of Isfara. He and his wife bought a dilapidated house, converted the living room into a small chapel, and planted the first church in that part of the world.

But not everyone was happy about this. The local newspaper started printing "hit piece" articles about Sergej, his church, and his former life of crime. "There is no place in Isfara for Sergej and those like him," said the articles. And then someone accepted an implied challenge to stop the young church. On Monday evening, January 12, 2004, while Sergej prayed inside the small chapel, a masked assailant gunned him down. Nevertheless, the church continues to this day.

Sadly, Sergej Besserab's story isn't unique. Every day believers across the world are persecuted for their faith. Every day the world shows its animosity toward those who love Christ. But are you surprised?

Lord, I pray for my brothers and sisters across the world who suffer because of their faith. May we all stand strong together. Through Christ, amen.

Swing Set Discipleship

If anyone has material possessions and sees his brother in need but has no pity on him, how can the love of God be in him? (1 John 3:17).

Scripture: **1 John 3:16-24**
Song: **"The Servant Song"**

"Wow, Daddy!" exclaimed my 4-year old daughter. "Now I have two swing sets in my backyard."

"Yeah, isn't that great?" I replied, wiping sweat from my face. "I guess so," she said, less than enthusiastically.

I had just finished putting together my second swing set in two years. (Why does it take so many nuts and bolts to assemble those things?) As I placed my tools back in the shed, I could tell my daughter had something on her mind. "Katherine, what's wrong?" I asked.

"Well, I've got two swing sets," she thoughtfully answered. "But my friend Jimmy, who lives down the street, doesn't have any in his backyard. Do you think I could give him one of mine?"

Later that afternoon, my wife and I (and Katherine too) picked up the smaller swing set and carried it down to Jimmy's house. I don't know who was more excited— Katherine, about giving a wonderful gift, or Jimmy, about getting his first swing set. Wait! I was the most excited of all, seeing my daughter teach me how to be a practical disciple of Jesus.

Lord, all good things in my life have come from Your hand. Help me share them with a cheerful heart, at a moment's notice. In Jesus' name, amen.

Whiner or Winner?

We also rejoice in our sufferings, because we know that suffering produces perseverance (Romans 5:3).

Scripture: **Romans 5:1-11**
Song: **"Praise Him! Praise Him!"**

I thought I was a strong person, but I soon learned differently. A friend had invited me to her exercise class, and after just a couple visits, I developed significant soreness. The instructor's take on the situation? "You're finding your weak points," she said. "Just keep working, and your endurance will improve over time."

My goal was to be slimmer and stronger, but discomfort wasn't part of the plan! I became discouraged and began grumbling, until I realized: I have a choice; I can be a whiner or be a winner. The instructor encouraged me to focus on the hoped-for results, not the temporary pain.

Any of us can grow weary of the pain that comes with life's trials. And it's always tempting to complain and look for the easy way out. Paul tells us in Romans 5, though to stay the course and allow the tough times to strengthen our weaknesses. Then one day our reward will be to share in God's glory. That's what I call winning!

God, I'm grateful for the many ways You encourage me each day. When I focus on the struggles, though, help me recognize their perseverance—producing potential. And keep my eyes always on You, the one who provides strength for the journey. I pray through my deliverer, Jesus. Amen.

March 12–18. **Connie Coppings** is a minister's wife and freelance writer in Nicholasville, Kentucky. She enjoys playing the piano, cooking, and gardening.

Settle, and Stay Close

Settle matters quickly with your adversary who is taking you to court. Do it while you are still with him on the way, or he may hand you over to the judge (Matthew 5:25).

Scripture: **Matthew 5:21-26**
Song: **"Moment by Moment"**

Ralph Waldo Emerson said, "For every minute you're angry, you lose 60 seconds of happiness." And we know that, if left unresolved, anger can lead to physical and emotional ill health. Suppressed anger is often the culprit behind headaches, stomach disorders, elevated blood pressure, and even heart attacks. So why would someone hold onto this destructive emotion?

I worked as a counselor for several years, and I was amazed at how much time and energy people devoted to keeping anger alive. One client remarked, "I like the feeling of power my rage gives me." A minor disagreement had sparked his initial anger, but years later it had become a raging inferno.

Admitting to God when we're wrong is the first step to our freedom. Then we can move forward and "settle matters" with our fellow human beings. Jesus points to the very practical results of taking action with our anger. It may well keep us out of jail; it will definitely keep us closer to Him.

O Lord, forgive me for the times I've allowed anger to control my words and actions, making an adversary of a potential friend. May my heart be filled with Your love each minute of this day. In the name of Jesus, amen.

Love That Serves

Jesus said, "Simon son of John, do you truly love me?" He answered, "Yes, Lord, you know that I love you." Jesus said, "Take care of my sheep" (John 21:16).

Scripture: **John 21:15-19**
Song: **"I Will Serve Thee"**

I held my nephews and niece when they were just a few days old. My heart felt such love for them, and I prayed they would grow up to be followers of Jesus Christ. I told them "I love you" many times, but it was important they see those words in action as they grew. I spent time with them, attended significant events in their lives, and supported their dreams over the years.

Our Scripture today shows Peter affirming his love for Jesus with strong words. Three times he was questioned; each time he replied, "You know that I love you." Jesus' response in each instance seems to ask a deeper question, however: "You say the words, Peter, but are you willing to demonstrate their truth through service to me?"

We love many things, don't we? We love our favorite team, we love our pets, we love chocolate, and we love recognition. But if we wish to know what it means to love Jesus, we can always go back to His masterful ever-so-direct description. It's simple, really: "Take care of my sheep."

Gracious God, I am humbled by the depth of love You exercised in the sacrifice of Your own beloved Son for me. Please help my love today reflect the one who first loved me. In the name of my precious Savior I pray. Amen.

Love That Shares

Command them to do good, to be rich in good deeds, and to be generous and willing to share (1 Timothy 6:18).

Scripture: **1 Timothy 6:11-19**
Song: **"Give of Your Best to the Master"**

Have we forgotten the word *share?* It seems most messages coming from the media these days tell me, "You deserve it all; deny yourself nothing." Maybe that's why storage containers fill my closets and garage. Do I look to these things for a sense of security?

We share anytime we give our time, labor, or possessions; however, when we add a grateful heart to our actions, we come closest to the command of Scripture in our passage today. Knowing that God feeds us, we can offer meals to the hungry; knowing He shelters us, we can work to build someone else a home. One Christian woman even gave her kidney, knowing that a friend would shortly be without any!

I am so thankful that God has shared His love in the gift of His Son to me. What better example of what it means to share? And what better motivation to switch off the television commercials for a while and close those ad-filled magazines pages? They promise me security—if only I will get that next precious bauble. God tells me my greatest happiness comes through giving.

Gracious Lord, I know You can use only what I'm willing to share. So give me a grateful and generous heart. Keep my eyes on the security that comes in knowing You. In the name of my Savior, Jesus Christ, amen.

Best of Both Worlds

Dear friends, let us love one another, for love comes from God. Everyone who loves has been born of God and knows God. Whoever does not love does not know God, because God is love (1 John 4:7, 8).

Scripture: **1 John 4:7-12**
Song: **"The Bond of Love"**

I loved receiving gifts as a child. I thought about them even before I received them; and once I opened them, I would spend countless hours playing with my new things. Occasionally, one of my sisters would show interest in what I had, and "sisterly love" would be put to the test.

In the church, we are brothers and sisters in Christ, and our relationships there, too, are often tested. But God is love, and He calls us to be loving with one another.

A wonderful way to express our love for fellow believers is to pray for them—whether they know we're doing so or not. It actually treats them with the kind of personal regard that God holds toward us. Writer Richard Foster put it like this in *Celebration of Discipline*: "We do not pray for people as 'things' but as 'persons' whom we love. If we have God-given compassion and concern for others, our faith will grow and strengthen as we pray."

So . . . we can exercise love while strengthening our own faith? To me, this is the best of both worlds!

Lord, show me any unloving attitudes I may be holding toward my brothers and sisters in Christ. You have bestowed your loving acceptance upon me; help me do the same for those around me. In Christ's name, amen.

Family Resemblance

Love is made complete among us so that we will have confidence on the day of judgment, because in this world we are like him (1 John 4:17).

Scripture: **1 John 4:13-17**
Song: **"O Perfect Love"**

From the day I was born, people have commented on how much I look like my father. At reunions and other family get-togethers, people would say, "You are so much like your dad!" He was a humble Christian, and I was proud to be identified with him. His words and actions demonstrated his love for me, and I found great confidence in them. Long after his death, that love continues to affect my life.

I've counseled with people who tell me they can't remember anyone ever telling them they were loved. How sad! Like a garden without water, they struggle to grow and become what God would have them be. Because they can't seem to feel themselves beloved, they have trouble extending love to others.

Each day we come in contact with people longing to be shown they are valued—longing, really, to have a glimpse of the loving God. Thankfully, as "adopted" children of God's family (see Ephesians 1:5), we can show them what the Father is like in our words and deeds. We simply express our family resemblance.

O God, I grieve for those who feel unloved. Make my heart a vessel of Your love, pouring out to those in need. Through Christ, amen.

God's Perfect Love

There is no fear in love. But perfect love drives out fear, because fear has to do with punishment. The one who fears is not made perfect in love (1 John 4:18).

Scripture: 1 John 4:18-21
Song: "O How I Love Jesus"

My husband and I said vows on our wedding day, promising to love each other "in sickness and health, for richer or poorer." In other words, we'd try to act lovingly, no matter what was happening in our lives. Over the years, I've noticed our love flowing within words of encouragement, through special cards, or in smiles that convey "I believe in you."

When difficult times arise, we try to talk things through. Having built our relationship on love and respect, we can approach each other without fear. No, our love isn't perfect, but our marriage is in the hands of God, the one with perfect love for us.

Romans 5:8 says, "While we were still sinners, Christ died for us." How radical—to be loved *before* I'm able to be lovable! He allows me the freedom to approach Him, confess my sin, and know that I have no reason to fear His rejection. God does that for us and calls us to do our best at treating one another just that way. Which makes me wonder: am I waiting for anyone in my world to "clean up first" before I'll treat him or her with kindness?

Father, *I need never fear to coming before You in my sinfulness. You came for just my type of person—the imperfect ones! In Jesus' name, amen.*

Am I a Living Lure?

Come ye after me, and I will make you to become fishers of men (Mark 1:17, *King James Version*).

Scripture: **Mark 1:16-20**
Song: **"I Want to Be More Like You"**

This verse reminds me of an advertisement I saw for rattling fishing lures that glow in the dark. Fish come to such a lure from far away because they can hear and see the lure. In similar fashion, as Christian "fishers of men," our lives must provide a stark contrast to the world around us. In fact, our words and actions ought to reflect those of Christ himself. The apostles spent time with Jesus and opened their hearts to Him that He might become a part of their lives. As a result of Christ living in them, thousands were drawn to a new life.

We, too, can spend quality time with Jesus. He has placed us in a darkened world to be a shining light for Him, a glowing lure. So today I'll pause to consider: is my life attractive to the seekers around me? Are people drawn to me—to Christ in me—when they long for truth? Oh, may my life glow with His radiating love!

Dear God, *help me reflect Your life and Your love, not in any forced or phony way, not with superspiritual platitudes, but in all genuineness with a real willingness to listen, to care, to reach out with practical encouragement. In all of this, may You be glorified. I pray this prayer in the name of Jesus, my Savior and Lord. Amen.*

March 19–25. **Barb Haley** is a teacher and freelance writer who lives with her husband in San Antonio, Texas.

Biblical Bookkeeping

For God so loved the world, that he gave his only begotten Son, that whosoever believeth in him should not perish, but have everlasting life (John 3:16, *King James Version*).

Scripture: **John 3:16-21**
Song: **"Beneath the Cross of Jesus"**

A Christian young man worked as a banker in the days when accounts were kept by hand in a big leather ledger. One day this banker thought about God's Book of Life and imagined a page with his name at the top. As he watched God total the sum of his sins, he realized he could never pay the debt.

But God promptly took the pen and transferred the complete debt to the account of Jesus Christ. Thinking God was finished, the banker was further amazed when God proceeded to credit his account with the total righteousness of Jesus Christ (see Philippians 3:9).

Love can mean so many things in our world today. But God's love goes beyond all we can imagine, for His love calls us to be what we could never become on our own—a perfect creature in the likeness of His Son. And since we can't produce that marvelous work by our own effort, He gives us His indwelling Spirit to accomplish it, from beginning to end.

No, we will not perish but have everlasting life. Because He loves us just that much.

God, I'm amazed at the work You've done for me and also within me. Let its excellence shine through in my world today! Through Christ, amen.

Soli Deo Gloria

I have glorified thee on the earth: I have finished the work which thou gavest me to do (John 17:4, *King James Version*).

Scripture: **John 17:1-5**
Song: **"Lord, Prepare Me to Be a Sanctuary"**

Johann Sebastian Bach, the famous composer, once said, "All music should have no other end and aim than the glory of God and the soul's refreshment." The titles of his works usually began with "J.J." (*Jesus Juva*, the Latin for "Jesus, help me") and ended with "S.D.G." (*Soli Deo Gloria*, or "to God alone, the glory"). Bach apparently didn't consider his compositions to be his work alone. He prayed for God's help and then gave credit where credit was due. Really, what do any of us have to offer God that God hasn't already given us?

The situation reminds me of a small child who wishes to buy her father a birthday present. She innocently asks for the money and later joyfully delivers the gift. In the same way we can joyfully return to God the fruits of all His goodness toward us, the exercise of all the gifts He's given. It doesn't matter whether we travel as missionaries or clean office buildings or write beautiful orchestral pieces. Let us make our goal one thing on this earth: to finish the work He gave us to do.

Father, Your Son, Jesus, lived to glorify You, and that is how I also wish to live. I offer my time, my talents, and my will for Your use. Work through me to accomplish the tasks You have set before me. And bless the work of my hands that it might lead others to You. In Christ's name I pray. Amen.

What a Start!

If the Spirit of him that raised up Jesus from the dead dwell in you, he that raised up Christ from the dead shall also quicken your mortal bodies by his Spirit that dwelleth in you (Romans 8:11, *King James Version*).

Scripture: **Romans 8:9-17**
Song: **"Bring Your Vessels, Not a Few"**

A missionary tells of being given a car that wouldn't start without being pushed. For two years, the man enlisted neighborhood children to get the car going and then had to either park on a hill or leave his engine running once he got the car started.

When it came time for the missionary to move on, he passed the car on to the man who would take his place. The new owner promptly looked under the hood, tightened an engine cable, and started the car with no problem at all. For two years, the power had been there, and only a loose connection had kept the missionary from putting it to work.

Paul says the same powerful Spirit who raised Christ from the dead dwells within us even now. The Holy Spirit enables us to put to death all those impulses that work against His will and frustrate our own joy. By this Spirit—and only through Him—we've gotten our start in God's kingdom. Now we can move forward with Him always.

Dear Father, *You sent Your Spirit to empower me for the life You've called me to live. Thank You in the name of Jesus, my Savior. Amen.*

Daddy Will Carry It

Because ye are sons, God hath sent forth the Spirit of his Son into your hearts, crying, Abba, Father (Galatians 4:6, *King James Version*).

Scripture: **Galatians 4:1-7**
Song: **"I Know Whom I Have Believed"**

Young Corrie ten Boom once asked her father, "What is sex sin?" Not answering, he instructed her to carry his case—full of watches and spare parts. "It's too heavy," Corrie responded.

"Yes," he said. "And it would be a pretty poor father who'd ask his little girl to carry such a load. It's the same way, Corrie, with knowledge. Some knowledge is too heavy for children. When you're older and stronger, you can bear it. For now you must trust me to carry it for you."

"I was more than satisfied," Corrie remembers. "Wonderfully at peace. There were answers to this and all my hard questions. But now I was content to leave them in my father's keeping."

Life is tough, and our minds often swirl with questions for *Abba,* our "Daddy" in Heaven. *Why don't You heal me? Why did You let her die? Why don't You help me find a job?*

God carries the answers. He loves us; He knows our limits. Could we leave our heavy questions for a moment today and simply relax in His presence?

Abba, I come to You as a child—full of questions, doubts, and worries. Fill me with Your peace as I surrender them all to You. Through Christ, amen.

Stable Priorities, Changing World

This is love for God: to obey his commands (1 John 5:3).

Scripture: **1 John 5:1-6**
Song: **"Change My Heart, O God"**

When Truett Cathy opened his first Chick-fil-A restaurants during the days of segregation, he disregarded public opinion and hired employees without racial consideration. Doing the right thing was important to him.

"I believe the Bible to be a road map for our life and a blueprint for our life, and we could do very well to not only read the Bible, but put the Bible into practice," Cathy says. Today he does just that. Forfeiting millions of dollars, he closes all 1,200 of his restaurants every Sunday, believing the day ought to be reserved for rest rather than business.

"I'd like to be remembered," he says, "as one who kept my priorities in the right order. We live in a changing world, but we need to be reminded that the important things have not changed, and the important things *will* not change if we keep our priorities in proper order."

John the apostle tells us that we show God our love by obedience, even in a changing world that demands our time and attention. As for me, I'm inspired to take a minute sometime today to examine my priorities.

Heavenly Father, do continue to speak to me through Your Word, revealing areas in my life that I have not yet surrendered to You. Transform my heart and make me what You created me to be. In the holy name of Jesus, my Lord and Savior, I pray. Amen.

Yes, You May Know

I write these things to you who believe in the name of the Son of God so that you may know that you have eternal life (1 John 5:13).

Scripture: **1 John 5:7-13**
Song: **"How Can We Sinners Know?"**

I looked at the question again. "Would you go to Heaven if you died today?" The answers included *Yes, No,* and *I'm not sure.* A seventh-grader in a parochial school, I had become a Christian years before. I loved God and tried to keep His commands. But was that enough? Marking my answer, I turned in my test.

I'll never forget that day. All but two of the students had marked *I'm not sure.* My teacher walked us through the Scriptures. "We are all sinners in need of God's grace," she said. "God is so good! He provided for our forgiveness through the death of His own Son, Jesus." After a little more explanation, she concluded by reciting our Scripture verse for today, stressing the KNOW.

We prayed a prayer of thanks and belief. Then we wrote the following in the covers of our Bibles: "I rededicate my life to Christ today. I believe He is the Son of God. Therefore, I now have eternal life. If I were to die today, I would spend eternity with my Lord and Savior."

Dear God, Your grace is unfathomable, too much for me to comprehend. Yet in the waters of baptism, You have extended it to me with all the benefits of forgiveness and acceptance in Your family. How I praise You in this moment of quietness! In the name of Jesus, Son of God, I pray. Amen.

A "Living" Stone?

As you come to him, the living Stone—rejected by men but chosen by God and precious to him—you also, like living stones, are being built into a spiritual house to be a holy priesthood, offering spiritual sacrifices acceptable to God through Jesus Christ (1 Peter 2:4, 5).

Scripture: **1 Peter 2:4-10**
Song: **"Because He Lives"**

As a child, I felt so important sitting by my father in his old Ford dump truck. Having made arrangements with retired farm owners, Pa rumbled up dirt roads, backed up to crumbled stone walls, and loaded the rocks he later sold to masons and builders. New England is stone-wall country, and I still enjoy driving scenic Route 169, passing one wall after another.

The first epistle of Peter (whose name Simon, Jesus changed to Rock), reminds me of my native rocky countryside, especially when I read the words "living stones." But I wonder, isn't that a contradiction in terms?

Upon closer inspection, however, I realize: it's all about Jesus! He is the one who rose from the dead, alive forevermore. Knowing Him as my Savior and Lord, living my daily life in His love and power, I too become a "living stone."

Gracious Father, *today keep me aware of my identity in the living Lord Jesus. For I pray in His name, with all thankfulness. Amen.*

March 26–March 31. Having retired from 30 years of classroom teaching, **Blanche Gosselin** is now "refired" in the areas of prayer, Bible teaching, and writing.

Builder at Work

Every house is built by someone, but God is the builder of everything (Hebrews 3:4).

Scripture: **Hebrews 3:1-6**
Song: **"His Name Is Wonderful"**

"We've decided to build our retirement home now, while we're young and able to make the mortgage payments," my nephew told me. He and his wife had found the right builder and eagerly anticipated the completion of their dream house.

The Bible has a lot to say about houses. The prophet Nathan assures David, "The LORD himself will establish a house for you" (2 Samuel 7:11). "Unless the LORD builds the house, its builders labor in vain," states Psalm 127:1. And Hebrews 3:4 tells us that God is a builder—"the builder of everything."

In the Bible the word *house* sometimes refers to a building; elsewhere it means a household, a community of people related by blood or common responsibilities. In our passage, "God's house" refers to His obedient children.

That's where you and I come in. Jesus was a faithful Son over God's house, carrying out the Father's plan of salvation. He began a new family, God's household of redeemed believers. As we fix our thoughts on Jesus, we gain much more than a dream house. The heavenly home awaiting us is more real than anything in the world.

Master Builder, I fix my heart on Jesus, knowing You will complete in me what You've begun. All praise to You, in Christ's name. Amen.

Embarrassing? No!

When the chief priests and the teachers of the law saw the wonderful things he did and the children shouting in the temple area, "Hosanna to the Son of David," they were indignant (Matthew 21:15).

Scripture: **Matthew 21:14-17**
Song: **"Hosanna, Loud Hosanna"**

For years Rita taught first grade. Whenever we met for lunch, she'd regale me with stories of student antics. Being quite creative, Rita devised all kinds of learning fun and also used her own brand of time out. In a corner, hidden by an upright piano, was a small stool; any offender knew that to sit there, away from all activity, was just no fun.

One day the school supervisor, Mrs. Jordan, visited Rita's class. All seemed to go well, and Rita felt she had passed the test. Then, as the visitor prepared to leave, one little, squeaky voice piped up from the corner: "Mrs. Jordan, I bet you don't know who's behind the piano."

Children can be embarrassing at times. But Jesus didn't seem to mind. "Let the little children come to me, and do not hinder them, for the kingdom of heaven belongs to such as these," He said (Matthew 19:14). As He entered Jerusalem on a humble mount, how pleased Jesus must have been to hear jubilant "hosannas" ring from the lips of innocent children, their praise a far cry from the indignation of His religious enemies.

Father God, Your Son called us to humble ourselves as little children. By Your grace, initiate that change of heart in me. In Christ I pray. Amen.

Marvelous Mercy (for Losers)

The stone the builders rejected has become the capstone; the LORD has done this, and it is marvelous in our eyes (Psalm 118:22, 23).

Scripture: **Psalm 118:21-28**
Song: **"Praise to the Lord, the Almighty"**

It was our final high school men's basketball game. Two county rivals tied for . . . last place. Only a few seconds to go, with the scoreboard showing the game tied up at 50 points each. But all of our starters had fouled out! On the court: pigeon-toed, undersized Kevin and his lackluster second-stringers.

Suddenly, the ball flew high into the air, right into Kevin's upraised hands. A little lay-up—the winning basket! I still remember the uncontrolled applause as Kevin's teammates hoisted him into the locker room.

That unforgettable scene taught me something important about appearances and reality. Jesus, the capstone, was never a second-stringer, but He did know the pain of rejection. Yet He accomplished the most awesome feat in cosmic history—the salvation of the lost . . . of the losers.

When I consider this amazing reality, my heart swells with thanksgiving. Every day becomes a marvelous mercy in my eyes.

Gracious Heavenly Father, thank You for providing in Jesus the perfect capstone for the building of Your kingdom. May I never take for granted the marvelous accomplishment of Your divine deeds on my behalf. I pray this prayer in the name of Jesus, my Savior and Lord. Amen.

Why a Donkey?

Those who were sent ahead went and found it just as he had told them. As they were untying the colt, its owners asked them, "Why are you untying the colt?" They replied, "The Lord needs it" (Luke 19:32-34).

Scripture: **Luke 19:28-34**
Song: **"I Surrender All"**

Do you see the rich symbolism here? We might ask, after all, why Jesus would enter Jerusalem—for His final week on earth—riding an unused, unbroken donkey. Why not choose a strong horse, emblem of might and honor, the mount of kings, officials, and generals?

Yet Jesus himself planned His entrance into the holy city, and in so doing, He fulfilled prophecy: "Rejoice greatly, O Daughter of Zion! Shout, Daughter of Jerusalem! See, your king comes to you, righteous and having salvation, gentle and riding on a donkey, on a colt, the foal of a donkey" (Zechariah 9:9).

The meaning? Horses represented war; Jesus was coming to restore peace between creator and wayward creatures. He needed the donkey, but many onlookers missed the point. They expected a warlike leader to free them from Roman rule.

Of course, Jesus is often "missed," going unrecognized in our lives. Let us turn to Him in this moment. He's right here with His peace.

God of Peace, let me bring Your Word to others, not in a spirit of conflict, but with the mind of the prince of peace. In His name I pray. Amen.

Give, or Sleep?

They brought it to Jesus, threw their cloaks on the colt and put Jesus on it. As he went along, people spread their cloaks on the ground (Luke 19:35, 36).

Scripture: **Luke 19:35-40**
Song: **"Give Me Thy Heart"**

In biblical times, the cloak served as an essential outer garment—usually a large square of cloth with two arm-holes—worn over other clothing. An average person owned only one such precious wrap. "If you take your neighbor's cloak as a pledge, return it to him by sunset, because his cloak is the only covering he has for his body. What else will he sleep in?" (Exodus 22:26, 27).

I imagine the crowd as Jesus enters Jerusalem: those who fetched the requested donkey throw their cloaks upon it and help Jesus mount. The procession moves on; people spread their cloaks on the road before Him. . . .

I want to call out, "Wait a minute! Think about what you're doing. You're going to need that cloak to keep warm this very night!"

Nevertheless, this throng of disciples "began joyfully to praise God in loud voices for all the miracles they had seen: 'Blessed is the king who comes in the name of the Lord!'" (vv. 37, 38). So I ponder: is there indeed more joy in selfless, sacrificial giving than in a comfortable night's sleep?

God of Heaven, serving You wholeheartedly because of who You are is the greatest joy of my life. I praise You in Christ's name. Amen.

DEVOTIONS®

*T*hose who
seek the LORD
lack no good
thing.

—Psalm 34:10

APRIL

Photo © Díamar

Gary Allen, Editor

Devotions® is published quarterly by Standard Publishing, 8121 Hamilton Avenue, Cincinnati, Ohio, 45231. A division of Standex International Corporation. © 2006 by Standard Publishing. All rights reserved. Topics based on the Home Daily Bible Readings, International Sunday School Lessons. © 2003 by the Committee on the Uniform Series. Printed in the U.S.A. All Scripture quotations, unless otherwise indicated, are taken from the HOLY BIBLE, NEW INTERNATIONAL VERSION®. NIV®. Copyright © 1973, 1978, 1984 by International Bible Society. Used by permission of Zondervan. All rights reserved. Where noted, Scripture quotations are from the following, used with permission of the copyright holders, all rights reserved: *King James Version (KJV)*, public domain. *New American Standard Bible (NASB)*, © 1960, 1962, 1963, 1968, 1971, 1972 The Lockman Foundation. *The New King James Version (NKJV)*, Copyright © 1982 by Thomas Nelson, Inc.

The First and the Last

"I am the Alpha and the Omega," says the Lord God, **"who is, and who was, and who is to come, the Almighty"** (Revelation 1:8).

Scripture: **Revelation 1:1-8**
Song: **"Jesus Is Coming Again"**

Exiled on the island of Patmos, John received from God a prophetic vision: the revelation of, and from, Jesus Christ. John assures all believers: "Blessed is the one who reads the words of this prophecy, and blessed are those who hear it and take to heart what is written in it, because the time is near" (v. 3). The book of Revelation centers on the sovereignty of God, on the primacy of Jesus, and on the certain judgment God will execute on all evil—including Satan himself.

In our passage today, using the imagery of the first and the last letters of the Greek alphabet, Jesus declares that He is the beginning and the end, the originator and the consummator, of all things. Therefore, I can rely on His powerful presence, now and in the future. Such knowledge is almost too wonderful for me to grasp! In silence, I meditate on this truth, sincerely thanking the divine author and finisher of my faith.

Lord, grant me a thirst to know more fully the alpha and the omega of my life. And guide me each day, in wisdom and love, as I await the coming of Your glorious kingdom. Through the Lord Jesus Christ, I pray. Amen.

April 1. Having retired from 30 years of classroom teaching, **Blanche Gosselin** is now "refired" in the areas of prayer, Bible teaching, and writing.

Bread for Life

He took bread, gave thanks and broke it, and gave it to them, saying, "This is my body given for you; do this in remembrance of me" (Luke 22:19).

Scripture: **Luke 22:7-23**
Song: **"We Plow the Fields and Scatter"**

Because I live in a city, I rarely think about the origin of the food that ends up on my local supermarket shelves. Two years ago, however, on a summer train trip to Wisconsin, I had ample opportunity to view the "amber waves of grain" growing in high-plains states where so much of our food originates.

As our train threaded through Montana and North Dakota, I marveled at how vast—how lonely—this landscape appeared. In the midst of acre upon acre, brimming with wheat, oats, and barley, only an occasional tractor, trailing its plume of smoke, puttered through the scene.

Would I be able to endure the loneliness of farming? In spite of the solitude, would I take comfort in knowing that my solo efforts would, in time, feed many?

I also wonder, did Jesus, at that holy Thursday meal, facing His difficult, singular task just ahead, take comfort in knowing that the bread of His body would, in time, give eternal life to multitudes?

*Thank You, **Father,** for the bread of life, given for me. Help me always remember the source of my soul's nourishment. In Jesus' name, amen.*

April 2–8. **Phyllis Nissila**, of Springfield, Oregon, teaches high school English and community college GED and citizenship classes.

Sacrificial Masterpiece

Christ died and returned to life so that he might be the Lord of both the dead and the living (Romans 14:9).

Scripture: **Romans 14:7-12**
Song: **"I Gave My Life for Thee"**

Having been punched, whipped, and kicked, Jesus slumps—torn, bleeding, and gasping for breath. The ragged chant of His accusers—"Crucify Him! Crucify Him!"—pierces His ears. Then He glimpses someone twisting a thorn-studded branch into a grotesque mockery of a crown for His skull. All the while, the clank of hammer and nails punctuates the horror.

Jesus waits, alone, as unfettered evil closes in. Even His disciples have left Him.

Yet He is *not* alone.

Where time stands still, an invisible crowd, robed in white, surrounds the scene. We are from every nation, denomination, and era; our ranks stretch beyond Jerusalem into eternity. Each in our own way, we worship the perfect Lamb, the Lamb of God, now awaiting His sacrificial altar, our altar.

Lord of both the living and the dead! Yes, beyond time Jesus summons strength, shoulders the cross, and works an eternal masterpiece as He ascends the hill of our salvation.

God and Father of my Lord Christ, how can I thank You for the work of atonement You planned for me from eternity? I can only bow my knee and my heart in this moment of gratitude. In the name of my Savior, amen.

While Still Dark

Early on the first day of the week, while it was still dark, Mary Magdalene went to the tomb and saw that the stone had been removed from the entrance (John 20:1).

Scripture: **John 20:1-9**
Song: **"In the Garden"**

From all accounts, Jesus, You rose early that morning. By the heavenly power that brought Your dead body to life, You left the dark of the cave for the dark of the day, the promise of the first Easter morning not yet purpling the sky.

Magdalene was yet to bring her ministrations. The disciples were yet to race to the tomb. It was just You, alone, at the dawn of the day that split time.

Scriptures indicate Your frequent desire for solitude. I wonder, did You, even then, want a little time to yourself? Before the acclaim and controversy of the new era, did You want to check on Your mother as she slept, no doubt a fitful sleep, thick with grief? *(Soon, Mother, soon.)*

Did you gaze on Peter, too, so lately devastated by denying You, so constantly loved by You? *(Soon, Peter, soon.)*

Did You visit Gethsemane once more, that place where the full impact of Your sacrifice bled through Your pores? And did You stand one last time—trembling and triumphant—at Golgotha? I know this: You rose early, Jesus, in the fullness of time, to accomplish all.

Father, *while it is yet early, I draw near to You. Fill my heart with love for Your Son and for those He loves. In His precious name I pray. Amen.*

In Failure, Fellowship

"They have taken my Lord away," she said, "and I don't know where they have put him." At this, she turned around and saw Jesus standing there, but she did not realize that it was Jesus (John 20:13, 14).

Scripture: **John 20:10-18**
Song: **"Never Alone"**

Mary Magdalene's first post-crucifixion glimpse of Jesus certainly wasn't what she expected. She looked for Him in the grave; she found Him in the garden. In fact, she thought He was the gardener.

Until He spoke her name—"Mary."

The confusion was understandable. The last time Mary saw Jesus, His battered body had just been removed from the cross so that she and the others could prepare Him for burial. Her last view—through eyes blurred with tears, no doubt—was of His lifeless body wrapped in burial linens and laid on a stone slab. In other words, her last, lingering view of Jesus was at the scene of His seeming defeat.

And now He was here. Transformed. Alive!

Plagued by the twin torments of guilt and regret, we often linger at the "grave" of our own seeming defeat. It is hard to see Christ glorified here, too, hard to recognize Him in the midst of our failure. But He is here, as well, alive and inviting our fellowship. And He knows us each by name.

Dear God, help me to remember the promise of Your Son never to leave me—even when I stumble, even when I fall. For this, I am eternally thankful. In Christ's holy name I pray. Amen.

Power Within

Again Jesus said, "Peace be with you! As the Father has sent me, I am sending you." And with that he breathed on them and said, "Receive the Holy Spirit" (John 20:21, 22).

Scripture: **John 20:19-23**
Song: **"Peace, Perfect Peace"**

As the disciples broke bread on that first Easter evening, I imagine them recalling the last three years with Jesus, recalling the power: how they tasted superb wine from a water jug, saw a dead man stumble from his tomb, and heard the shouts as demons fled.

Yet having been in the midst of all that power wasn't enough to shake the grip of anxiety here and now, not enough to soothe the sting of cowardice.

Afraid of Christ's enemies, the disciples kept hushed tones, locked doors, close guard. I imagine the tension: *Where is He? What do we do now? If our enemies find us, what will they do?*

Then Jesus amazes them again. In one physics-defying instant, doors still bolted, He appears in their midst. Perhaps more amazing, He extends not condemnation for cowardice, but peace; not criticism for doubt, but proof of His reality by showing His pierced hands and side.

And He gifts them with the power they long for—the Holy Spirit, the power within that would revolutionize their world and revolutionizes ours.

Thank You, **God,** *for the peace that flows from You. May I walk in Your ways today. Through Christ my Lord, amen.*

April 7

Faith-Building in Progress

[Thomas] said to them, "Unless I see the nail marks in his hands and put my finger where the nails were, and put my hand into his side, I will not believe it" (John 20:25).

Scripture: John 20:24-31
Song: "Falter Not"

The first time my husband and I saw our house, it was little more than a foundation and a frame. Yet we could still envision the completed structure and appreciate its unique design. Amid the lumber stacks, cable coils, and rolls of pink insulation strewn about and covered in sawdust, the building looked wonderful to us, and we knew it would eventually be a warm and inviting home.

Like our house in progress, Thomas, doubts on display, was a believer in progress. But he wasn't the only one in need of finishing touches. Peter, for example, was still recovering from a glaring miscalculation of loyalty. And the other disciples, intimidated by the enemies of this "spiritual project," were behind schedule in the construction of the new church. Their faith foundations also needed serious shoring up.

Jesus responded by offering Thomas a hands-on opportunity to build his faith. Jesus also provided the rest of the disciples—and us—with many other signs and miracles, that our faith also might be completed, right on schedule (see Philippians 1:6).

*Remind me, **Lord,** to keep a hard hat and a soft heart in my spiritual construction zone. Through Christ's name I pray. Amen.*

Blessed Reassurance

When I saw him, I fell at his feet as though dead. Then he placed his right hand on me and said: "Do not be afraid. I am the First and the Last. I am the Living One; I was dead, and behold I am alive for ever and ever!" (Revelation 1:17, 18).

Scripture: **Revelation 1:9-12, 17, 18**
Song: **"Leaning on the Everlasting Arms"**

I recall once entering a busy airport terminal and imagining what it might be like to one day enter the temple in the new Jerusalem to see Jesus. I envisioned a similar scene, an excited, bustling crowd. I heard shouts and laughter, saw tears and smiles as people, like those around me in the terminal, anticipated greeting their beloved one, the Son of God.

As soon as my mind's eye focused on Jesus, however, I caught my breath. In a split second, I realized I'd never be able to stand under my own power at such an extraordinary event. Face-to-face with the one through whom all things were made—how could I possibly maintain my footing?

Like John on Patmos, I too would surely fall at His feet "as though dead." However, I imagine Jesus reassuring me too, as He did with John. "Do not be afraid," He'd say then, even as He reassures me now when I sometimes lose my footing over life's ordinary trials and challenges.

*Thank You, **Lord,** for Your reassurance, for Your help in all circumstances. And thank You, especially, for the vision of Your awesomeness that comes through to me today in Your Word. Through Christ Jesus, amen.*

The Fledgling

The LORD is good to all, and His mercies are over all His works (Psalm 145:9, *New American Standard Bible*).

Scripture: **Psalm 145:8-12**
Song: **"God Will Take Care of You"**

The homely fledgling squawks incessantly. After falling from its nest, it calls to the parent. The tiny bird flaps its wings in an attempt to reach safety; however, those small wings just can't work a self-rescue.

Quickly, the plump mama robin darts down to feed its baby a bite of worm. The young bird quiets down, hops close to mama, and follows her along a hedge to hide. This act of care and provision repeats itself throughout the afternoon until the sun settles below the horizon.

As I watch this scene unfold on my front lawn, I consider how God provides for all His earthly creatures—and that includes me. When life causes me to stumble and fall, the Lord reaches to care for me with everlasting mercy. He hides me in the shadow of his wings (see Psalm 17:8).

When our lives tremble with chaotic circumstances, erratic emotions, or rocky relationships, may we look to this merciful Lord. He hears and responds, quieting our souls as we rest in Him.

O Lord, I thank You for taking such good care of Your creation. Help me to know and sense Your presence, even when I feel alone and desperate. Grant me Your mercy each day. In Christ's name, I pray. Amen.

April 9–15. **Susanne Scheppmann** lives in Nevada with her husband, Mark. She is an author and speaker for Proverbs 31 Ministries.

For a Moment, Revere Him

The fear of the LORD is the beginning of wisdom; all who follow his precepts have good understanding. To him belongs eternal praise (Psalm 111:10).

Scripture: **Psalm 111**
Song: **"O Master, Let Me Walk with Thee"**

Thunderstorms once terrified my young son. Now he loves loud firecrackers. My little boy once feared high bridges too. Now he rides the highest and jerkiest roller coasters. He enjoys the thrill of fear when the metal car slides down the heights and races around a tight corner.

Fear comes in many forms and meets us at various places. Some fears can paralyze us into immobility; others may well enhance our lives. The fear of the Lord is an enhancer.

What is fear of the Lord? It isn't a trembling in your shoes in dread of what God is going to do next. Rather, it's the reverent honor we render to our all-powerful king. Such fear not only acknowledges His power over our lives but also His unfailing love for each of us.

According to the psalmist, reverence for God starts us on the path to wisdom. And this godly wisdom gives us the ability to make good decisions on a daily basis. I would like to walk that path today. Will you join me in a moment of reverence?

Dear God, *let me fear You in a way that opens my heart to Your incomparable wisdom. Give me understanding as I read Your Word and seek to obey it. In the name of Jesus, my Savior, I pray. Amen.*

Aching Arms

In him and through faith in him we may approach God with freedom and confidence (Ephesians 3:12).

Scripture: **Ephesians 3:7-13**
Song: **"Still, Still with Thee"**

Justin, my toddler nephew, whimpered away from me. He feared coming into outstretched arms for a squeeze from his adoring aunt. Instead, he darted away to Mom's familiar lap. My arms ached to hold this strawberry-blond cherub; he wouldn't come within reach of me.

It made me realize how often I fear a kind of closeness with God. If I draw close, will He ask me to do something outside my comfort zone? Will He call me to let go of something dear to me? Or even worse, perhaps God is displeased with me. Does He then stand ready to exact punishment?

The words of two apostles confront my anxious thoughts. Paul tells me I can approach God with freedom and confidence. Then James encourages me with, "Come near to God and he will come near to you" (4:8).

The next time I want to shy away from God, I hope to remember what a fatherly hug He's extending to me, always. Even when He calls me to repent, He does it from His fathomless love. I like to think His arms ache for me, even now.

Father, because of Jesus, I may approach You with a joyful heart. Let nothing hinder me from developing a closer relationship with You, my loving heavenly Father. In the name of Jesus, amen.

What's in a Name?

There is none like Thee, O LORD; Thou art great, and great is Thy name in might. Who would not fear Thee, O King of the nations? Indeed it is Thy due! (Jeremiah 10:6, 7, *New American Standard Bible*).

Scripture: **Jeremiah 10:6-10**
Song: **"Blessed Be the Name"**

Do you know Shania Twain's real name? This pop music diva's actual given name is Eileen. The music industry thought "Eileen" didn't evoke a superstar image, though—hence the change.

I'm fascinated by names. I like the way you can guess someone's generation just by knowing his or her first name. For example, Brittany rings of Generation X. However, Ebenezer recalls to our minds a century gone by. Another fascination: celebrities may be known just by their first names—think of Elvis, Tiger, or Cher.

The Lord's name is above all other names, disclosing supremacy in all things. What images come to your mind as you read these names of God: Father, Lord God Almighty, Christ Jesus, Savior, the Lamb, Abba, and Sovereign Lord? All of these names reflect certain truths about our mighty God and—thankfully!—they define who He is in our relationship with Him.

So what's in a name? Everything, if we speak the names of our God.

Lord of All, *thank You for revealing yourself to me through Your many wonderful names. In Christ I pray. Amen.*

Just like Father

Be imitators of God, as beloved children (Ephesians 5:1, *New American Standard Bible*).

Scripture: **Ephesians 4:25–5:2**
Song: **"Take My Life and Let It Be"**

"You sound just like your mother!" remarked a friend of the family. This was news to me. My mother passed away when I was young, and I have no memory of her voice. Yet her tone and inflections come through in my adult speech. Somehow, many years ago, perhaps my young ears listened and then imitated my mother's words.

Just as we mimic our parent's words, as children of a heavenly Father we should sound like Him. Hmm, but what does He sound like?

Thankfully, the Bible provides a few examples of God's speech patterns. Ephesians 4 calls us to be kind, compassionate, forgiving, and encouraging. It also reveals communication that is clearly unlike God's, such as slander, bitterness, or any unwholesome speech. Mimicking the good isn't always easy for me to accomplish every day!

Yet I recall a children's song, "Practice Makes Perfect." It persuades hearers to keep improving their behavior until it becomes a habit. Will you practice godly speech patterns with me today? Then one day we will no doubt hear, "You sound just like your Father!"

Heavenly Father, *teach me to pattern my speech in a manner that sounds like Your heart. Remind me to be kind and encouraging with my words today and always. I pray in the sweet name of Jesus. Amen.*

Wired Tired?

You have persevered and have endured hardships for my name, and have not grown weary (Revelation 2:3).

Scripture: **Revelation 2:1-7**
Song: **"Art Thou Weary?"**

"You look tired," says a concerned friend. My response? I puff up with pride, wearing my exhaustion as a badge of honor. I know sometimes I wrongly perceive my tiredness as spirituality, especially if I've been overly busy with kingdom work. Then I excuse my fatigue by saying, "This is the way God made me. He wired me tired."

But has the Lord really called us to lives of weariness? He certainly wants us to persevere, but Christ also called His disciples to refresh and renew themselves: "Come with me by yourselves to a quiet place and get some rest" (Mark 6:31). Here's what I find truly remarkable: the disciples were busy doing wonderful things for God, yet Jesus called them away to a *better* venture—to rest for a time.

I needed a daily reminder of this truth, so I pasted Isaiah 40:31 on my mirror: "Those who hope in the LORD will renew their strength. They will soar on wings like eagles; they will run and not grow weary, they will walk and not be faint." How do these words encourage you?

God, help me to realize that my weariness—even from my attempt to serve You—is hardly a badge of honor. Nudge me to rest and to restore myself from the busyness of daily life. Call me away that I might simply be still and enjoy being in Your presence. In the name of my Lord Christ, amen.

How Worthy!

Thou art worthy, O Lord, to receive glory and honor and power: for thou hast created all things, and for thy pleasure they are and were created (Revelation 4:11, *King James Version*).

Scripture: **Revelation 4**
Song: **"All Things Bright and Beautiful"**

"All things bright and beautiful . . . the Lord God made them all." Cecil Alexander created this familiar hymn refrain in 1848 while staying in Ireland's spectacular Markree Castle. The nobility of this old stone fortress, coupled with the beauty of the surrounding landscape, urged her to inscribe words that would stand the test of years. And these are, indeed, memorable words sparked by her awe of the Lord's creative hand.

It makes me consider: how often do I neglect the myriad evidences of God's handiwork in my life? Life passes by in a scurry of daily activities. However, His creation calls out to me to slow down for a moment of enjoyment and wonder. Look! A hummingbird whizzes by my window. The wet fragrance of newly mowed grass wafts through the screen. Sips of steamy jasmine tea revive my afternoon. God bestows these graces as a reminder to stay aware of His marvels on earth.

Yes, today I will slow down a bit. Praise will flow from my tongue to the Lord God who made all things. How worthy He is!

Lord, I praise You for the beauty of creation. The flowers, the animals, the sunshine, and moonlight declare Your magnificence. In Jesus' name, amen.

Those Blessed Beetles

They cried out to the Lord in their trouble, and he delivered them from their distress (Psalm 107:6).

Scripture: Psalm 107:1-9
Song: "Enough"

I was a sophomore in college when my family's financial burdens started weighing heavily upon me. My parents had three children in college, and Dad had health problems. We were in debt.

I'd seen God answer prayers in my life, but this was overwhelming to me. With the medical bills and college expenses piling up, the situation seemed hopeless. I didn't know anywhere else to turn, but to God. I asked for the money to cover it all.

Why are we surprised when God answers our big requests? I certainly was. We discovered beetles in the trees on our farm, so after selling the trees from 60 acres, we could pay all the bills! But, you see, we weren't in the tree-growing business and would never have thought of selling those trees. Except for those blessed beetles.

God is a bit more creative than we are, isn't He? I considered this entire unfolding of events to be quite miraculous. For this I know: He answers when we cry out to Him.

Father, You are so good. You are faithful. Your love endures forever. Forgive me when I forget just who You are. In the name of Jesus, amen.

April 16–22. **Carol Bradfield** has taught Sunday school and numerous small-group Bible studies. She and her husband, Jim, live in LaGrange, Georgia.

A Clean Fix

Let us draw near to God with a sincere heart in full assurance of faith, having our hearts sprinkled to cleanse us from a guilty conscience (Hebrews 10:22).

Scripture: **Hebrews 9:11-15**
Song: **"Nothing but the Blood"**

"Mom, the sink's leaking again."

"That's it! I'm calling the plumber," Mom said.

Dad had tried numerous times to fix those leaking pipes, slathering plumber's cement all over. (I'm sure he must have used his ever-at-hand gray duct tape too.) The leaks kept coming back, though, awaiting a proper fix.

The plumber and his helper arrived. After replacing the pipes, the assistant, John, said, "Miss Eva, you'll save yourself a lot of money, if you call us before your husband tries to help."

The pipes had rusted on the inside, and the rust was wearing through to the outside. Dad's surface fixes only helped for a time; the plumbers fixed all the previous problems in one attempt. Now Mom had new kitchen pipes, good inside and out.

Jesus does something similar within all who love Him. He corrects all of our cover-ups, our futile attempts to right our wrongs. He clears away all the surface fixes and goes straight to the internal cleansing we need.

Abba, thank You for doing such a great work for me and in me. Thank You for the blood of Christ that justifies me and then frees me from sin. Help me keep my heart pure and my conscience clear today. In Jesus' name, amen.

No Turning Back

I press on to take hold of that for which Christ took hold of me (Philippians 3:12).

Scripture: **1 Peter 1:13-21**
Song: **"Follow Me, the Master Said"**

"I'll take the grilled chicken salad with fat-free ranch dressing," Pam said.

After the waitress left, I asked her, "Why don't you celebrate with a big pasta dish?" Pam had reached her weight-loss goal, having lost 20 pounds and droped two sizes. She looked fantastic.

"I still want to be careful. I worked too hard, and I don't want to gain any of it back!" she replied.

"I guess that means we're not splitting a dessert," I said. She rolled her eyes, laughed, and shook her head.

For four months, Pam planned meals and walked around her neighborhood. She obediently followed the plan and determinedly said no to many and various temptations. She kept focusing on the envisioned results. And the results were indeed spectacular—a new appearance and a new attitude.

Pam's experience reminds me of the scriptural principle before us today: Let us stay alert, follow Christ's plan, say no to the things that so easily weigh us down, and focus on the goal—becoming more like Christ.

O Father, thank You for such a priceless and wonderful gift, the gift of Your Son. Keep me from going back to my old ways and old loves. Help me press on, through Christ who strengthens me. Amen.

Let the Music Begin!

He put a new song in my mouth, a song of praise to our God; many will see and fear, and will trust in the LORD (Psalm 40:3, *New American Standard Bible*).

Scripture: **Psalm 40:1-5**
Song: **"I Will Sing of the Mercies"**

"I'd never heard people sing like that," my friend Jennifer said. "As a musician, it intrigued me. They really *meant* what they were singing."

I listened as Jennifer told me about the first time she'd visited a particular church. She was 25, and her sister had invited her. That was also intriguing because her sister had been as wild and rebellious as Jennifer was.

Church was nothing like Jennifer had expected—not just the music, but the people too. The way they treated each other, how they loved each other . . . it all drew her back to the services, week after week.

Jennifer had long viewed Christianity's claims with skepticism. Yet, because those believers sang with such heartfelt intensity and loved one another so deeply, she decided to investigate further. She started reading the Bible, looked into its historicity and authority, opened her heart to its callings. Before long, she had entered the waters of baptism.

It all began with the music.

Heavenly Father, Your wonders are many. Your thoughts are too great for me. Your mercies are new every morning. Help me not only to sing of Your mercies but also to declare them daily. In the name of Christ, amen.

Heartfelt Affection

It is right for me to feel this way about all of you, since I have you in my heart (Philippians 1:7).

Scripture: **Philippians 1:3-11**
Song: **"Bind Us Together"**

"So, how long have you two known each other?" a new acquaintance asked my suite mate Carla and me. It was the October after we started college, and without hesitation we both replied, "Since August." We were as surprised as everyone else at our simultaneous answer.

Carla and I thought alike and often spoke together like that, sometimes stating whole sentences in unison. The summer before attending college, each of us had prayed for a best friend. We were each other's answer to prayer. We lived in the dormitory together for four years, through good times and bad.

I've been out of college for almost 15 years now, and every time I think of Carla, it is with thanksgiving and affection. Although we don't see each other often, she's in my heart and will always be a special friend.

I am thankful for Paul's words in this passage, and I can understand them more powerfully when I put faces to them, faces of those whom God has placed in my life. I don't think Paul would mind if I used his prayer on their behalf—and let them know of my intentions.

Dear Lord, I thank You for the wonderful people You have placed in my life. May I not only remember them but also remember to pray for them. In the name of the Father, the Son, and the Holy Spirit, I pray. Amen.

Earning the Position

We pray . . . that you may live a life worthy of the Lord and may please Him in every way (Colossians 1:10).

Scripture: **Revelation 5:1-5**
Song: **"Worthy Is the Lamb"**

"So, how did you arrive at your current position?" I asked the architect seated at our banquet table.

"I was with a firm in the Midwest when an employment agency called and asked whether I'd be interested in this job. The position required licensing in several states, which I had, along with experience in a specific industry, which I also had."

"How many other candidates also met the criteria?"

"Only two or three others, as far as I know. Our qualifications arose from the work we'd been doing to that point. My previous jobs required the licenses. I was blessed to be one of the few who had what was required for this position."

Very few had what was required for such a specialized job. In Revelation, I find another specialized job—that of breaking the seals and opening the scroll. No one in Heaven or earth could do it except Christ. He alone was worthy, having earned the right through His triumph over sin and death. So consider this: if He has earned the right to such a great position in Heaven, what has He earned the right to do in and through our lives?

O God, show me any part of my life that does not honor You. Your Son died for me; help me to live for Him. In His name I pray. Amen.

A Worthy Lord

From Him and through Him and to Him are all things. To Him be the glory forever. Amen (Romans 11:36, *New American Standard Bible*).

Scripture: **Revelation 5:11-14**
Song: **"Blessing, Honor, and Glory"**

I stepped to the counter and ordered my meal "to go" at the busy fast-food restaurant. When I got back in my car, though, I noticed I had no fork . . . or salad dressing. I went back; the counter lady seemed genuinely embarrassed. "I'm sorry. I must have overlooked them," she said. "I try to double-check to make sure I haven't left anything out." I thanked her, knowing that being in a hurry makes it easier for any human being to leave something unintentionally undone.

In Revelation, John tells us Christ is worthy to receive many things: power, riches, wisdom, might, honor, glory, and blessing, not just for now but forever. The elders, living creatures, and angels were *intentional* as they praised Him.

But are we? How often do we take the time to "double-check" our hearts, lifestyles, and praises? Do we intentionally give Him all of the things the heavenly hosts say He is worthy to receive?

Almighty Creator and Lord of my life, You are worthy of power and riches. You are full of might and wisdom. Help me intentionally and continually give You all the praise You deserve. I pray this prayer in the name of Jesus, my all-worthy Savior. Amen.

Nov. 1 '10

They'll Know

We have heard of your faith in Christ Jesus and of the love you have for all the saints (Colossians 1:4).

Scripture: **Colossians 1:3-8**
Song: **"They'll Know We Are Christians by Our Love"**

Have you Googled today?

The Internet search engine called Google™ is now so well known that its name has become a common verb. Like many successful companies, Google™ used advertisements and other promotions to establish a brand that represents its product with a single word.

As Christians, what is our brand? For what are we known? Just think how powerful our witness would be if the label of Christian became synonymous with love! And not just love as a concept or feeling, but love as an action verb.

Of course, we are not a business, and love isn't a sales technique that we can use to attract people to our church. We love because Christ loved us and because it is what God calls us to do. Love is one way of manifesting His mercy and grace in our daily lives and expressing it to everyone we come in contact with. It asks for nothing in return. It was happening in the ancient city of Colosse. Could it happen your town too?

*Thank You, **Lord**, for loving me. Grant me boldness and creativity as I seek to share Your love with the people in my life. Through Christ, amen.*

April 23–29. **Beth Huber** is a pianist and piano teacher as well as a freelance writer and editor. She resides in Chester County, Pennsylvania.

Look Up

I will lift up mine eyes unto the hills, from whence cometh my help (Psalm 121:1, *King James Version*).

Scripture: **Psalm 121**
Song: **"Jesus, Lord, We Look to Thee"**

In the past when people asked my opinion or advice about ethical matters, I would begin my response by saying "If it were me . . ." or "Well, I would. . . ." It's as if I were presenting myself as an expert, somebody with all the moral answers. But I came to realize that God's perspective on right and wrong might hold a little more weight! He is the expert with all the answers.

So I've been making an effort to stop using those phrases. I now try to direct people's eyes upward to God when they're struggling with a tough quandary or facing a decision-making challenge. As I seek to filter all of life's choices and situations through the truth of the gospel, I want to help others do the same thing.

That's really where we need to look, isn't it? Up to the hills, up to Heaven itself, where God sits enthroned in glory. Yet it gives me a thrill to know that this same Lord of all chooses to dwell within me as well. What an awesome Lord we have! He is our help and He is our hope.

Gracious God, when I face times of confusion or trouble, may I look to You for the way through. And when I advise others, may I encourage them to keep their focus on You as well. Thank You that we can rely on the truth of the gospel and the wisdom of Your Word. All praise to You, in Christ's holy name. Amen.

Everyday Blessings

I lie down and sleep; I wake again because the LORD sustains me (Psalm 3:5).

Scripture: **Psalm 3**
Song: **"Great Is Thy Faithfulness"**

Traveling in a foreign country can be unsettling. Everything is so different! The unfamiliar language, the new food, the "strange" customs—all force us to rethink every move we make. The simplest, formerly routine actions now seem to require extra effort. Ordering a beverage, finding a restroom, and even crossing the street suddenly require an added measure of awareness, concentration, exploration, and discovery.

What if we approached this day as if we were in a foreign country? What if we took the time to notice every small comfort and provision with fresh eyes, with new appreciation for God's grace and care? He is behind these everyday blessings of life that we take so much for granted. Every breath, every heartbeat—every hour of every day—is a gift from the Lord who sustains our being. "His compassions never fail. They are new every morning; great is your faithfulness" (Lamentations 3:22, 23). As fellow travelers, as pilgrims in this foreign land, let's give thanks for His great faithfulness.

Heavenly Father, I am so grateful for all the blessings that You supply every day. Forgive me for the times when I take those things for granted. I pray for an attitude of gratitude and a spirit of thanksgiving for Your faithfulness and all that You provide for me. In Jesus' name, amen.

Whom Shall I Fear?

Fear the LORD, you his saints, for those who fear him lack nothing. The lions may grow weak and hungry, but those who seek the LORD lack no good thing (Psalm 34:9, 10).

Scripture: **Psalm 34:1-10**
Song: **"Great and Wonderful"**

Some Bible translations use words other than "fear" in Psalm 34:9, including "honor," "revere," "respect," and "worship." Dictionary definitions of *fear* reflect those ideas but also include the phrases "anxiety caused by real or possible danger" and "to expect with misgiving."

That kind of fear is something we might have trouble reconciling with our understanding of God as a loving and gracious Father. Yet God also loves justice, provides discipline when it's necessary, and allows us to face the negative consequences of wrong choices. That kind of fear can prevent us from falling into sinful attitudes, words, and actions.

Christian author Elisabeth Elliot wrote, "The more we learn to fear God, the less we fear anything else." When we are in right relationship with the Lord, when we honor His authority, our day-to-day fears and anxieties lose their lion like power to bring us down.

*How awesome and powerful You are, **Mighty God!** Thank You for reminding me that when I fear You—when I give You the honor and authority You deserve—I have no need to fear anything or anyone else. I bow down before You in worship and praise. In the name of the Father, the Son, and the Holy Spirit, I pray. Amen.*

The Best Offense

Because you have kept My command to persevere, I also will keep you from the hour of trial which shall come upon the whole world, to test those who dwell on the earth (Revelation 3:10, *New King James Version*).

Scripture: **Revelation 3:7-13**
Song: **"Who Is on the Lord's Side?"**

Perseverance is one of those unsung, underrated character qualities. It implies a sense of plodding or treading water, making little if any visible progress. That just doesn't seem very thrilling or impressive, does it? And yet, according to this passage from Revelation, that type of endurance is going to be rewarded by God.

Consider the role of the defense in a sport like football. In my own limited understanding of the game, I've always appreciated the glory of the big offensive plays. To my untrained eye, those dramatic plays are easier to understand and get excited about. (In fact, I've always felt that the teams should be running touchdowns every few minutes in order keep the game action packed.)

But a friend recently gave me some insight into the value of the defensive role. He described the strategy, teamwork, courage, and determination necessary for a successful defense. Denying victory to the opposition can prevent the defeat of our team. As they say, "The best offense is a good defense."

Dear Lord, *I pray for a greater appreciation of a persevering defense against evil. Please give me courage, faith, and strength. Through Christ, amen.*

The Power of One

I looked and there before me was a great multitude that no one could count, from every nation, tribe, people and language, standing before the throne and in front of the Lamb. They were wearing white robes and were holding palm branches in their hands (Revelation 7:9).

Scripture: **Revelation 7:1-3, 9, 10**
Song: **"To the Lamb"**

In 1999 the world's population reached six billion people. To get a handle on that enormous number, think about this: In 1972, the *Pioneer 10* spacecraft lifted off into space, and it took 25 years to reach the distance of six billion miles from earth, with round-trip communications at that point taking more than 18 hours (at the speed of light, 186,000 miles per second).

Now picture the size of the crowd worshiping at the feet of the Lord as He sits on His throne in Heaven. Try to imagine the number of believers over the entire scope of human history past, present, and future. The sights and sounds of that experience are unfathomable—the splendor of God, the mass of diverse peoples, the echoes of praise and worship.

It is an awesome thing to belong to the family of God! There we will all be, along with every tribe, every people, every language represented. That is the glory, supremacy, and majesty of our Lord. That is the power of One.

God, I can hardly imagine the glorious spectacle of all believers worshiping You. What a wonderful day that will be! Through Christ my Lord, amen.

Touch of God

The Lamb at the center of the throne will be their shepherd; he will lead them to springs of living water. And God will wipe away every tear from their eyes (Revelation 7:17).

Scripture: **Revelation 7:11-17**
Song: "He Touched Me"

The sense of touch is said to be the first sense we experience in the womb and the last sense we lose before we die. While the other four senses (sight, hearing, taste, and smell) are located in specific areas, the sense of touch encompasses the entire body. Research has shown that babies who are frequently touched and held will fuss less, sleep better, and even have stronger immune systems as adults. That's how important touch is to human beings.

Our Scripture verse for today conveys the image of an affectionate, personal Lord who touches us. He goes beyond making sure our sorrows cease; He touches our faces, gently wiping away our tears like a parent comforting a child.

Our God is spirit, so we can't know His literal, physical touch. But He is not removed or distant. Through the comfort of the indwelling Holy Spirit—and through loving friends, our family, and church members—we do indeed experience the touch of God in our lives.

*Thank You, **Father,** for this beautiful picture of Your tender kindness. I long for the time when there will be no more sadness. Thank You, too, for the comfort You give me in this life. In the holy name of Jesus, my Lord and Savior, I pray. Amen.*

What to Do with Grace

Tell those who have been invited. . . . Come to the wedding banquet (Matthew 22:4).

Scripture: **Matthew 22:1-14**
Song: **"Come, Let Us Use the Grace Divine"**

This parable tells us what to do with grace by telling us what *not* to do with it. Do not turn down its invitation to attend God's banquet. Show up for the feast of God's lavish blessings. As the roll is taken at the table of God's bounty, answer when your name is called.

Grace is given to be accepted. The biblical record is clear about that. A woman taken in adultery, a tax collector up a tree, a hopeless paralytic let down through a hastily torn up roof—all of them discovered it. A man whose sight had gone, a man who never had any, a woman who got her dead son back. They accepted grace.

And then there's the disciple who vehemently denied Jesus but was restored and commissioned by Jesus to feed His lambs. It's all the same for them. It's all the same for us. Grace is given to be received.

Respond affirmatively to God's creating grace that gives life. Say yes to God's saving grace that offers eternity. Receive the sustaining grace that keeps you each day.

*Your grace is everywhere, **O God,** and I am most grateful. I open my heart today to receive every offer of Your goodness. Through Christ, amen.*

April 30. **Phillip H. Barnhart,** retired minister, has written 13 books, compiled 5 others, and contributed numerous articles to various publications. He lives on Perdido Bay in Florida with his wife, Sharon.

My Prayer Notes

DEVOTIONS®

Gary Allen, Editor

*T*he grace of
the Lord Jesus
be with God's
people.

—Revelation 22:21

MAY

Photo © Díamar

Devotions® is published quarterly by Standard Publishing, 8121 Hamilton Avenue, Cincinnati, Ohio, 45231. A division of Standex International Corporation. © 2006 by Standard Publishing. All rights reserved. Topics based on the Home Daily Bible Readings, International Sunday School Lessons. © 2003 by the Committee on the Uniform Series. Printed in the U.S.A. All Scripture quotations, unless otherwise indicated, are taken from the HOLY BIBLE, NEW INTERNATIONAL VERSION®. NIV®. Copyright © 1973, 1978, 1984 by International Bible Society. Used by permission of Zondervan. All rights reserved. *New American Standard Bible (NASB),* © 1960, 1962, 1963, 1968, 1971, 1972 The Lockman Foundation. *The Contemporary English Version (CEV).* Copyright © 1991, 1992, 1995 American Bible Society. Used by permission. All rights reserved.

A Song to Sing

They were singing, "Lord God All-Powerful, you have done great and marvelous things. You are the ruler of all nations, and you do what is right and fair (Revelation 15:3, *Contemporary English Version*).

Scripture: **Revelation 15:1-5**
Song: **"Majesty"**

When we belong to God, we have a song to sing, a song of testimony to the greatness of God in our lives. It is a song of grace and glory that counters philosopher Friedrich Nietzsche's taunting of the church: "They would have to sing better songs to make me believe in their Redeemer." We sing wonderful songs because we have a wonderful God. Our music starts on earth and ascends to heaven on the wings of our love for Him and our faith in His promises. Like those John saw in his vision, we play our instruments and lift our voices in praise.

When we belong to God, we do not keep our music inside us. We let it out every day, in every way. Just as the Israelites sang a song of deliverance to God, we sing a song of thanksgiving to the one who made us, died for us, and keeps us company throughout the day.

All-Powerful Lord in Heaven, You have done such great things! All Your ways are right and fair, as You extend perfect justice combined with infinite mercy. How can I keep from singing Your praises? In the name of Jesus, Lord and Savior of all, I pray. Amen.

May 1–6. **Phillip H. Barnhart,** retired minister, is also a prolific writer, contributing articles to various publications. He lives in Florida with his wife, Sharon.

Bow Now!

The kingdom of the world has become the kingdom of our Lord and of His Christ; and He will reign forever and ever (Revelation 11:15, *New American Standard Bible*).

Scripture: **Revelation 11:15-19**
Song: **"I Exalt Thee"**

In New York's Rockefeller Center stands a famous bronze statue of the Greek god Atlas carrying the globe of the world on his mighty shoulders. He is bending forward, straining greatly under the tremendous weight. Every muscle and tendon stands out in agonizing relief. Just across the street, at Saint Patrick's Cathedral, is another statue depicting the Christ child. Here the baby Jesus serenely and effortlessly holds the globe of the world in the palm of His tiny hand.

God—not *a* god—is in charge. The control knob is in His hand; His management holds sway throughout the cosmos. And if the entire universe is already His kingdom, then it makes sense to await the coming day announced in Revelation 11:5. Then, visible to all, Christ will reveal himself as sovereign ruler of the world as well.

He holds back for a while, letting human will have its say. But He will not restrain himself forever, as Revelation powerfully reminds us. The question is, am I bowing my knee to this sovereign ruler *now*, so it won't be a shock when I must do it *then*?

Sovereign Lord, throughout the whole universe, all things are under Your authority. I acknowledge: that includes me too. Through Christ, amen.

Raise Your Praise

Praise the LORD. Praise the LORD from the heavens, praise him in the heights above (Psalm 148:1).

Scripture: Psalm 148:1-6
Song: "Oh! Say, but I'm Glad"

A minister had just started his Sunday sermon when thunder roared in the heavens, lightning flashed across the sky, and rain poured down in pounding torrents. Always one to recognize God's blessings in everything, the preacher said to the congregation, "Isn't God wonderful? While all of us are sitting in here, dry and comfortable, He's out in the parking lot washing our cars!"

Great reasons to raise our praise to God pop up everywhere. No turn of the head or touch of the heart escapes the call to thanksgiving for the excesses of God's grace. We could go on for an hour, lifting up every word of thanksgiving for what God does for us, and still remain far from exhausting our inventory of praise. The psalmist clearly felt the impact of God's goodness as well. He plumbs the depths of vocabulary and syntax to find phrases sufficient to honor Him.

The primary *focus* of the spiritual life is what God does for us and who God is to us. The foremost *obligation* of the spiritual life is to express our gratitude.

Dear God, I raise my praise to You for the full cupboard of my life and the adventures with You in my journey. Because of Your bounty, I come to You with a hallelujah heart and an amen attitude. I fall down before You, overwhelmed by Your blessings. In the name of Christ, amen.

Don't Hold That Applause!

Let them praise the name of the LORD, for his name alone is exalted; his splendor is above the earth and the heavens (Psalm 148:13).

Scripture: **Psalm 148:7-14**
Song: **"O for a Thousand Tongues"**

During the opening ceremonies of a state fair, the governor was honored with a 19-gun salute. When the emcee explained to the crowd that a 21-gun salute would mean the president was in attendance, a bright 8-year-old girl asked her grandfather what it would mean if it had been a 100-gun salute. "I don't know, honey," he said.

She responded, "It would mean *God* is in town!"

God is always in our town. Let us take up the psalmist's invitation and respond accordingly, as Arturo Toscanini once did when he visited the Grand Canyon. A companion watched as the great conductor stood motionless, contemplating the miracle of what stretched before him. Suddenly, after a long and silent meditation, the maestro burst into applause.

What God does for us each day is what might be called "shouting news." Breath of life, vista of opportunity, gift of skill and talent, touch of friends and family—the list goes on and on, and each item deserves and demands our exuberant response.

Magnificent God, *You give me so many reasons for praise! You bring gifts to me in such a variety of creative ways, and I am grateful for each of them. In the holy name of Jesus, my Lord and Savior, I pray. Amen.*

You're the Greatest!

The twenty-four elders and the four living creatures fell down and worshiped God who sits on the throne (Revelation 19:4, *New American Standard Bible*).

Scripture: **Revelation 19:1-5**
Song: **"The Great God of Heaven"**

God is larger than our concepts of Him, and no finite dogma or creed can capture God's infinite vastness. God is not even in space; space is in God. He sits at the head of creation, high and holy on the throne of dominion. And like the elders and creatures of our verse today, wherever we turn we must acknowledge the ultimate power and boundless presence of God. God minus the world equals God. The world minus God equals nothing.

At the funeral of Louis XIV, the cathedral overflowed with those who came to pay their tribute to a monarch they perceived as great. The room was dark, save for one candle illuminating the king's golden casket.

At the appointed time, the court preacher stood to address the people. He reached from the pulpit and snuffed out the single candle that had been placed there to symbolize the greatness of the king amid all else.

Then from the darkness came four words, "God only is great."

Infinite and Sovereign God, I come to bow down before Your magnitude and magnificence. I open my mouth to say what I think of You but cannot speak. You are so much more than mind can reflect or tongue can recite. Let this silence reveal my thankful heart. Through Christ I pray. Amen.

Where to Kneel

I knelt at the feet of the angel and began to worship him. But the angel said, "Don't do that! I am a servant, just like you and everyone else who tells about Jesus. Don't worship anyone but God" (Revelation 19:10, *Contemporary English Version*).

Scripture: **Revelation 19:6-10**
Song: **"For the Healing of the Nations"**

Soon after signing the Emancipation Proclamation, Abraham Lincoln took a trip up the river to Richmond. When he got off the boat on the river bank at the edge of the Confederate capital, a group of former slaves recognized him from half-remembered pictures they'd seen over the years. One of the men ran several yards to where Lincoln stood with his advisers, knelt directly in front of him, and attempted to kiss his shoes. But the president spoke quickly and graciously. He said, "Do not kneel to me. You must kneel only to God."

Imagine if, on the day that happened, the apostle John could have watched from Heaven. He might recall the angel's word of caution to him, too, and heartily approve of Lincoln's words.

All of us humans stand before God on level ground, created excellently, loved equally and fully. Misguided human will makes some of us slaves and some of us rulers . . . for now. In the kingdom to come, we will all be free—at liberty to worship our Lord forever, side by side.

God, You reign among all peoples and circumstances. And I, among my fellow servants, kneel before You. All praise to You, in Jesus' name. Amen.

He's All in All

As I have often told you before and now say again even with tears, many live as enemies of the cross of Christ. Their destiny is destruction, their god is their stomach, and their glory is in their shame (Philippians 3:18, 19).

Scripture: **Philippians 3:17-21**
Song: **"Be Thou My Vision"**

John's heart attack struck at noon, and by 4:30 doctors had placed two stents into a main artery, assuring much better cardiac blood flow. Three days later he returned home with a new lease on life—but still facing battles with his addiction to cigarettes.

In the following days, John realized how much of his life, night and day, centered around his smoking habit. Trying hard to quit, he didn't know what to do with his hands, his time, his thoughts; he felt a great loss of control.

I feel for John, knowing that we are all addicted to some finite "god" in one way or another. The challenge of life is to free ourselves from what some have called the false infinites that demands inordinate affection. The apostle Paul writes that as long as these earthly things are so important to us, God remains less than our all in all.

Father God, when I am weak, I ask for strength. When I am tired, I ask for rest. When I fail to put You first, I ask for intervention. I am not in control, and I give thanks that You are! Through Christ my Lord, amen.

May 7–13. **Geneva Rodgers** is a rural grandmother embarking on her third career of writing. She's active in her church and views every day as a new beginning.

Hourly Battle

He must reign until he has put all his enemies under his feet (1 Corinthians 15:25).

Scripture: **1 Corinthians 15:20-28**
Song: **"Jesus Shall Reign"**

John is in his second week of battle against those cigarettes that likely contributed to his heart attack. I'm cheering him on, but he finds it no easier to quit today than when he started. It's an hourly fight . . .

Across town, Sarah stands in her kitchen, preparing the evening meal, and her battle rages too. It's in her smell, taste, and touch as she handles the food. There's that leftover piece of pie on the counter, ice cream in the freezer, gravy to taste for seasoning—and what tempting mashed potatoes! It's a regular boxing ring here, and Sarah, fighting in the heavyweight class, fights hard . . .

And here's Jane. Her good friend has just dropped by for a little gossip session. Jane has tried to conquer the habit but wants so badly to share what she overheard in the post office about the Smiths. It's a *war!*

Have you learned yet that willpower doesn't work against those kinds of internal enemies? Yet if we can sit still with our temptations long enough, we'll sense a deeper "I want" bubbling up in our hearts. We want *Him,* the source of our deepest longing, the one who won't let us go until He reigns within, free and clear.

Dear Father, *waiting in Your presence, I feel the pull of this habit. Let Your "pull" within me be stronger just now. In Jesus' name, amen.*

It's Not About Me

We make it our goal to please him, whether we are at home in the body or away from it (2 Corinthians 5:9).

Scripture: **2 Corinthians 5:1-10**
Song: **"Lord of the Dance"**

One more word about my friend John: he loves God, attends church, prays, and studies his Bible. But he fails to realize that abusing his lungs with smoke hardly pleases God. His focus is on himself at the moment—how hard it is to quit, how much he's giving up, how scary the prospects if he doesn't stop. That load gets pretty heavy on a daily basis. What are the chances he can continue?

Will, on the other hand, has taken a different approach. He knows without a doubt he can't quit on his own. He acknowledges his weakness and seeks daily strength from God and loving encouragement from God's people. I've noticed that his load seems to lighten each day. What are the chances he will continue?

These bodies of ours aren't really about us. They're about our stewardship, our call to stay fit for God's work through us. (I, too, need much help there!) With John and Will, and all my brothers and sisters in Christ, I come before God to humbly confess my failures. But I also come to renew my fondest hope: that I might please Him.

None of us knows how long our bodies will last. But to please Him—*whether here or there*—what a great goal!

Father, You have given me this body to keep ready for Your service. Help me to care for it as You care for me and my friends. In Christ, amen.

One Step at a Time

By faith Abraham . . . considered him faithful who had made the promise (Hebrews 11:11).

Scripture: **Hebrews 11:10-16**
Song: **"My Faith Looks Up to Thee"**

My daughter, a physical therapist, tells stories of patients struggling to regain their health after suffering strokes, automobile accidents, and other crises. She's a nurturing, caring soul, but often these patients begin to dread her appearance in their doorways. Why? Because they know whatever she has in store for them that day will likely hurt. No pain, no gain.

The therapy may involve just lifting an arm, taking a small step, pushing a ball, or simply trying to sit up. But the early treatments usually hurt, nevertheless.

And they hurt my daughter's heart! She feels her patients' pain as they try so hard. But she also knows that weeks later much of the pain will be replaced by the joy of freer movement and better coordination. That's when she's greeted with smiles (and an occasional piece of pie). They had faith in her ability; they persevered in the promise of regained health.

In our relationship with God, our hurts are just as real, just as painful. He is faithful, though, and calls us to have faith in His saving ability. We are rewarded with wholeness, fullness, a complete turn around.

God, You made me Your child. Now help me take each step toward becoming in practice what I am in position. Thank You, in Jesus' name. Amen.

What Kind of Life?

The heavens will disappear with a roar; the elements will be destroyed by fire, and the earth and everything in it will be laid bare. Since everything will be destroyed in this way, what kind of people ought you to be? You ought to live holy and godly lives (2 Peter 3:10, 11).

Scripture: **2 Peter 3:10-18**
Song: **"Amazing Grace"**

It had been such a good day. Lots of friends had called to visit. Lots of news had flown over the wires; sadly, most of it was hearsay. But Jane was elated to know that she was the hub of the group, the confidante of all. She would listen, absorb, and eventually pass on certain "information" to whomever she thought needed to hear.

Things came to a screeching halt at the post office later in the afternoon. As circumstances would have it, all four friends were there as Jane entered. Their faces were not pleasant, and their bodies quickly turned inward to close her out. Apparently Jane's gossip had somehow trampled on the feelings and reputations of her friends. It wasn't supposed to happen, but it did.

As we consider Peter's words in our verse, each of us must look at our lives to see what Jesus will find there when the earth and heavens finally melt away. What He sees—now and *then*—ought to be holy and godly lives.

*Renew my heart, **O God,** that I might walk ever closer to You. Make my actions loving and self-giving, and cloak my words in kindness. Your Son, Jesus, is my best example! In His name I pray. Amen.*

Let Him Hear Your Cry

Before they call I will answer; while they are still speaking I will hear (Isaiah 65:24).

Scripture: **Isaiah 65:17-19, 23-25**
Song: **"I Want to Be Ready"**

Sarah is 76, a beautiful 76 years old. She doesn't know why she's been so blessed with good health, a sharp mind, her original teeth, and very few ailments. Sarah is afraid of dying . . . and also afraid to let anyone know it.

Chad, 33, divorced, had found a supportive Bible study group. He called for help, for peace, for meaning. Just recently he told several friends he felt his time on earth was short. He had finally gotten his life in order and was content. Chad died this past week.

A child dies in an auto accident, a nursing home resident turns 100, a father of three succumbs in a fire, and a fiancée is raped and killed. Their stories all appear together in my newspaper, and I know I could search my whole life to make sense of these puzzling patterns. Yet I must content myself with this: only God can know my own readiness, when my spirit is "done" and ready to leave this earthly existence. We can theorize, we can mathematize, we can philosophize. But until the cry of our heart is surrender, perhaps we have not yet called to Him.

Loving Father, on bended knees I cry out to You for the peace that passes understanding. I cry for joy at Your patience with me and Your continued love. How I thank You for hearing me! And I do want to be ready for Your call to service, whatever it may involve. I pray in Jesus' name. Amen.

Worth the Fight

He will wipe every tear from their eyes. There will be no more death or mourning or crying or pain, for the old order of things has passed away (Revelation 21:4).

Scripture: **Revelation 21:1-8**
Song: **"When We All Get to Heaven"**

It's now been six weeks. John, Sarah, Will, and Jane have all walked rocky paths, fought daily battles, lost hope and regained hope, lost strength and found strength. They encountered ferocious warriors and ministering angels in their walks with God. They grew, sometimes two steps forward and one step backward.

Nevertheless . . . progress! Each has broken another dubious chain of command on their spirits, giving God more room to operate in their hearts. Were they successful in each battle? No. But they dared to fight, knowing the prize was worth the struggle. The tears and pain, the death—and all the old things—will soon pass away. Knowing this, we, like them, can take the next step forward.

When we think of a whole "order of things" passing from the scene, we may assume we're required to take giant leaps of faith each day. But God is patient with us. He knows we can usually manage only the next small step in front of us. He waits, He encourages, He picks us up when we fall. If tears need wiping away, He's there for that too. What awesome love!

O Precious Father, when my road seems too rough to travel and my load too heavy to carry, turn my gaze heavenward. In Jesus' name, amen.

Exercise Those Muscles!

I keep asking that the God of our Lord Jesus Christ, the glorious Father, may give you the Spirit of wisdom and revelation, so that you may know him better (Ephesians 1:17).

Scripture: **Ephesians 1:15-23**
Song: **"There Is Power in the Blood"**

Muscles are an amazing part of God's creation. They are elastic, snapping back when exerted. All they do is shorten and lengthen, but these organic rubber bands are responsible for every bodily movement.

But have you ever pulled a muscle? I started a strength-training exercise program using weights a few years ago. When I first worked one of the upper-body machines, I discovered how weak my arm muscles were and how quickly they became sore. Ouch!

Yet after a few months of strength training, I realized how much easier the arm machine had become. I could push harder and faster because the more I used my muscles, the better they worked.

Perhaps Paul had this concept in mind when he prayed that the Ephesians would learn to know God better. These believers could "exercise" their belief in God's own "muscle"—the power that raised Christ from the dead.

Almighty God, *thank You for exerting Your power in the resurrection of Your Son. Give me discipline to exercise a daily life of prayer so our fellowship might grow stronger and deeper. Through Christ I pray. Amen.*

May 14–20. **Jane Cook** is the former White House Deputy Director of Internet News Services for President George W. Bush. She lives in Alexandria, Virginia.

Crediting the Creator

The sun will no more be your light by day, nor will the brightness of the moon shine on you, for the LORD will be your everlasting light, and your God will be your glory (Isaiah 60:19).

Scripture: **Isaiah 60:18-22**
Song: **"God of Wonders"**

My little boy loves to watch videos from a popular series for babies and toddlers. His favorite part is the puppet that acts as tour-guide narrator. The puppet introduces each new concept, such as the sky or a new color or the next number. Then the puppet steps out of the picture so the child can view videos of the sky or different colored scenes.

Even as young as 4 months, my son would coo with delight whenever the puppet appeared. Like most movies, these videos end with credits. They show the name and face of the puppeteer who gave form and function to the puppet. My son is still too young to understand that someone is guiding the puppet. But someday he will distinguish the creator from the creation.

In Genesis we learn that God created the sun to guide us by day and the moon to give us light at night. He gave the sun and moon their form and function. Isaiah reminds us that when life's "video" is over, it is the puppeteer, not the puppet, who deserves our recognition and praise.

Magnificent Creator, I praise You for Your glorious creation of the earth and sky. You are a God of far-flung wonders, yet You promise to stay close to me in deep communion. I offer my praise through Your holy Son. Amen.

Digging for Reality

Since we are receiving a kingdom that cannot be shaken, let us be thankful, and so worship God acceptably with reverence and awe (Hebrews 12:28).

Scripture: **Hebrews 12:22-28**
Song: **"Rock of Ages"**

Can you imagine proving the existence of an imaginary place? That is exactly what German archaeologist Heinrich Schliemann accomplished in 1870. He uncovered Troy, the ancient city of Homer's *Iliad*. Because Homer described Troy as a seaside town, historians concluded it was an imaginary place, since no seaside city or ruins existed in the region.

Schliemann proved the doubters wrong. He studied Homer's descriptions and eventually discovered the ruins of Troy buried inland, below other cities, in western Turkey. Clearly, although Troy was once a thriving city, it could be shaken and destroyed. Uncovering its ruins only proved its existence, not its invincibility.

Some people think Heaven is as imaginary as the Wizard's oz, Santa's workshop at the north pole or Alice's wonderland. All of these places disappear as soon as we close a book or turn off the television set. The book of Hebrews, however, promises us that we are receiving a real kingdom that cannot be shaken. Our response is to worship its king.

King of kings, I can't fathom the immensity of Your kingdom, which is and is yet to be. May I worship You in an acceptable way, with reverence and awe for Your solid invincibility. In the name of Jesus I pray. Amen.

Incremental Glory

We, who with unveiled faces all reflect the Lord's glory, are being transformed into his likeness with ever-increasing glory, which comes from the Lord, who is the Spirit (2 Corinthians 3:18).

Scripture: **2 Corinthians 3:7-18**
Song: **"He Leadeth Me"**

Several years ago Washington, D.C., residents witnessed a series of unveilings when the city became home to a new major league baseball team. To build a fan base, the new franchise sponsored a series of press events over many months. At the publicity kick off, the mayor hit a home run when he unveiled the team's name: the Washington Nationals.

A few weeks later he unveiled the team's colors and uniforms. Soon the streets and subways were filled with red T-shirts and caps boasting a curly *W*. Then a spokesperson walked around town in an egg costume to encourage fans to guess the identity of the team's mascot. When the egg hatched, out came a costumed eagle, delighting young children. Opening-day crowds proved the effectiveness of this incremental strategy.

God employs a kind of unveiling strategy with us. He doesn't make one announcement and then exit the stage. Instead, He provides us with frequent unveilings of His love, plan, and purpose for us—an ever-increasing glory.

Lord, thank You for giving me daily opportunities to grow and become more like You. May I respond in trust and obedience. In Jesus' name, amen.

Radiant Rebirth

It [Jerusalem] shone with the glory of God, and its brilliance was like that of a very precious jewel, like a jasper, clear as crystal (Revelation 21:11).

Scripture: **Revelation 21:9-14**
Song: **"By the Grace of God We'll Meet"**

Ruby and sapphire mining turned a Blue Ridge Mountain town in North Carolina into a commercial diamond in the 1870s. For years these gemstones brought a sizable profit, but the town eventually lost its sparkle when synthetic minerals replaced the commercial need for authentic stones. So, one by one the mines closed.

Years later the mines opened again, this time for tourism. Mine owners sold buckets of stoney dirt, promising visitors they could keep whatever jewels they found there. The stones were washed and held up to the sun; anything that sparkled was a precious find. When these folks began taking their newfound gems to jewelry stores to turn them into rings and necklaces, the town was reborn.

Similarly, Revelation predicts that another town will be reborn because of sunlight. The new Jerusalem will sparkle like a precious jewel, with the Son of God as its light source. Whether it's a jewel, a town, or a human being, wiping away some mud and reflecting the Son delivers a radiant rebirth.

Lord, give me a makeover; wipe off any debris and hold me up to Your light. By the power of Your indwelling Spirit, may I reflect even a fraction of Your brilliance today. Thank You, in Jesus' name. Amen.

Living Temple

I did not see a temple in the city, because the Lord God Almighty and the Lamb are its temple (Revelation 21:22).

Scripture: **Revelation 21:22-27**
Song: **"Behold the Lamb"**

One of my favorite buildings in Washington, D.C., is the National Cathedral. This Gothic marvel sits atop the capital city's highest hill. I love the symbolism of its cross-shaped floor plan, towering stained-glass windows, pointed arches, sky-high ceiling, giant bells, and flying buttresses. All of these characteristics encourage visitors to worship, pray, and sing to the Lord.

Most church buildings use architecture and interior design to point us toward God. A white, wooden church building in the countryside makes a simple statement about the call to a simple liftestyle. Another building's full-scale fountain pours forth a picture of the river of life. Some congregations display banners on their worship wall, the bright fabrics emblazoned with various names for God or truths of His character.

Revelation tells us the new Jerusalem will not have a temple though. The Lord himself will be its temple. No longer will we need visual symbols and architectural inspirations to motivate us to worship. The Lord's presence will be closer to us than a ring on our finger.

*You are the great architect, **God,** the builder of Your temple. Show me how to worship You in spirit and truth each day, with a sincere heart and dedicated priorities. In the name of Your Son, my Savior, I pray. Amen.*

Heavenly Imprint

They will see his face, and his name will be on their foreheads (Revelation 22:4).

Scripture: **Revelation 22:1-5**
Song: **"On My Heart Imprint Thine Image"**

When I was pregnant, my son's soccer like kicks bonded me to him before his birth. And although my husband is grateful that it's the *woman* who actually bears the child, he also needed a way to bond with his son. Would the little guy at least *look* like him?

When Austin was born, we immediately compared his tiny features to our own baby pictures. Austin's nose and ears are near duplicates of mine, but his most dominant features scream "I look like my daddy!" His forehead, hairline, hair color, skin tones, mouth, eyes—and even the dimple above his upper lip—clearly came from my husband.

Five days after Austin's birth, my husband was holding him in a doctor's office waiting room. Another patient commented that Austin looked exactly like his dad. My husband just beamed because from Austin's forehead to his toes, he bears his father's likeness.

God promises us in Revelation that from our foreheads on the outside to our hearts on the inside, we will bear our Father's imprint. How much more will our heavenly Father beam when we arrive to see His face.

Father, thank You for loving me so much that You placed Your birthmark on my forehead. I seek to return Your love today! In Jesus' name, amen.

Trading My Sorrows

You will grieve, but your grief will turn to joy (John 16:20).

Scripture: **John 16:17-24**
Song: "Trading My Sorrows"

The death of our newborn son devastated me. A year later, I was pregnant again, but fear grew within me too. What if this child contracted the same illness as our son's? I couldn't bear the thought of burying another child. I certainly didn't want to miss the miracle of this pregnancy; however, I found it hard to see past my pain.

With a heavy spirit, I forced myself to attend a praise service at our church. The words of Psalm 30:5b spoke to my frightened soul, "Weeping may remain for a night, but rejoicing comes in the morning." As I began repeating that verse, I sensed God asking me to do that very thing, to give Him my sorrow so He could exchange it for His joy.

That thought became my theme throughout the pregnancy and birth of our new son, whom I now refer to as my "joy boy." This new life is a constant reminder to me of how God delights in exchanging for joy our most disappointing and painful life experiences.

Comforting Father, thank You for this life of adventure with You, filled with all forms of joy and sorrow. I don't expect You to remove every source of suffering while I'm on this earth. But I do look forward to the day when eternal joy is my settled home. Through Christ I pray. Amen.

May 21–27. **Stacy Rothenberger,** mother of five, homeschools, works part-time as a speech language therapist, and enjoys writing and speaking about what God is teaching her along the way.

Why, Lord?

In this world you will have trouble. But take heart! I have overcome the world (John 16:33).

Scripture: **John 16:25-33**
Song: **"Through It All"**

"Why, Lord? Why can't my life be going as I had planned? My marriage isn't everything I expected. My kids aren't perfect. Even my friends and family have disappointed me!"

God allowed me to finish my long tirade of complaints before I sensed a tender and gentle reply: "But if everything had gone as you had planned, our intimacy wouldn't have matured. As a result of those disappointments and struggles, you are learning to depend on me. Instead of making demands, you are receiving what is given. Continue clinging to me. I will never leave you or forsake you."

Have you found these things true in your own life? In the times I've stopped complaining, and offered thanks in the midst of tough circumstances, I've experienced a renewed closeness to God. He allowed me to learn something new about myself, about others, and about His character. Yes, on the spiritual journey, hindsight is clearer than the road ahead; we're called to walk by faith. But take heart! Instead of complaining, praise Him for another opportunity to see His power revealed.

Lord, thank You for the powerful lessons hidden in each trial I face. Remind me to take heart and trust You in every situation. In Jesus' name, amen.

Bearing with One Another

Be completely humble and gentle; be patient, bearing with one another in love (Ephesians 4:2).

Scripture: **Ephesians 4:1-6**
Song: **"Cast Thy Burden Upon the Lord"**

He did it again. How could I forgive my husband for making (what I thought was) a poor decision? The Bible instructs us to "[bear] with one another in love," but what, exactly, does it mean?

I went to my dictionary and found that bear with can mean "to exert pressure or effort on." I hadn't thought of it that way before. Armed with this rather obscure definition, I felt I could at least approach my husband with my concerns rather than stuffing them into the pit of unresolved conflict.

Later, I came across another definition that surprised and encouraged me even more: "to give birth to." By my willingness to withstand, endure, support, approach, and exert, God could eventually give birth to something new—in me and in my relationships at home.

Just as a pregnant woman bears down to bring forth new life, God was allowing me the opportunity to bear with my husband in love. The result: new life sprang up within our marriage.

Dear Lord, thank You for bearing with me in love! Help me do the same for others, especially with my husband and other family members. Please breathe new life into every relationship plagued with conflict today. In the holy name of Jesus, my Lord and Savior, I pray. Amen.

Well Suited Now!

Clothe yourselves with compassion, kindness, humility, gentleness and patience. . . . And over all these virtues put on love, which binds them all together (Colossians 3:12, 14).

Scripture: **Colossians 3:12-17**
Song: **"Make Me a Blessing"**

A battered T-shirt, a mismatched pair of socks, a winter scarf, and fuzzy earmuffs—each item became a memorable teaching tool for my young children. The lesson: the importance of putting on the Lord Jesus Christ.

You see, being cooped up together for seven days a week could tax anyone's KQ (kindness quotient), and I needed something to help my children remember to model Jesus. So I labeled each item with a characteristic of Jesus. The socks were "kindness" and "gentleness," for without these it could be easy to tread on others as we climb the ladders of our own success. "Humility" and "patience" went to the earmuffs; without their covering we might hear things that make us irritable. The warm scarf symbolized "compassion," which needs to be draped over those who are hurting.

Finally, the well-worn T-shirt, symbolizing "love," was placed over all of these godly characteristics. As my children put each item on, it was as if they were actually clothing themselves with Jesus' righteousness. They were now well suited to model God's love to others.

Heavenly Father, *keep clothing me with the best of virtues that I might learn to model Your life to others. In Your loving name I pray. Amen.*

Properly Prepared

Behold, I am coming soon! Blessed is he who keeps the words of the prophecy in this book (Revelation 22:7).

Scripture: **Revelation 22:6-11**
Song: **"What If It Were Today?"**

"I'll be right over." Panic jolted me into action. My new friend mustn't see my house in such disarray! But how could I clean up the mess before she arrived? I began hiding things, shoving toys under the sofa, slamming pans into the oven and squeezing dirty clothes into dresser drawers. I even sprayed window cleaner into the air, in hopes of achieving a just-cleaned aura.

By the time she arrived, I was exhausted. And instead of enjoying our visit, I worried. What if I missed something? Would she see through my squeaky clean facade? (And what if she inadvertently took a look under the sofa?)

Jesus is coming back. In fact, He'll "be right over" (we just don't know exactly when). Instead of waiting until the last moment, we can be practicing an interior preparation, day by day. Developing a little more compassion. Opening to a deeper sense of peace, a less harried run at success. I would like to be ready with a free and joyful heart to greet my heavenly visitor when He arrives. Or, will I go to Him first?

Father, I desire to live each day in hopeful anticipation of Your Son's return. Show me the kinds of preparation that would please You most—and give me the will to put them into practice. Come, Lord Jesus. Amen.

A Sacrifice of Praise

My reward is with me, and I will give to everyone according to what he has done (Revelation 22:12).

Scripture: **Revelation 22:12-16**
Song: **"We Bring the Sacrifice of Praise"**

As a new Christian I struggled with the thought of meeting God face-to-face when I died. Would I have to hang my head in shame? I hadn't led anyone to Christ, my tithing was minimal, and I failed to reflect Jesus on many occasions. I seemed to possess nothing of significance to offer Him.

God used my biggest fear, the death of a child, to help me understand what it means to offer a sacrifice of praise. In Hebrews 13:15 we are encouraged to "continually offer to God a sacrifice of praise." A sacrifice always requires a death. It may not include a physical death but may involve the death of a desire, death of an ideal, or death of a dream. If pain weren't involved, it wouldn't be a sacrifice.

God was providing me an opportunity to offer Him a sacrifice of praise *in* and *through* my pain. Even though my heavy heart didn't want to rejoice, I deliberately chose to do so. God taught me that my response to this trial could someday be transformed into a crown of righteousness (see 2 Timothy 4:8), a crown I'll gladly lay at His feet.

Dear God, I offer my praise for the free gift of salvation. Yet I know You call me to good works as Your grateful child. Give me the wisdom and strength to serve You well. In the name of Jesus my Savior I pray. Amen.

Amen!

The grace of the Lord Jesus be with God's people. Amen (Revelation 22:21).

Scripture: **Revelation 22:17-21**
Song: **"God of Grace and God of Glory"**

"Mom, do you know what the last word of the Bible is?" My 8-year-old son had me stumped, so he smiled as he answered his own question, "Amen."

Most of our prayers end with this simple word, but what does it mean? We decided to look up the definition and found that it means "May it be so." Four simple words.

Suppose we really meant our amens? Would we live differently? For example, when I read a verse such as Philippians 4:4—"Rejoice in the Lord always"—if I say amen to that, may it be so, then I don't have any excuse for not praising God at all times.

And what about Revelation 22:20 where Jesus says, "Yes, I am coming soon"? Amen, may it be so.

If I took seriously every word in the Bible, and lived as if it were so, how much of my doubt, fear, worry, anger, and self-centeredness could I easily let go? That grace-filled life Jesus promised me—how I could live it!

May it be so.

Dear Lord, may it be that You will find me faithful and waiting for Your return. In the meantime, may I share to a hurting and needy world the grace You have lavished on me. Amen, amen, amen, may it be so. I pray in Your most precious name!

Too Messy?

Rescue the weak and needy; deliver them from the hand of the wicked (Psalm 82:4).

Scripture: Psalm 82
Song: "More Like the Master"

The other day I was driving to church when traffic slowed considerably. In the closed lane ahead was a familiar red car, now dented and smashed on one side. Instantly I recognized the driver who was talking to police officers along the roadside. We had just given money to this driver for engine repairs—on a now totaled car! In my frustration, I made a choice not to stop. Everyone was OK, so rather than offering assistance or comfort, I hurried on to church.

In the busyness of daily life, it is sometimes easy to turn away from the needy. We find quite rational reasons to stay uninvolved because we are busy with family or work, lack financial resources, or feel that folks should be able to meet their own needs. What's more, other people's problems can often complicate our own lives! Yet it is just such forms of complication that make the call to service what it is: an often inconvenient giving of our self—the whole of us—including our schedules and plans.

God, may I refuse to turn away from people in need when it seems too messy to get involved. Renew my compassion, in Christ's name! Amen.

May 28–31. **Karen Lusby** is a Colorado girl—born and raised amid the beautiful mountains and clear, blue skies.

No Faking It!

Our offenses are many in your sight, and our sins testify against us. Our offenses are ever with us, and we acknowledge our iniquities (Isaiah 59:12).

Scripture: **Isaiah 59:9-15**
Song: **"Come Ye Sinners, Poor and Needy"**

When I confronted my teenage son with a missed curfew, he replied defensively "I wasn't late *on purpose;* I fell asleep. Besides, other kids are doing much worse things than I am!" How like us human beings to minimize or justify our wrongdoing!

Sadly, sin separates us, not only from one another but from God. When Israel sinned, the prophet Isaiah called the nation to repentance. Their sins were many, but God would redeem and bless the people if they sincerely and honestly owned up to their misdeeds. The principle holds for all of us: No matter our offense, we can confess our sin and be cleansed with God's forgiveness.

How much easier it would have been for my son to say "Sorry, Mom; I was wrong." Rather, he sought redemption without the necessary step of confession. Yet the two always go together. The apostle John clearly affirms: "If we confess our sins, he is faithful and just and will forgive us our sins and purify us from all unrighteousness" (1 John 1:9).

Father, help me to be perfectly genuine with You—no hiding, no faking, no covering up. How thankful I am that You call sinners into fellowship with You! Through the name of Jesus, amen.

Ruinous Disobedience

If you do not obey these commands, declares the LORD, I swear by myself that this palace will become a ruin (Jeremiah 22:5).

Scripture: **Jeremiah 22:1-5**
Song: "Joy Unspeakable"

Two young college-age Christians recently chose to date one another. With excitement, they deliberately asked their family and friends to hold them accountable to God's standards in their relationship. They are committing to physical purity as an act of obedience, claiming 1 Corinthians 6:13 as their guiding principle: "The body is not meant for sexual immorality, but for the Lord, and the Lord for the body." Although challenging in today's world, their obedience is joyful for them.

In contrast, I chose disobedience when young and dating. I tested God's limits rather than trusting His Word. In hindsight, I regret opting for instant gratification (with its resulting misery).

Through the prophet Jeremiah, God long ago made clear the benefits of following His commands. And the blessings are many: wisdom and guidance for daily life, encouragement, hope, comfort, purity, freedom, peace, protection. And, of course, we avoid the ruin of living only for ourselves.

Almighty Lord in Heaven, *my heart is sometimes weary with disobedience. In those times, give me strength and courage to turn toward You. I know Your help is available, if I will only accept it. I pray this prayer in the precious name of Jesus. Amen.*

Sometimes Walking Alone

Do two walk together unless they have agreed to do so?
(Amos 3:3).

Scripture: **Amos 3:1-10**
Song: **"Faith Is the Victory"**

For years I'd heard debates on how to stay in fellowship within the church while disagreeing on points of theology. The answer was to focus on Jesus Christ and on spreading the gospel rather than giving energy to divisive disputes. However, some issues have become so nationally visible that they are now splitting churches.

For example, in more than one denomination, the idea of expanding the definition of marriage seems to hold some appeal for certain members. And thus the orthodox must decide whether to walk together (and perhaps work for renewal from within) or walk away. I heard one national church leader recently recite what God asks in Amos 3:3, "Do two walk together unless they have agreed to do so?" Holding his Bible high, he said, "Those who do not uphold this—I will not go with them." I admire a person like that, one who knows that a line can be crossed by others, beyond which he cannot go.

The principles apply to all. If we align ourselves with those who have walked away from God, we are surely witnessing to our agreement with them. And we walk on dangerous ground.

O Lord, keep me walking close to You this day that I might discern truth from error and always delight in Your ways. Through Christ, amen.

DEVOTIONS

*T*he ways of the
LORD are right;
the righteous
walk in them.

—Hosea 14:9

JUNE

Photo © Liquid Library

Gary Allen, Editor

New Start Available

The LORD has sworn by the Pride of Jacob: "I will never forget anything they have done" (Amos 8:7).

Scripture: **Amos 8:4-8**
Song: **"Amazing Grace"**

When my children were betrayed by a friend, they responded angrily: "That was unfair! I'll *never* be his friend!" Betrayed by an office colleague, I was hurt and vowed never to trust her again. When we're treated unfairly, we can hardly believe it, and we nurse our hurt.

God doesn't hold onto hurt in self-destructive ways as we so often do. However, He does remember the unfaithfulness of His people as He calls them back, over and over, to His heart of love.

How it must have hurt when Israel breached its covenant with Him! In Amos's day, the nation engaged in empty religious ritual, abusing the poor and needy. God abhors such evil; He knows and remembers the pain it causes. But we can be thankful for this: He extends the opportunity for repentance. He consistently provided warnings so the people could see their sin, repent, and receive the great blessing of forgiveness. A new start lay ahead for them, just as it does for you and me.

Dear Lord, when I am hurt and eager to judge, let me forgive as I have been forgiven. Remind me of Your mercy. I pray these things in the precious name of my Savior, Jesus Christ. Amen.

June 1–3. **Karen Lusby** is a Colorado girl—born and raised amid the beautiful mountains and clear, blue skies.

Brick by Brick

Though you have built stone mansions, you will not live in them (Amos 5:11).

Scripture: **Amos 5:10-15**
Song: **"Mansion Over the Hilltop"**

I once took great pride in being self-sufficient. I wore my apparent independence like a comfortable, well-loved sweater, a favored possession that I pulled out of the drawer and put on whenever I felt vulnerable or wasn't in complete control. Although I had given my life to Christ, I unwittingly held on to my sweater-of-sufficiency as a kind of armor of relational protection.

Slowly, over time, my sweater became tattered with age and use. I married, became a parent, divorced, and remarried. Then, months after taking a lucrative but stressful job, I was diagnosed with a potentially debilitating autoimmune disease. I couldn't protect myself from the sickness. Emotionally exposed and vulnerable, I turned to God and sought answers.

I learned that my protective sweater was really a "stone mansion" sheltering my heart. God lovingly dismantled it, brick by brick. How difficult it was to let go! Yet, finding my sufficiency in Him, how could I ever go back to the old way of being? As the apostle Paul put it in 2 Corinthians 3:5, "Not that we are competent in ourselves . . . but our competence comes from God."

Father, I know I'm often stubborn, wishing to run my own life without interference. But be my sufficiency this day. Through Christ, amen.

Openhearted?

"Even though you bring me burnt offerings and grain offerings, I will not accept them. Though you bring choice fellowship offerings, I will have no regard for them" (Amos 5:22).

Scripture: **Amos 5:20-25**
Song: **"Here I Am to Worship"**

Sunday services in our congregation begin with contemporary music worship followed by the minister's sermon. I like the music because it helps me prepare my heart to hear the scriptural message.

Recently our worship minister stood before the church and expressed his concern that our worship had seemed to become routine for us. Were we just going through the motions? Were our lips expressing what was truly in our hearts?

He challenged us gently, inquiring whether our familiarity with the service had caused us to become less than genuine. In response, we put music aside for a month during Sunday services. Instead, we worshiped together through prayer and sharing Scripture with one another.

How easy to become complacent! As God's people found long ago, when life is always the same, when worship is predictable and giving becomes routine, our hearts can drift from God. Thankfully, He knows our hearts. He keeps knocking there until we open wide once again.

My Father, God, I seek to worship and praise you with an authentic heart, open to all Your wisdom, guidance, and care. Help me to avoid being complacent with You when life is routine. I pray in Jesus' name. Amen.

The Kids Are Watching

He did evil in the sight of the Lord, as his fathers had done; he did not depart from the sins of Jeroboam the son of Nebat, which he made Israel sin (2 Kings 15:9, *New American Standard Bible*).

Scripture: **2 Kings 15:8-12**
Song: **"Father in Heaven, Who Lovest All"**

"One more minute and I'll have the bolt off this gate."

Samuel looked past his dad, afraid the police would show up. Yet he loved the feel of adrenaline pumping through him. When he was younger, he'd hated the fact his father was a thief. He laid in bed every night not knowing whether Dad would be in jail or at home when he woke up. Now Samuel understood the rush his father felt every time he made off with something valuable. What could be easier than working two hours a week to support his family? He knew stealing was wrong, but he just didn't want to stop.

Our parents play a huge role in how we think, don't they? When Israel had kings, the people could never know whether a king would "turn bad." But to make matters worse, a son would often follow in the footsteps of an evildoing dad. It's no different today. The children are watching us; they will pick up our ways, for good or ill.

Father, thank You for being my example of what an earthly parent should be. Today and always, may I follow only You! Through Christ, amen.

June 4–10. **Darlia Hill** lives and writes in Grand Junction, Colorado. Her three children have blessed her life immensely since she lost her husband in 2004.

No Need to Stumble

Whoever is wise, let him understand these things; whoever is discerning, let him know them. For the ways of the LORD are right, and the righteous will walk in them, but transgressors will stumble in them (Hosea 14:9, *New American Standard Bible*).

Scripture: **Hosea 14**
Song: **"Gentle Shepherd, Thou Hast Stilled"**

Water cascades over the rocks, foaming and frothing in the small pool below on its journey down the mountainside. Mist swirls over the creek as the roar of rushing water shuts out all other sounds in the forest.

Then I see a doe walking amid the fast-moving creek, each step sure and graceful. Her fawn rushes into the water, too, but ignores the path her mother took. The little one, on spindly legs, stumbles over the rocks with each step. By the time she reached her mother, her little hooves must have been bruised and sore.

When we take our eyes off the one who leads us, we lose our footing. We trip over pebbles and twigs in our way—all the daily troubles we encounter. But according to Hosea, we can walk a righteous path without stumbling. The problems won't go away, but we won't need to face them with hopeless despair. God is there with us. He leads us through the creek beds of our crises, over the mountains, through the streams, onward to glory.

Dear Father, *thank You for being my guide, for holding my hand as I follow the path You've placed before me today. In Jesus' name, amen.*

Our Humble God

I led them with cords of a man, with bonds of love, and I became to them as one who lifts the yoke from their jaws; and I bent down and fed them (Hosea 11:4, *New American Standard Bible*).

Scripture: **Hosea 11:1-5**
Song: **"At Thy Feet, Our God and Father"**

A vast desert lies behind and before me, and the sun shows no mercy as it burns into my skin. My legs no longer hold me, so I fall to my knees for a rest. My canteen is a lifesaver on this rigorous wilderness trek. Water is no longer simply a need but the difference between living and dying.

But suppose I'm without water or food, languishing in a hot, dry desert? I have felt that way at times, spiritually thirsty, longing for a sense of the Lord's care. Yet I'm sure He wants to lead us out of our deserts, just as the prophet tells us. For God is always there to offer us living water, the fellowship of His presence. With Him, every desert will come to an end.

He cares about us enough to "bend down" to feed us. What an amazing thing! When the load we're carrying threatens to overwhelm, He asks us to give it to Him. He is just that humble in His great love.

Dear Father, thank You for not leaving me in the desert places of my days. I am so grateful that You bend Your love to me, even when I fail to look to You for help and guidance. Today, may I leave all my struggles with You and drink deeply from the wellspring of Your goodness. Through Christ, amen.

Hear the Bugle?

My people are bent on turning from Me. Though they call them to the One on high, none at all exalts Him (Hosea 11:7, *New American Standard Bible*).

Scripture: **Hosea 11:6-11**
Song: **"Our Guilt Do We Confess Today"**

The snowpacked earth held the weight of the burro and the shivering man. At least there weren't any storm clouds in the Colorado sky—and just three more miles to go before Daniel would reach the next town. He'd made this loop through the mountains many times in the past four years, being the only preacher in the 1870s who made it to the few remote mining towns. As he entered the center of each town, he blew his bugle and then headed to the saloon to hold services. There he would call hardened miners to repent and be baptized in Christ's name.

Many realized this "mountain minister" brought the answer they'd searched for. The Lord he proclaimed became more precious to them than any riches they'd hoped for in the hills.

That is how I want Christ to be for me, today and always. Unlike the people of Hosea's day, I want to hear Him when He calls. And I hope that someday we two will be so close that even His most gentle whisper will be as a trumpet call to my ever-listening spirit.

O God, thank You for ministers who faithfully preach Your Word, even in the most difficult places. Help me to hear Your call through them and turn my heart to Your goodness and guidance. Through my Lord Jesus, amen.

A Land Without God

Listen to the word of the LORD, O sons of Israel, for the LORD has a case against the inhabitants of the land, because there is no faithfulness or kindness or knowledge of God in the land (Hosea 4:1, *New American Standard Bible*).

Scripture: **Hosea 4:1-5**
Song: **"Lord, Thou Hast Greatly Blessed Our Land"**

Another program filled with the sad things we do to each other. I listen to a story about a father who tried to take his own son's life. I turn off the television set.

Has the kindness left our land? We call a baby in its mother's womb a "mistake" and do away with it. When someone is sick without much hope for recovery, we begin considering euthanasia. When men or women grow "too old," we take them away from us to be cared for by strangers.

And what about the knowledge of God in our land? We've made prayer in schools illegal. We've banned the Ten Commandments from public display in our courts of law. Are we trying to erase God as if He never existed?

Have we become like Israel of old? Yet then, as now, God preserved a faithful remnant. May we be in that number! May we desire more of God each day, not less. Only then will faithfulness, kindness, and godly knowledge bloom once again in our midst.

God, thank You for loving the sinners of this world, those just like me. Now help me be an ambassador for You, an agent of change for the good in my culture. In the name of the Father, the Son, and the Holy Spirit, amen.

Already Favored

The thief enters in, bandits raid outside, and they do not consider in their hearts that I remember all their wickedness (Hosea 7:1, 2, *New American Standard Bible*).

Scripture: **Hosea 7:1-7**
Song: **"Thus Speaks the Lord to Wicked Men"**

"Brandon, they won't know if you don't tell," Kyle said, laying the stolen video game on his bed. "I deserve this game; Mom and Dad promised it to me months ago."

As Kyle threw his shirt in the corner, a pack of cigarettes fell out, and Brandon picked them up. "Now you're smoking? You know Grandpa died of lung cancer."

"That was him, not me." Kyle grabbed the cigarettes. "In fact, I think I'll smoke one right now."

Brandon backed to the door. "If you won't tell them you're stealing and smoking, then I will."

"Go ahead. You just want to be their perfect child. I'll never be that." Kyle slammed the door shut.

None of us will ever be that perfect child, neither for human parents nor for our heavenly Father. Yet God sent prophets like Hosea to tell us that God sees and cares about what we do. And when the time was just right, He offered us the perfection of His Son, Jesus. In Him and His strength, we can carry out good works that please Him—not to earn His favor, but because we already have it.

Father, forgive me for not considering how my sins make You feel. Thank You for the forgiveness that comes through Christ. In His name, amen.

Our Lighthouse

Return to your God, observe kindness and justice, and wait for your God continually (Hosea 12:6, *New American Standard Bible*).

Scripture: **Hosea 12:5-10**
Song: **"They That Overcome"**

Waves crashed upon a rocky shore as a lone figure sat in the sand, his head resting on bent knees. "How did I lose everything so fast?" Matt wondered. He thought the money he provided as breadwinner of the family would be enough. Now his family life lay in pieces around him. The corporate prestige and power that had once mattered so much now meant nothing. If only he could have back the family he'd neglected for so long. But they were miles away, living in a different state.

Matt had loved God as a boy but thought he'd out-grown Him. Now he realized he needed God to shine His light upon him and guide him home. He'd go to his family and ask their forgiveness.

Matt knew it might be a long time before his wife and kids would believe he really was a changed man. But he'd wait—continually wait in God's presence—knowing his life was secure only in that harbor of heavenly peace.

Lord, thank You for never giving up on me. I often make foolish plans, poor decisions, and self-destructive choices. But in Your mercy and goodness You stay close nevertheless. So in the next crisis that awaits me, give me grace and courage to wait patiently for Your guidance and to carry out Your will as You reveal it. In the name of Jesus, Lord and Savior, I pray. Amen.

Soon, in Heaven

You answer us with awesome deeds of righteousness, O God our Savior, the hope of all the ends of the earth and of the farthest seas (Psalm 65:5).

Scripture: **Psalm 65:1-8**
Song: **"Only Trust Him"**

A strong hurricane bore down on the Florida coastal town. Preparation time had ended, and now the people headed inland to seek safety.

A television reporter spotted one family cramming their car with all the belongings they could squeeze in. He approached the mother and asked her what she was feeling. "Hope," she replied. "We've done as much as we could to protect our house and our land. But this is such a powerful storm, we have no idea what may happen to it. It might be all gone when we get back, and we may have to start all over again. But right now there's nothing more to do. Now we can only hope."

No one knows what tomorrow holds. One of life's storms may be bearing down on us. Or sunny skies may be waiting to burst forth from gray clouds. But in all circumstances, our ultimate hope rests in our precious Savior. He has promised to be with us forever—in storms now, in Heaven soon.

Dear God, *no matter what troubles may come, I know You will never leave me. I place my hope in You for now and for eternity. In Christ, amen.*

June 11–17. **Jeff Friend**, big fan of the Baltimore Orioles, is also an award-winning writer and speaker who lives in Largo, Florida, with his wife, Nancy.

Worthy Example

**Following the example of his father Uzziah, Jotham did what
was pleasing to the LORD** (2 Kings 15:34, *Good News Translation
in Today's English*).

Scripture: **2 Kings 15:32-36**
Song: **"Let My Life Be a Light"**

As we sat around the table counting the money collect-
ed in the morning service, I came upon two little offering
envelopes that jingled with the sound of coins. The envelopes displayed the names of young sisters and the word
"Tithes" written across them in childlike scribblings.

When I opened the envelopes, four pennies fell from
each and plopped on the table. I stared at the little pile of
coins. I had been opening envelopes for several minutes,
pulling out checks and paper money without a thought.

But these eight pennies held my attention. Was it silly
for a child to give four cents? Not at all! Their parents had
taught them about tithing, and the children were simply
following the example of obedience to God.

The amount of the girls' contribution may seem insig-
nificant, but the spiritual foundations being built into
their lives are a matchless gift of love to them. I am sure
God receives their offering with pleasure—and with joy in
Mom and Dad's good work.

*Heavenly Father, may I live following good examples that are pleasing to
You. I thank You for placing godly people in my path. May I be an
example to others as You give me opportunities each day. In Jesus'
name, amen.*

Ready, Set, Go

I heard the voice of the Lord saying, "Whom shall I send? And who will go for us?" And I said, "Here am I. Send me!" (Isaiah 6:8)

Scripture: **Isaiah 6:1-8**
Song: **"Send Thou, O Lord, to Every Place"**

As the preschool teacher gathered the children around her, looking into all the eager faces, she softly said, "I have a very special job for someone to do." Before she could speak another word, each child shot up an arm and started waving it excitedly. Each hoped to be selected for the special task.

"But I haven't even told you what the job is!" said the teacher. "What if it's something hard, or something you don't like to do?" Not a hand went down, and the children continued to call out to their teacher. The details didn't matter to them. All they knew was that this beloved woman was asking for a volunteer; they simply wanted the chance to please her.

When the Lord said, "Whom shall I send?"(Isaiah 6:8). Isaiah immediately responded, "Send me!" Although he didn't know what he was going to be sent to do, he jumped at the opportunity to serve his Lord. And for good reason. There is a sense in which, whatever we are doing, if we have turned our hearts to God's presence in it with us, we will find joy there. Have you found it so?

__Holy God,__ I make myself available to serve You today, joyfully saying, "Here I am!" Through Christ the Lord, I pray. Amen.

God's Got You Covered

"My favor will shine on you like the morning sun. . . . I will always be with you to save you; my presence will protect you on every side" (Isaiah 58:8, *Good News Translation in Today's English*).

Scripture: **Isaiah 58:6-12**
Song: **"Surround Me, O Lord"**

Whenever the president of the United States appears in a public place, he's surrounded by secret service personnel. They watch for signs of trouble and are ready to respond at the first hint of something amiss. They blend in with the crowd and draw little attention to themselves.

They are trained to go to any lengths, even sacrificing their own lives, if necessary, to ensure the president's safety. Because of their presence, he can move about freely, without fear.

We also live in a world of danger. Yet God protects us on every side. What does that mean, in practical terms? For one thing, even though we cannot see Him, He constantly watches over us. But He ensures our safety in a deeper way than the guardians of a human president—not by sanitizing our existence or by denying any physical harm to us in our fallen world. He aims higher. In all situations, even our most painful ones, He seeks to grow our souls in holiness. His good and great goal is to prepare us for eternity. What an awesome protection!

Lord, *how thankful I am that You guard my soul against attack, that you protect my faith in You. Bring me home safely! Through Christ, amen.*

The Comforter Has Come

Comfort, comfort my people, says your God (Isaiah 40:1).

Scripture: **Isaiah 40:1-5**
Song: **"The Comforter Has Come"**

As the result of a venomous spider bite, I had 12 surgeries over six years and suffered extreme pain during most of that time. Finding it difficult to express to my family what I was going through, I would often become frustrated. It just seemed that no one could truly understand my situation.

During this time I learned the supreme value of comforting words and deeds. My family and friends would do whatever they could to soothe my suffering, both physically and emotionally. Although they could not help bear my pain—and they really couldn't understand it or feel it the way I did—they were able to encourage and support me in all kinds of practical ways.

The Israelites had endured years of hard times, and God had heard their cries of grief. Finally He proclaimed that it was time for them to be comforted and encouraged out of their misery.

God is also aware of our sufferings, even when we may think we're struggling alone. And there is, indeed, a time for those sufferings to come to an end. God has appointed that time. Be assured; relief is on the way.

God, You have promised a day when every tear will be wiped away. In the meantime, give me the peace of Your presence and the comfort of Your indwelling Spirit. In Christ's name I pray. Amen.

Delight in the Best

"Stop bringing meaningless offerings! Your incense is detestable to me. New Moons, Sabbaths and convocations—I cannot bear your evil assemblies" (Isaiah 1:13).

Scripture: **Isaiah 1:10-14**
Song: **"I Am Thine, O Lord"**

When I played football in high school, I found our coach to be very demanding. As we prepared for the upcoming season, he would run us through a variety of training drills every day. The first couple weeks we practiced with such great intensity that we could hardly lift our arms and legs by the end of the day. But every afternoon it was the same drills, over and over again.

Coach soon realized we were only doing those drills because we had to, not because we wanted to become better players. Truth be told, we just wanted the pain to end for that day.

After one particularly lackluster drill, Coach called us together and vented his frustration. "If any of you are just going to walk through this practice, then get off the field right now!" he bellowed. "I'm sick of this laziness!"

God does not want our half-hearted attempts to worship Him. He's not interested in lackluster routines. But He's *very* interested in you and me. I'm sure that's why He constantly invites our sincere worship and praise. What delight He must know when we give Him our best!

Father, You are worthy of my sincere worship. May my offerings be acceptable in Your sight. In the name of Your Son, my Savior, I pray. Amen.

Keeping It Simple

"Stop doing wrong, learn to do right!" (Isaiah 1:16, 17).

Scripture: **Isaiah 1:15-20**
Song: **"Trust and Obey"**

We're bombarded by slogans these days, those catchy little phrases advertisers use to highlight the main features of their products or services. Marketers spend a lot of money developing those cute ditties to help consumers understand and remember a basic concept.

Likewise, we tend to greatly condense information. After reading a 300-page novel, we may simply tell a friend, "It was about a man and his dog trapped in the mountains." We certainly left out a few details, right? But our friend at least caught a glimpse of the plot.

In Isaiah we find such an example of a basic concept God wants us to understand. It is nicely condensed, easy to remember: stop the wrong; do the right. What could be easier to recall? (The difficulty comes in the details.)

God constantly called the Israelites to trust Him and worship Him with sincere hearts. And Jesus' message was to repent of our sins and follow Him. Not difficult concepts, but impossible to carry out under our own power. Thus, centuries later, the apostle could say in Galatians 2:20: "I no longer live, but Christ lives in me. The life I live in the body, I live by faith in the Son of God, who loved me and gave himself for me."

Great God, sometimes I tend to lose sight of the essence of Your Word. Help me simply focus on doing what is right today. In Jesus' name, amen.

God's Invitation

"He has brought me to his banquet hall, and his banner over me is love" (Song of Solomon 2:4, *New American Standard Bible*).

Scripture: **Luke 14:15-24**
Song: **"Jesus Is Calling"**

One December, several years ago, I decided to host a fancy Christmas party. I planned the menu and decorated the house with all the trimmings of the season. I could picture my friends laughing and enjoying themselves around the beautifully decked-out Christmas tree.

When I called my friends to invite them, one by one they . . . declined! One was ill, another was having surgery, and another would be out of town. All gave excellent excuses, but, to say the least, I was quite disappointed. Never again would I plan a party until I was sure my friends could attend.

I didn't think of inviting the poor or the lonely into my home. Yet Luke tells us that is exactly what the Lord did (the man in the parable represents Jesus). He invited the people to come, but they were all too busy.

God still goes out into the highways and byways to call the poor and the lost. I was lonely and hurt when He called me to His banquet table. I will be forever grateful.

Father God, I want to be at Your great banquet in Heaven. Prepare me so I will be ready when You send out the invitations. In Jesus' name, amen.

June 18–24. **Marty Prudhomme** has been writing and teaching Bible studies for the past 20 years. She leads a friendship evangelism ministry called "Adopt-a-Block" for her church in Covington, Louisiana.

Day of Rejoicing

Surely our griefs He Himself bore, and our sorrows He carried
(Isaiah 53:4, *New American Standard Bible*).

Scripture: **Isaiah 25:6-10**
Song: **"Rejoice Today with One Accord"**

Several years ago I went on a mission trip to the Philippines where I constantly saw children begging in the streets, even at midnight. In the city of Manila, thousands of people live in a gigantic garbage dump. It's referred to as Smokey Mountain because of the fires that continually smolder under the mound. The citizens of this horrific city live in cardboard houses and survive off the trash. Many die of disease and hunger.

I was amazed to find so many people on Smokey Mountain who had faith in God. They know what it means to trust the Lord for their very existence. And they long for the day when their suffering will end, when their sorrow will be defeated forever.

Not everyone suffers like these people of the Philippines, but many of us are emotionally neglected, brokenhearted, abused, and wounded. Isaiah tells us about a day when the Lord of Hosts will prepare a lavish banquet for all of us who look to Him. All of God's people will rejoice together and be glad in His salvation. What a day of rejoicing that will be!

Father, I believe there will be a day when heartache, and sorrow, and suffering will cease forever. Give me the will to help those who suffer until then. I pray through my deliverer, Jesus Christ the Lord. Amen.

Good News for Now

He began to say to them, "Today this Scripture has been fulfilled in your hearing" (Luke 4:21, *New American Standard Bible*).

Scripture: **Isaiah 61:1-6**
Song: **"Spirit of the Living God"**

As I was growing up, at times depression would overwhelm me. I hoped marriage would rescue me from my troubles, but my problems became even more difficult. Often I felt hopeless, unloved, wondering, "Is this really all there is to life?" I didn't know that Jesus was my way out of this downward spiral.

Jesus stood in the synagogue 2,000 years ago and proclaimed that Isaiah's prophecy was fulfilled in Him. He was called to bring good news to the afflicted and to give a spirit of praise to those who mourn. I know there was no time limit to His heavenly mission, because I still remember the day I accepted Jesus' gift of salvation. He began healing my depression and my marriage. Now I can praise the Lord for my husband, children, and grandchildren. Yes, Jesus is still restoring lives.

Only He can repair our broken hearts. If we allow Jesus to take our junk, He will make something beautiful. The Spirit of the living God dwells in all who will receive His salvation. The Scripture is fulfilled in our hearing—now.

Lord, thank You for the gift of salvation. Help me comfort those who mourn and long for wholeness. I want to bring them the good news of Your grace so they will praise You forever. Glory to You, in Christ's name! Amen.

Known by Joy

"Their descendants will be known among the nations and their offspring among the peoples. All who see them will acknowledge that they are a people the LORD has blessed" (Isaiah 61:9).

Scripture: **Isaiah 61:7-11**
Song: **"Therefore the Redeemed of the Lord"**

My friend Shannon grew up with an abusive father who terrorized her family. At 13 years of age, she fought her way out of the house with a baseball bat, rescuing her mother and younger sister in the process.

When I first met Shannon years ago, she was serving as head of our local pregnancy crisis center. She was so much fun to be around that laughter followed wherever she went. Since that time, she has traveled for several years teaching children and adults God's Word in Indonesia, the Philippines, and Mongolia. Though the people of these nations live under terrible oppression and fear, Shannon can relate to their sorrows: "I know God can heal a wounded heart; He healed mine."

I believe God calls each of us to rise above our circumstances, relying upon His provision of daily strength. In fact, Isaiah tells us that God's people will be known among the nations because of their rejoicing in the Lord. They will be like a well-watered garden with seeds springing up into praise before all the earth. What a powerful image of our witness for Christ!

Dear Lord, *no matter what heartache comes into my life, I rejoice in Your presence with me. Thank You, in Jesus' name. Amen.*

Blessings Come Back

In their prayers for you their hearts will go out to you, because of the surpassing grace God has given you. Thanks be to God for his indescribable gift! (2 Corinthians 9:14, 15).

Scripture: **2 Corinthians 9:10-15**
Song: **"The Gift of Love"**

Four months ago I began an "Adopt-a-Block" ministry in my community. With a team of volunteers, we introduced ourselves to the people on Slemmer Road by distributing Easter baskets. The residents were a little puzzled, but we soon made friends. We didn't carry Bibles or talk in religious language. We simply explained that God cares for them, and so do we. Returning weekly, we prayed for them and brought food to the sick and needy. Soon we began to see answered prayers in their midst. One man even gave his neighbor a car.

Last month I had a stress test and angiogram. One of the families whose lives had been changed by our outreach effort phoned to let me know they were praying for me every night. I know God heard those prayers—they certainly gave my heart a boost.

God tells us to minister to others' needs and that they in turn will bless God and us. What a wonderful way—through blessing our neighbors—to add a few trinkets to the heavenly treasure chest.

Good and merciful God, may I always see others through Your eyes of compassion. Use me as a vessel to pour out Your love to the hurting and the lost in my world. In the name of Your Son, my Savior, I pray. Amen.

Come, Be Satisfied

"Why spend money on what is not bread, and your labor on what does not satisfy? Listen, listen to me, and eat what is good, and your soul will delight in the richest of fare" (Isaiah 55:2).

Scripture: **Isaiah 55:1-5**
Song: **"Springs of Living Water"**

My daughter-in-law and I have the same love for chocolate—all kinds of gooey chocolate confections, candy bars, and ice cream. When we first met, I coaxed her into the family with chocolate cakes. During my childhood, when there was no money for extras, I could never get enough chocolate. I remember standing outside the ice cream parlor begging Mom for a cone.

Today, I can buy all the chocolate I want, but it makes me gain weight. So, you see, I'm never satisfied.

Many people try to fill their lives with substitutes for genuine spiritual life. They "self-medicate" their soul-hurt, their deep longings, with things that temporarily dull the pain. These only fill the gap for a few moments; afterwards, there's a price to pay. Have you been there?

Isaiah says we can be content with the abundance God provides. It may not seem like gourmet food at first glance. But as we settle down in peace before the Lord, we find a table spread with just the right food for nurturing life within us. He gives living bread, himself, forever.

Lord, *may I never be disappointed with Your daily provision in my life, for You know just what I need. In the name of Christ I pray. Amen.*

Bitterness, Good-bye

"As the heavens are higher than the earth, so are my ways higher than your ways and my thoughts than your thoughts" (Isaiah 55:9).

Scripture: **Isaiah 55:6-11**
Song: **"Higher Ground"**

One night, while on a mission trip to Panama, I met a woman named Mary. Several years before she had lost her 6-year-old daughter to cancer. Her husband left her soon afterwards because he couldn't handle the grief. Now Mary was very bitter; everyone could see it on her face. In fact, bitterness and anger had consumed her life for a long time. And she wanted nothing to do with God anymore, assuming He had cruelly taken her child away from her.

A friend of Mary's virtually dragged her to our church service one night. She heard this message: God sees the hurts of our hearts. She heard that God was calling her to give up the bitterness, for He was pouring out His compassion on her hurting soul. Though everyone in town could see only her bitterness, He saw her grieving heart.

Mary suddenly realized that God's ways were not her ways. She called on Him while He was near and received His transforming love that night. Mary let go of the bitterness in her heart and began a new life.

Dear Lord, I know that human sin has brought much pain and suffering into our world—and that You're allowing it to continue for a time. But it still hurts. Nevertheless, lift my eyes to my neighbors today. Give me the courage to help ease their pain in some small way. In Jesus' name, amen.

Clinging to the Rock

Thou shalt fear the LORD thy God; him shalt thou serve, and to him shalt thou cleave, and swear by his name (Deuteronomy 10:20, *King James Version*).

Scripture: **Deuteronomy 10:12-22**
Song: **"Rock That Is Higher Than I"**

My fingernails dug into the leather of the saddle horn as my horse plunged down the riverbank, bucking frantically. I could see more rocks than water, so I clung to what I had, desperately.

Is it like that between God and us? He invites His people to cleave to Him, to stick close and form an unbreakable bond with Him. He knows we'll face times of desperation more serious than landing headfirst in a river. Therefore, He promises never to leave us (see Hebrew 13:5).

Sometimes my first reaction to difficulty is to pull away from God. "Why me?" I ask. Why must I face financial insecurity, physical or emotional pain? Yet, in those times, I hear His invitation to cleave. I hear Him whisper His promise—not that I might have a better life, but that I might have a better relationship with Him. After all, cleaving, joining, and staying close result in companionship. And what could be better than companioning with God?

God of relationship, thank You for being my Rock to cleave to when the rocks of life's trials threaten to loosen my grip. In Christ I pray. Amen.

June 25–30. **Ron Silflow** works as an educator in the area of human and animal biotechnology. He resides in Bozeman, Montana, with his wife, Laura. His passions include being with his three children, caring for people, and journaling.

In Great Distress?

Wherefore lift up the hands which hang down, and the feeble knees; and make straight paths for your feet (Hebrews 12:12, 13, *King James Version*).

Scripture: **Hebrews 12:6-12**
Song: **"No Other Name but the Name of Jesus"**

I've just read the Bible story in which King David and his men came back to their city and found it burned to the ground. The city's families had been taken captive, including the wives and children of David and his men. It was so bad that there was talk of stoning David for the lack of protection while he was away. Yet here's the statement that sticks with me so powerfully: "But David found strength in the LORD his God" (1 Samuel 30:6).

David didn't deny the reality of great distress. Instead, he used it as a good reason to look to a higher source than himself for courage. He had to let go of the weight of self-reliance and look to God. When our hearts are heavy, our hands will hang down.

When our hearts look up, our hands can arise in surrender, in trust, in courage. As the great preacher Charles Spurgeon once said, "The refiner is never far from the mouth of the furnace when his gold is in the fire, and the Son of God is always walking in the midst of the flames when his holy children are cast into them."

*You are my strength, **Almighty God of glory,** when I am weak. Lift up my head and hands before You when distress fills my days. And set my feet on a solid path. Through Christ my Savior I pray. Amen.*

Jealous Love

Woe to them that devise iniquity, and work evil upon their beds! when the morning is light, they practice it, because it is in the power of their hand (Micah 2:1, *King James Version*).

Scripture: **Micah 2:1-5**
Song: **"Saviour, Thy Dying Love Thou Gavest Me"**

I arrived at the high-school social late and quickly scanned the room for the girl I was to meet there. No sign of her. Had she tired of waiting and returned home? Then my eyes caught her talking to another boy, their eyes locked on to each other, oblivious to my presence as they walked into a nearby garden, hand in hand. My face flushed red, my heart sank, and, 30 years later, I still feel the jealous crush.

Despite many warnings, God's people, during the time of Micah, were becoming more openly rebellious. God was about to manifest a part of His nature that is inseparable from His spirit of love: His righteous jealousy. "For thou shalt worship no other god: for the Lord, whose name is Jealous, is a jealous God" (Exodus 34:14, *KJV*). Of course God is the only one in the universe with the right to be jealous of worship. Why? Because He's . . . *God!*

The wonderful thing is that God is jealous for our fellowship, which is for our good, for our best. He loves us so much that He guards this relationship with His life. The cross of Calvary proves it.

Loving, jealous God, *forgive me for turning elsewhere for satisfaction in life. You gave Your life for my love. Thank You, in Christ's name. Amen.*

No Hiding Here!

Then shall they cry unto the Lord, but he will not hear them: he will even hide his face from them at that time, as they have behaved themselves ill in their doings (Micah 3:4, *King James Version*).

Scripture: **Micah 3:1-7**
Song: **"I Lay My Sins on Jesus"**

To be chastened by God is, to say the least, unpleasant. To have Him hide His face, though, is unbearable. Chasten us, judge us, but, O God, please don't abandon us!

Yet He cannot look on our sin. Therefore, like David, in repentance we cry out, "Cast me not away from thy presence; and take not thy Holy Spirit from me" (Psalm 51:11, *KJV*).

So often the pressures of life and the guilt of our sin lead us to question God . . .

"Are You really enough for me?"

"Do You have what it takes to carry me through?"

"Will You turn Your face from me?"

The good news chimes in at just this point: Because our sin was placed on Jesus when He hung on the cross, God hid His face—once and for all. Christ not only bore the judgment for the world's sin, He was abandoned by the Father so we would be accepted. When we come to God in repentance, we hear the resounding reply to our deepest plea: "No, I will not turn my face from you!"

Father, how I love You for the mercy of Your saving plan! How I praise You for my forgiveness! Glory to You, through Christ the Lord. Amen.

Inconvenient Surrender

Therefore shall Zion for your sake be plowed as a field, and Jerusalem shall become heaps, and the mountain of the house as the high places of the forest (Micah 3:12, *King James Version*).

Scripture: **Micah 3:8-12**
Song: **"Come, O Come, Thou Quickening Spirit"**

Have you noticed? God's plow will turn your life upside down. The purpose of His plow is to prepare good ground to receive His good seed. Good ground plus good seed lead to good fruit.

Is your ground wild and untamed? Or, perhaps, has your ground recently produced a fruitful crop? To the plow, it doesn't matter. The plow will bury what can be seen on the surface and reveal what has been hidden.

Saul, apprehended by Jesus, had his life turned upside down on the road to Damascus. What was visible on Saul's surface—a life of persecuting Christ's followers—got buried by this miraculous encounter. What had been hidden in Saul's depths, Christ brought to the surface, "for [Saul] is a chosen vessel unto me, to bear my name before the Gentiles" (Acts 9:15, *KJV*). What a transformation! His name even changed. Now he was Paul, the apostle.

I want my heart to be ready for that plow in coming days. It isn't an easy surrender. It might be uncomfortable, might be inconvenient. But it's the only way to grow.

O Lord, move upon my heart today and prepare me to be a more productive fruit bearer in Your kingdom. Through Christ I pray. Amen.

Walk in His Paths

Let us go up to the mountain of the LORD, and to the house of the God of Jacob; and he will teach us of his ways, and we will walk in his paths (Micah 4:2, *King James Version*).

Scripture: **Micah 4:1-5**
Song: **"The King of Love My Shepherd Is"**

It looked like my grandpa was teaching me to braid a three-strand rope from baling twine. But he was teaching me much more. He was teaching me of God's ways. As we braided, he spoke of lives being entwined together. He talked about the entwining of a husband and wife with Christ.

I held in my hand a three-strand rope. In my mind I saw a picture of a Christ-centered marriage relationship—"a threefold cord is not quickly broken" (Ecclesiastes 4:12, *KJV*).

What an invitation! God calls us to take a journey in His *paths*, not highways. Paths of learning. Paths of companionship and intimacy.

Can you recognize the path God has you on at the moment? He doesn't promise our paths will be easy. But He invites us there anyway, because He's been there before and will lead us now. There is great intimacy in that kind of walk with Him.

My Lord and shepherd, I join You for the journey on Your paths. I thank You that I can declare, like the psalmist, "Though I walk through the valley of the shadow of death, I will fear no evil: for thou art with me" (Psalm 23:4, KJV). In the name of Your Son, my Savior, I pray. Amen.

My Prayer Notes

DEVOTIONS

*T*he earth will
be filled with the
knowledge of the
glory of the LORD.

—Habakkuk 2:14

JULY

Photo © Stockbyte

Gary Allen, Editor

God's Goodness

O my people, what have I done unto thee? And wherein have I wearied thee? testify against me (Micah 6:3, *King James Version*).

Scripture: **Micah 6:3-8**
Song: "Within the Veil"

"God, if You are good, then why . . . ?" Like me, you've probably asked this question many times, under many difficult circumstances. Is it OK to question of God, "Are you good?" David said, "I had fainted, unless I had believed to see the goodness of the Lord in the land of the living" (Psalm 27:13, *KJV*). David got his answer, and we each long to hear our answers, individually, from God. Why? Because it is difficult to hold to the goodness of God when our circumstances scream differently. This was a problem in Micah's day, and it still plagues us too.

I am comforted by the fact that God invites such questioning, just as He invited the ancient Israelites to "testify against" Him. So join me in responding to God's invitation to meet with Him in every circumstance—whether we are joyful or in pain, whether confident or confused. As you plead for His response, let Him answer you personally. He has shown us His love by saving us through Christ's blood. He will reveal His goodness right where our hearts need Him today.

O Lord, You have shown me what is good: to walk humbly with You each moment. That is my desire this day. Through Christ, amen.

July 1. **Ron Silflow** loves to journal his conversational relationship with Jesus. He and his wife, Laura, live in Bozeman, Montana. They have three children.

Pie in the Sky?

I would have lost heart, unless I had believed that I would see the goodness of the LORD in the land of the living (Psalm 27:13, *New King James Version*).

Scripture: **Psalm 27:7-14**
Song: **"God Will Take Care of You"**

Ministers are sometimes accused of preaching a "pie in the sky" brand of Christianity. The downtrodden are encouraged to keep their focus on Heaven and all the blessings to come in the afterlife. For most of us, though, as precious as that blessed hope is, it's not enough just to imagine it coming to pass . . . someday. We need hope for *today*, assurance that God is working on our behalf in the here and now. David was a man after God's own heart, but even he admitted he would have lost heart if he couldn't count on seeing God's goodness here on earth—in the land of the living.

Ironically, it may be easier to have faith for life beyond the grave. We may have to press in closer to the Lord to gain that same assurance for our daily walk in this life. When we draw close to Him, He will draw close to us, and we will see His goodness at work in our lives to give us the strength we need today.

God of all goodness, thank You for Your promise to be with me every step of the way, in this life and in the life to come. In the name of Jesus, my Savior and Lord, I pray. Amen.

July 2–8. **Rosalie M. LoPinto** is a freelance Christian writer. She lives in Riverside, Rhode Island, and works with several ministries in the area of communications.

Whom Do You Trust?

Stop trusting in man, who has but a breath in his nostrils. Of what account is he? (Isaiah 2:22).

Scripture: **Isaiah 2:12-22**
Song: **"No One Ever Cared for Me Like Jesus"**

Ancient Egyptians believed their kings, the pharaohs, were actually gods. They also believed their own continued existence in the afterlife was connected to that of the pharaohs, and thus gave great care to preserving their rulers' bodies after death. Mummification was crucial because one could only survive in the afterlife as long as the body survived.

We Christians view things differently! We know our spirits will remain when our bodies have returned to the dust. And we don't rely on another human being to usher us into the afterlife. Yet in this life we still sometimes place people on pedestals, looking to them for our own survival. We expect politicians to fix this troubled world, ministers to mend our wounded hearts, friends to cure our loneliness, and spouses to meet our deepest needs.

In reality, it is the prince of peace, the healer, the friend of sinners who sticks closer than a brother. He is the lover of our souls, in whom we can place our ultimate confidence. He is the only one on whom we can depend completely.

Lord, it seems easier to turn to the phone instead of the throne. Forgive me for all the times I look for answers from everyone else. Help me to remember to seek counsel from You, first and foremost. Through Christ, amen.

Heavenly Plans

The plans of the LORD stand firm forever, the purposes of his heart through all generations (Psalm 33:11).

Scripture: **Psalm 33:1-11**
Song: **"God Is Still on the Throne"**

In his book *1776*, David McCullough cites repeated instances when the colonial army survived almost certain defeat at the hands of the British by what seemed like divine intervention. Winds would shift, switching the advantage to the Americans. Or a sudden fog would keep them from detection by the British. Ultimately the Americans prevailed, and a nation was born.

For all its flaws, the United States of America has been a beacon of gospel light through much of its history. In fact, I believe God has allowed this nation to survive for His plans and purposes. Over the decades, thousands of missionaries have gone out from this land to every corner of the globe.

Whether for nations or for individuals, God's plans are indestructible. True, a certain amount of chance and probability infuse our fallen world for now. Yet we are never its victims, for all that enters our lives is only what God allows. Even more encouraging is this: "He who began a good work in you will carry it on to completion until the day of Christ Jesus" (Philippians 1:6).

*I thank You, **Lord,** that You knew me when I was in my mother's womb and You had a plan for me. I ask You now to fulfill Your purpose in me and through me, and I will give You all the glory. In Jesus' name, amen.*

Housecleaning

He . . . crushed the idols to powder and cut to pieces all the incense altars throughout Israel. Then he went back to Jerusalem (2 Chronicles 34:7).

Scripture: **2 Chronicles 34:1-7**
Song: **"Burn in Me, Fire of God"**

I don't like superficial cleaning jobs. Shoving things in closets, sweeping dirt under a rug, hanging clean curtains on dirty windows—that's not my thing. I never feel as if a house is really neat and clean until every window gleams and every closet displays order.

In our text, Josiah determined to utterly destroy every remnant of Israel's previous idolatry. He wanted to restore righteousness to the land, and he knew all of the evil reminders of Israel's sin had to be obliterated before he could restore the temple in Jerusalem.

If you're like me, you want your house to pass the "white glove test." But more importantly, you want your *life* to pass muster with your Lord. Let's take an inventory together in the week ahead. Anything needing to be cleaned up, straightened out—or even completely "crushed to powder"? I certainly want the temple of my body to be a clean and comfortable place for the Spirit of God to dwell.

Dear Lord, please show me if there is a habit or practice, or even a possession or a relationship, that shouldn't be in my life. Help me to be determined to destroy that which displeases You. I pray this prayer in the name of Jesus, my merciful Savior and Lord. Amen.

The Problem of Pain

The Lord within her is righteous; he does no wrong. Morning by morning he dispenses his justice, and every new day he does not fail, yet the unrighteous know no shame (Zephaniah 3:5).

Scripture: **Zephaniah 3:1-7**
Song: **"I Want to Be Like Jesus"**

"Why would a good God allow children to starve to death?" My friend Leif's question was nothing new. Human beings have struggled over "the problem of pain" since the beginning. Adam and Eve were the first to wonder about God's goodness and intentions.

A young Christian at the time, I offered up a quick and silent prayer before responding to my friend. "There is more than enough food in the world to feed every single person, with plenty left over," I said. "People starve because of the greed, hatred, and lack of concern for their fellow creatures." I don't know how you'd have answered, but I was as startled at my words as Leif apparently was. For the moment, at least, his latest assault on God's character had been squelched.

The point is, God is good—let's just settle the matter. We, on the other hand, are not always so good. We often fail to meet a need when it is in our power to do so. Much of the problem of pain results from our problem with sin.

Dear Lord, keep me from turning my eyes from the needs that swirl around me. Move me with Your compassion today! Through Christ I pray. Amen.

Can You Blush?

**Never again will you be haughty on my holy hill. But I will
leave within you the meek and humble, who trust in the name
of the LORD** (Zephaniah 3:11, 12).

Scripture: **Zephaniah 3:8-13**
Song: **"In My Life, Lord, Be Glorified"**

As a child, I loved Red Skelton. His funny and
poignant characters, like Clem Kadiddlehopper and Freddy
the Freeloader, could make me laugh and make me cry.
Commenting on the Freeloader, Red once said that Freddy
was "nice to everybody because he was taught that man is
made in God's image. He's never met God in person, and
the next fella just might be Him." Every night Red closed
his show the same way, "Good night, and God bless."

You can't listen to most of today's comedians for more
than a minute or two without realizing that Red would be
way out of his element in today's entertainment business.
Crudeness and vulgarity are the standard fare, served up
with arrogance but without shame. Jeremiah 6:15 refers to
such folks as those who "do not even know how to blush"
over their sin.

Today I'm asking myself: What do I find entertaining
and amusing? What am I willing to allow into my living
room—and into my spirit? And . . . do I still know how
to blush?

Father, help me remember today that You are present when I am watching
TV, listening to the radio, or hanging around the watercooler at work. Let
me recall that Your Spirit dwells within me. In Jesus' name, amen.

Treasure Hunt

"He will take great delight in you, he will quiet you with his love, he will rejoice over you with singing" (Zephaniah 3:17).

Scripture: **Zephaniah 3:14-20**
Song: **"May I Never Lose the Wonder"**

Let's be honest. For many of us, Bible reading can sometimes be a chore. Oh yes, we love the Word, and we know God wants to speak to us through it. Still there are days when it feels like a mandatory assignment.

Some years ago, I was having one of those days and feeling justly convicted. I put my Bible down and opened my heart to God. "Lord, make Your Word come alive to me," I prayed.

Returning to my Bible, I saw it for the first time—God sings! Not only does He sing, but I'm the *reason* He sings; He sings over me! The lover of my soul is so enthralled with me that He bursts into song. (Wouldn't you love to hear the song He is singing over you today?)

God's Word is full of precious jewels like that. If we live a hundred years, He will still be able to surprise us with some shining nugget of truth and wisdom we never saw before. Every time we read the Bible, we can approach it as a thrilling treasure hunt.

Lord of all truth and wisdom, show me something new in Your Word every time I pick it up. Thank You for this awesome book that nourishes me and helps me see You more clearly. Truly, it is the bread my soul requires, and nothing else can fill me so completely. In the name of the Father, the Son, and the Holy Spirit, I pray. Amen.

Waiting for God

Wait for the LORD and keep his way. He will exalt you to inherit the land (Psalm 37:34).

Scripture: **Psalm 37:27-34**
Song: **"It Is Well with My Soul"**

When I came home from the hospital to recuperate from cancer surgery, I was eager to get on with life. I wanted to pick up right where I'd left off. Reality set in quickly, however. I was weak; I was tired; I had no strength. When I sat down in my chair, I promptly fell asleep. It seemed I could do nothing that required even the smallest effort.

Time moved slowly. I felt bored and useless. Finally I struggled to my desk and began shuffling through bills and papers. *If I could just walk down the driveway to the mailbox. . . .* But my wife had to bring the mail to me.

I opened one of the cards she handed me. The cover displayed these words: "Be still, and know that I am God" (see Psalm 46:10). I stared at the words and let them sink in.

"Wait," I heard. "Wait for God's healing time, and savor this period of quietness. Wait for your body and your spirit to be restored. Listen to the voice that whispers when you wait. Then you will find the healing you need."

Patient God, teach me the importance of resting in the moment, for I am so prone to rush off and leave You behind. Give me the serenity that comes with pausing to hear Your voice. In the name of Christ, I pray. Amen.

July 9–15. **Drexel Rankin** served as an ordained minister for more than 35 years before his recent retirement. He and his wife, Patty, live in Louisville, Kentucky.

Are You Jesus?

To this you were called, because Christ suffered for you, leaving you an example, that you should follow in his steps (1 Peter 2:21).

Scripture: **2 Kings 23:31-37**
Song: **"I'm Gonna Live So God Can Use Me"**

The busy executive was rushing to catch his plane. He had almost given up living a *personal* daily life because of the great time demands of his *work* life—including speaking engagements along with all the administrative duties of his company. But on this particular morning, he had promised himself he'd try to at least act the part of a Christian as he went through this day.

By the time he had reached the airport terminal and checked his bags, he was running late. Charging down the concourse, he heard the last call for boarding. In his haste, he bumped into a small boy carrying several toys in his arms. The toys scattered across the waiting area.

The executive paused, saw the child in tears, and, with an inward sigh, remembered the promise he'd made to himself earlier. He stopped, picked up the child's toys, put them back in his arms, ruffled the lad's hair, and said, "I'm sorry."

The boy looked at the man with awe and said hesitantly, "Mister, are you Jesus?"

Lord, help me to be a shining token of Your love wherever I will be this day. May I reflect Your compassion to others. May I remind those whom I meet today of the love that You have for all people. Through Christ, amen.

Can You Detect Him?

Your eyes are too pure to look on evil; you cannot tolerate wrong. Why then do you tolerate the treacherous? Why are you silent while the wicked swallow up those more righteous than themselves? (Habakkuk 1:13).

Scripture: **Habakkuk 1:12-17**
Song: **"Immortal, Invisible"**

We human beings are tantalized by mysteries. Detective novels fascinate many of us, and even public television has a weekly program called, simply, *Mystery*.

God and His ways were a mystery to Habakkuk—and still are to us in many ways. The mystery of God, however, isn't so much *secretive* as it is *vast*. My wife and I rediscover this each time we visit another national park.

God's vastness encompasses the entire world, and it seems there just isn't enough time to understand it all. Yet answers are set before us everywhere—in nature, in science, in our own deeds. We too are each a part of God's mystery when we gather in worship, offer friendship to a stranger, or feed the hungry.

Echoing the prophet, our own "why's" will never cease, though. Not until the mystery is fully revealed when, as the Scripture says, we shall see Him face to face. For "now I know in part; then I shall know fully, even as I am fully known" (1 Corinthians 13:12).

Immortal, invisible God, in all the places You are, in all the things You do, in all the great and glorious mystery that is You, may I stand in awe today. In Christ's name, I pray. Amen.

Living with Questions

"The revelation awaits an appointed time; it speaks of the end and will not prove false. Though it linger, wait for it" (Habakkuk 2:3).

Scripture: **Habakkuk 2:1-5**
Song: **"Spirit of God, Descend Upon My Heart"**

My wife, Patty, is a more patient person than I am. I learn from her as she prepares her several gardens in our yard. The heat of the summer is now past as Patty plants the bulbs in the ground—tulips, daffodils, hyacinths. Carefully she chooses the right location. Gently she tamps the soil around them.

Through the cool days of autumn, into the first chilled days of winter, beneath the snow and the ice, those tubers will sleep in the darkness. The bulbs—and my wife—patiently wait for frozen days to pass. The ground will soon thaw, and sprouts will emerge.

This process of life parallels living for God. There is always a time of waiting in the darkness, living with questions that beg for answers. This was Habakkuk's situation when God encouraged him to hold on patiently.

Like the flowers of spring, I need that time for God to form me from within—to create something new and beautiful. In God's time, the answers to my questions will emerge in their own season.

Patient God, *teach me the secret of the planted seed—to wait on You. Give me Your gift of patience as I wait for You to form me as You wish. In the name of the Father, the Son, and the Holy Spirit, amen.*

The Eyes of a Child

"The earth will be filled with the knowledge of the glory of the LORD, as the waters cover the sea" (Habakkuk 2:14).

Scripture: **Habakkuk 2:6-14**
Song: **"For the Beauty of the Earth"**

Recently, my friend Jerry wrote about his little girl and the summertime dandelion season. He said that, like many people, he and his wife pay a lawn service to come to their home once a month to spray their yard. The service isn't cheap, but he thinks it's worth it to keep his lawn up to the standards of those who live around him.

But Jerry's 4-year-old daughter, Gracie, has a favorite yard in their neighborhood—the one down the street that is covered with dandelions. Gracie told her dad, "I hope we can have pretty little flowers like that in our yard some day!"

Oh, to see the world through those little eyes, to see the beauty of dandelions and to feel special because you're certain the sun is following you. I wonder how much of the glory of the Lord I miss on any given day. How much beauty, how much goodness? Maybe Gracie and all other children around us can teach us truly to see. I am sure that if we look closely enough we will see not only a wonderful creation but the face of the creator as well.

God of creation, I am thankful for the eyes of children who behold You in such a sincere and innocent way. Help me to learn from them as they teach me about seeing You everywhere in life. In the holy name of Jesus, my Lord and Savior, I pray. Amen.

In Silence

"The LORD is in his holy temple; let all the earth be silent before him" (Habakkuk 2:20).

Scripture: **Habakkuk 2:15-20**
Song: **"This Is My Father's World"**

Miss Graham, my first piano teacher, exercised infinite patience as she tried to teach me the rudiments of musical knowledge and performance. Among the concepts she attempted to clarify for me was the musical rest.

"Do you understand what a rest is?" she asked.

"A rest," I offered, "is a time filled with nothing."

Wrong answer!

She launched into an extended oration, explaining how the composer, in his genius, had placed the rest in a particular passage of the music to be part of the grand design of the composer's work. To the uneducated ear it might seem like "nothing" was happening. In truth, the composer used that silence to build the power of the music and to bring the entire score to a grand finale. "Something" was indeed happening in each silence.

I've pondered that lesson many times. A rest in a portion of human existence—silence—is hardly *nothing*. It is part of God's grand design. In the silence, if we listen closely with our hearts, we will surely hear something wondrous from on high.

Let me be still, O Lord. Let me push aside, at least for a time each day, the many swirling voices and noises that fill my mind. Today I want to hear Your whispers in the silence. In the name of Jesus, amen.

God for All Seasons

Though the fig tree does not bud and there are no grapes on the vines, though the olive crop fails and the fields produce no food . . . I will be joyful in God my Savior (Habakkuk 3:17, 18).

Scripture: **Habakkuk 3:13-19**
Song: **"Joy to the World"**

It came as a bit of a shock when the folks in the congregation opened their hymnals for the opening song: "Joy to the World." A Christmas carol in the middle of July? Was this a joke?

As their minister, I had chosen the hymn, not as a prank, but as a way to express the truth that rejoicing in the Lord knows no season. And it worked.

This was a song that we all knew, and we sang it boisterously, joyfully. In fact, there was spontaneous rejoicing—a praising of God that burst with life from deep within our souls. And why not? Christmas isn't the only season to sing gladly about God's coming in our midst.

Yet, as Habakkuk demonstrates, joy and happiness are not always the same. Circumstances can cause us deep pain and consternation, and we won't be happy about it. That's why happiness is usually a temporary, emotional condition based on "things going my way."

Joy is deeper. We can be joyful regardless of an unhappy situation. We have Christ within us. Even when those troubles seem to endure, He and His joy remain.

God who brings joy to heavy hearts, You are my God for all seasons. All glory to You, in the name of Jesus the king. Amen.

In the Sunshine, Draw Near

We must pay more careful attention, therefore, to what we have heard, so that we do not drift away (Hebrews 2:1).

Scripture: **Hebrews 2:1-4**
Song: **"Leaning on the Everlasting Arms"**

I find drifting in a rubber raft on a slow-moving river one of the most relaxing things to do. No white-water rapids for me! I just like to lie back, soak up sunshine, and watch dragonflies dart over the placid surface of the water.

Floating in a raft provides great summertime relaxation, but drifting away from church can sabotage our spiritual lives. Neglecting private devotional time or worship services can set us up to meander in the direction of our culture—which is often less than spiritually healthy.

Ask your minister and he'll probably tell you attendance and giving typically decrease during the summer months. But instead of sliding into a slump, I'm finding creative ways to keep God first this summer. My kids and I schedule outings so we won't miss services with our church. And picnics with small groups offer pleasant fellowship. I'm beginning to see that summertime is a wonderful season to draw near to the Lord.

Father, this summer I don't want to drift but to press closer and hear Your heart more clearly. I love You. Through Christ I pray. Amen.

July 16–22. **Patty Duncan** teaches fifth grade at Eugene Christian School, parents her teenage son, and spoils her two grandsons. She grew up in the Church of Christ in Cottage Grove, Oregon.

Coming Back to God

**If . . . My people who are called by My name humble them-
selves and pray, and seek My face and turn from their wicked
ways, then I will hear from heaven, will forgive their sin, and
will heal their land"** (2 Chronicles 7:14, *New American Standard
Bible*).

Scripture: **2 Chronicles 7:11-16**
Song: **"Prayer Is the Soul's Sincere Desire"**

Judy Buck, a busy second-grade teacher, mentors
young women in her church who want help. She studies
with them through a Bible course that provides an understanding of the Lord's work of redemption. Her effort provides a foundation for Christian living for new converts
or those returning to the church.

Sometimes Judy's students have moral issues; for
example, some may be living with a boyfriend before
marriage. "Some people think I shouldn't waste my time
with those young ladies," Judy says. But she disagrees.
More and more children and teenagers are growing up
with no Christian training and don't know how to choose
a godly lifestyle. Judy believes in loving them and helping
them find their way back to God.

God promised the Israelites that if they changed their
ways He'd forgive them and bring healing. He welcomes
wanderers home. We can do the same in His name.

*Father, help me embrace people with a warm welcome as they struggle to
find their way to a living relationship with You. Thank You for welcoming
me in just that way! I pray in the name of Jesus. Amen.*

Catch Him, Lord!

The LORD said to him, "I have heard your prayer and your supplication, which you have made before Me" (1 Kings 9:3, *New American Standard Bible*).

Scripture: **1 Kings 9:1-9**
Song: **"Eternal Father, Strong to Save"**

"My son, David, had gotten away with some things, like minor shoplifting," said my friend Kay, a single mom. "I could see a dangerous pattern developing, so I prayed for God to catch him if he got involved in anything that wasn't good for him. The next time, he was in handcuffs when I picked him up at the police station.

It seems David had gone joyriding with a friend who'd stolen a car. The police officer had no apparent reason to pull the boys over; nevertheless, he stopped them.

"I told David how I had prayed," said Kay. "He broke the law one more time, got caught again, and quit for good! David had a heavenly Father who knew everything he was doing and loved him enough to catch him!"

Kay had asked God to father her son, and God answered her prayers. Soon David was telling his friends he couldn't get away with anything. For me, the point is clear: as we watch teenagers testing their boundaries, we can pray for their heavenly Father's intervention in their lives. He does, indeed, hear our prayers.

Father, we who parent need Your help in extra measure during our kids' adolescence. Reveal Yourself to teens in a personal way, we pray, so they will choose to love You and live in Your blessing. In Jesus' name, amen.

It Never Entered My Mind

"They have built the high places of Baal to burn their sons in the fire as offerings to Baal —something I did not command or mention, nor did it enter my mind" (Jeremiah 19:5).

Scripture: **Jeremiah 19:1-6**
Song: **"Jesus Loves the Little Children"**

Since abortion became legal in the United States in 1973, approximately 40 million babies have died before birth. Worldwide, according to Planned Parenthood's research arm (the Guttmacher Institute), about 46 million babies were aborted in 1995, 26 million legally and 20 million illegally. The trend continues.

In Jeremiah's day, worshipers of idols burned their children in fire on public altars. Today the sacrifice of innocents occurs in private, in medical offices with doctors and nurses—who've been trained to heal and not harm—performing the deed. Even God's chosen people in Jeremiah's time sacrificed children to Baal, a god most closely resembling the love of money in modern times.

Sadly, today's women rarely abort their children for medical reasons—because of rape or incest or because their own health is in danger. Many are young or unmarried when becoming pregnant and often respond to pressure from others to just make their "problem" go away. It never entered God's mind that things should be as this.

God, for all who may regret terminating a pregnancy—assure them of Your abiding love and perfect forgiveness through Your Son. Comfort them all their days as You set them on the path of life. In Jesus' name, amen.

If You Choose to Break a Rule

"'Perhaps they will listen and everyone will turn from his evil way, that I may repent of the calamity which I am planning to do to them because of the evil of their deeds'" (Jeremiah 26:3, *New American Standard Bible*).

Scripture: Jeremiah 26:1-6
Song: "The Law of God Is Good and Wise"

In my fifth-grade classroom I post six basic rules, including "listening when others are talking" and "keeping your hands and feet to yourself." Next to the rules poster hangs another titled, "If You Choose to Break a Rule." It states the consequences of disobeying.

If students break rules, I write their names on the board as a warning and keep them inside from recess (five minutes for each mark I tally by their names after the warning). If the problem persists, or a student severely misbehaves—cheating or fighting—I call the parent later in the day. And in the case of a serious incident, I send the child to the principal immediately. Though I have it all planned out, I dislike enforcing rules and hate dealing with serious infractions.

Doesn't God feel the same way about us? He didn't want to bring disaster on the Israelites; He kept hoping they'd change their ways so He wouldn't have to discipline them. He provides boundaries for our good. Those boundaries discourage our straying from Him.

Lord, *it's hard to thank You for providing trouble when I go astray. But I know You're simply coaxing me back. Thank You, in Jesus' name. Amen.*

Rescued!

Thus says the LORD of hosts, the God of Israel, "Amend your ways and your deeds, and I will let you dwell in this place" (Jeremiah 7:3, *New American Standard Bible*).

Scripture: **Jeremiah 7:1-7**
Song: **"This World Is Not My Home"**

When I discovered slimy black mold growing on the walls of our water-heater closet, I feared the worst. I knew that our dentist's family had developed serious illnesses after exposure to a toxic black mold in their home. Testing confirmed my fears: stachybotrys, not the typical harmless black mold, contaminated our house also.

Overwhelmed, I sought advice from experts and followed their precautions. My son and I moved into an apartment, relieved to escape danger. We didn't mind the cramped quarters or close neighbors. In fact, it felt like a vacation because we were so thankful to God for rescuing us from illness. We lived there all summer while our manufactured home was demolished and replaced.

When God invited the Israelites to change their ways and dwell in the land with Him, He used a word meaning "to live in a temporary residence." I cherish owning my home, but when God moved us for a summer, I experienced His provision in a way I'll always remember.

O Lord of hosts, thank You for inviting me to live in Your ways, and dwell with You here on earth, while yearning for my permanent home in Heaven. Continue to prepare my heart for that glorious day! I pray this prayer in the name of Jesus, my merciful Savior and Lord. Amen.

Sick, or Getting Better?

"Will you steal, murder, . . . and offer sacrifices to Baal, and walk after other gods that you have not known, then come and stand before Me in this house?" (Jeremiah 7:9, 10 *New American Standard Bible*).

Scripture: **Jeremiah 7:8-15**
Song: **"Heart of Worship"**

My grown son, Amos, and I recently wondered aloud how Christians can live together out of wedlock and still come to church as if nothing were wrong. "They think God's cool with it," Amos said, and I sadly agreed. However, this popular picture of a permissive heavenly Father who smiles down at us without the hang-ups of old-fashioned morals hardly comes from the Bible!

We can hear the real God voicing real exasperation through Jeremiah. He cries out to His people who have lost their bearings in a corrupt culture, as so many have in our world today.

So what happens when the church gathers for worship? Are sinners present? Definitely. One hundred percent of the people in attendance fit that category. But working on issues differs from flaunting them. For example, our church offers loving support groups and classes for those battling addictions or struggling in other ways. Far from condoning the soul-sickness of sin, our churches can serve as hospitals for sinners who want to get well.

Father, You sent Your Son to come for sinners. Thank You for including me in that gracious rescue effort! In His name I pray. Amen.

Never Alone

The LORD upholds all those who fall and lifts up all who are bowed down (Psalm 145:14).

Scripture: **Psalm 145:13-21**
Song: **"Precious Lord, Take My Hand"**

The world watched, and the image remains imprinted on countless minds. Runner Derek Redmond had shattered Great Britain's 400-meter record but had missed the 1988 Olympics due to injury. Then, in 1992, he arrived in Barcelona ready to rock the world.

He didn't win the race, but what happened was much more memorable. Midway down his lane, Derek tore a hamstring muscle. He slowed, and then fell down. Tears streaming down his face, he struggled to his feet.

A commotion arose in the stands. A man fought past guards to get onto the track—Derek's father. "That's my son out there, and I'm going to help him," he said.

Jim Redmond put his arm around Derek's shoulders. "I'm here, son. We'll finish this together." Slowly, painfully, they walked 120 meters to the finish line while the crowd cheered.

That is the picture of our heavenly Father. When we fall, when we fail in our attempts to reach a goal, He lifts us up. Never, ever, do we run the race alone.

Father, thanks for lifting me back to my feet when I fall. Help me never be too ashamed to look to You for a new start. In Christ's name, amen.

July 23–29. **Darlene Franklin** lives with her mother in Denver, Colorado, where she discovered the greatest love of all—the God who loves "no matter what."

Man Hunt

"'Their leader will be one of their own; their ruler will arise from among them. I will bring him near and he will come close to me, for who is he who will devote himself to be close to me?'" declared the Lord (Jeremiah 30:21).

Scripture: **Jeremiah 30:18-22**
Song: **"Turn Your Eyes upon Jesus"**

The people of New Hampshire lost a beloved icon when the granite formation nicknamed "The Old Man of the Mountain" tumbled down in a rock slide in May 2003. The amazingly lifelike profile that graces their state quarter inspired one of my favorite stories, "The Great Stone Face" by Nathaniel Hawthorne.

In the story, the hero spends his life looking for a man who looks like the granite formation. He is sure that anyone with that majestic profile will match it in character. First one candidate, then another, disappoints. In the end, he discovers that he himself has the face that matches the mountain. After a lifetime of devotion, he resembles what he sought. Isn't this the idea in our Scripture today?

It happens that way in our spiritual growth. The more we seek the Lord and honor His character, the more we take on His qualities. It's the Spirit's work within us, moving us closer to that day when He will even "transform our lowly bodies so that they will be like his glorious body" (Philippians 3:21). What a complete work He does!

*Praise to You, **Father,** for making me into the likeness of Your dear Son! Yes, work mightily to conform me to His image. In His name, amen.*

Jump—for Rest

This is what the Lord says: "The people who survive the sword will find favor in the desert; I will come to give rest to Israel" (Jeremiah 31:2).

Scripture: **Jeremiah 31:1-9**
Song: **"My Faith Has Found a Resting Place"**

There comes a time for most of us when we feel as if we've jumped out of the frying pan into the fire. Like an ever-escalating novel, as soon as one disaster resolves, another appears. Have you been there recently?

Some years ago our landlady needed our apartment back, so we had to move. I looked for another apartment close to my place of employment but, for a long time, nothing worked out. I would have taken anything! But then, after making a list describing my *ideal* apartment—I found it! The biggest problem was that we'd now live farther away from my office than we'd been before.

That turned out to be just as well, though. A day after moving, I lost my job. I survived the sword of apartment hunting to end up in the desert of unemployment.

But that's where God gave me rest. He let me stay in the new apartment for five years before moving me to something even better. He led me to a new job and a new church, where great opportunities waited. If I had never jumped into the fire of the desert, I would never have experienced God's rest.

*When I wander in the desert, **God,** set up a campsite for me. Thank You for the kind of rest and peace only You can provide. In Jesus' name, amen.*

Baby Doll

"They will be like a well-watered garden, and they will sorrow no more" (Jeremiah 31:12).

Scripture: **Jeremiah 31:10-14**
Song: **"God, Who Touches Earth with Beauty"**

When the green thumbs were handed out, I must have been absent. My decidedly brown thumb has killed even the hardiest of plants. But when my daughter Jolene wanted to grow a nice houseplant in her apartment, a friend gave her a small botanical wonder that looked like a miniature palm tree. She called it Baby Doll and lavished love and care upon it.

The day came when Jolene had to leave her apartment for a few weeks, and she brought her precious plant to me. "Will you take care of Baby Doll for me?" she asked.

Chills ran up my spine as I envisioned the brown, shriveled stalks that would greet Jolene when she returned. Nevertheless, I put Baby Doll by my patio door and watered her once a week. She grew! Then she multiplied. Two miniature palm trees became four. Eventually, we added plants until half a dozen now crowd a small table, all of the leaves straining for the sun.

That's what God wants for us—lavish growth of our spirits. He lavishes love on us, calls us by a special name, waters us with the Living Word, and gives us everything we need to bear fruit in His kingdom.

Heavenly Father, *I am so thankful that You reproduce Your life in Your children. Help me grow and bear fruit for You. In Jesus' name, amen.*

This Computes!

"This is the covenant I will make with the house of Israel after that time," declares the Lord. "I will put my law in their minds and write it on their hearts. I will be their God, and they will be my people" (Jeremiah 31:33).

Scripture: **Jeremiah 31:33-37**
Song: **"The Law Commands and Makes Us Know"**

When I woke up this morning, I saw colored bugs going around in circles behind my closed eyelids. It was the pattern of a computer game I'd played before I went to bed. I often play it to relax at night. But apparently I play it too much, since the visual patterns were still implanted on my brain upon awaking.

Really, I'd rather have God's Word appear behind my eyelids when I awake in the morning. That would be wonderful, but what would it take?

I suppose I'd have to take seriously the GIGO principle that's so well-known among computer users: garbage in, garbage out. Whatever you feed into a computer, that is essentially what will come out, in spite of modifications; bad data always produces bad conclusions. Perhaps I could use the BIBO principle instead: Bible in, Bible out. The more I take in God's "data," the more His law will be written on my mind and flow out from my heart to others. That's a computation I can live with.

Lord, I praise You for revealing yourself in the Bible. Let me so immerse myself in Your written Word that it's the first thing I see in the morning and the last thing I see at night. Through Christ the Living Word, amen.

Putting Down Roots

"Build houses and settle down; plant gardens and eat what they produce" (Jeremiah 29:5).

Scripture: **Jeremiah 29:1-9**
Song: **"Brighten the Corner Where You Are"**

I grew up in Maine, the largest of the New England states, and it defined America for me. When I left for school in New Jersey and, later, Texas, I compared everything to Maine. Nothing measured up.

It took my college roommate to shake my thinking. "I try to find something good about every place where I live," she said.

Something good about the dry desert that was Texas? Surely she was joking. But I took her advice. I did enjoy the Fort Worth Zoo and then attended the Texas State Fair. When I moved to Arkansas, my children played in the Mississippi River. In Oklahoma, I learned more about our Native American heritage. In other words, wherever we moved became home. I learned to put down roots.

That was Jeremiah's advice to the Israelites, pining away for their homeland. "Build and plant, folks, because you're going to be here for a while!" Instead of pining for the past or dreaming of the future, suppose we get to work right where God has placed us today? Thankfully, wherever He is, there is peace and joy.

Gracious heavenly Father, I long to be Your servant—like the apostle Paul who was content in whatever state he found himself. Abiding in Your presence, I know it's possible. I pray in Jesus' holy name. Amen.

The Hiding God

"I will be found by you," declares the Lord, **"and will bring you back from captivity"** (Jeremiah 29:14).

Scripture: **Jeremiah 29:10-14**
Song: **"Open the Eyes of My Heart"**

Have you noticed there are times when God seems to play hide-and-seek? It happened for me when police arrested my teenage son for drug possession and he left home—for good. Hope deserted me. I had fought hard to make a good home for my children and now, *this!*

Where were God's promises? Where was God's love? Where was . . . God?

Looking back, I can now say: He was right there, waiting for me to seek Him. I found Him in a loving church family and amid a circle of marvelous, self-giving friends. His Holy Spirit carried my cries, which were too deep for words, straight to the Father's throne (see Romans 8:26).

God brought me back from that captivity of heart, slowly, over a period of years. My adult son is now a committed Christian soon to be married and no trace of his rebellious youth remains. We talk regularly.

It must be that when God seems to be hiding, He is doing extra teaching duty—diligently training us how to seek Him with all our hearts, the very best thing we could ever do with our lives.

Almighty God, when I can't find You as the Lord of the universe, let me seek You as my loving Father. In the name of Christ, amen.

Wait for God

The Lord longs to be gracious to you; he rises to show you compassion. For the Lord is a God of justice. Blessed are all who wait for him! (Isaiah 30:18).

Scripture: **Isaiah 30:15-19**
Song: **"Pass Me Not, O Gentle Savior"**

Tears clouded my vision as I stared at the results of the pregnancy test I'd just taken. This time I had been certain I was expecting, but I was wrong yet again. It was taking forever to start the family my husband and I so dearly wanted. Meanwhile, all around us, other couples were announcing their upcoming blessed events. I was genuinely happy for them, but I worried that we might never share in the great adventure of parenthood.

Several more months went by. Whenever a worry crept up on me, I turned it into a prayer. Then, finally, I saw that wonderful red line I'd been hoping to see on the test kit. A baby was on the way.

When our daughter, Honor, made her appearance, I knew that the wait had been well worth it. Only God could have given us such a gift. His graciousness overwhelmed me as I gazed into beautiful twinkling eyes. Never before had I considered the blessedness of waiting. Not until that very moment.

Lord, it's hard to wait when desires burn in my heart. Give me the courage to hold on, reminding me of the blessed rewards. In Jesus' name, amen.

July 30, 31. **Whitney Von Lake Hopler** has served as an editor for Crosswalk.com and for several newspapers and periodicals. She lives in Fairfax, Virginia.

Dismal Captivity

He was captured. He was taken to the king of Babylon at Riblah, where sentence was pronounced on him (2 Kings 25:6).

Scripture: **2 Kings 25:1, 2, 5-7**
Song: **"We'll Not Be Defeated"**

Just like Judah's King Zedekiah (whom the Bible says "did evil in the eyes of the Lord"), Saddam Hussein was captured after many in the free world condemned his deeds as Iraq's dictator. His sons were killed, and many of his soldiers scattered, just as things unfolded with Zedekiah.

Hussein had once reigned with great power, living in the splendor of luxurious palaces. But none of that could save him when it came time to reckon for his behavior. After U.S. forces invaded Iraq, Hussein was forced to hide in a filthy hole until they found him. He emerged shocked, broken, and defeated.

Those of us who follow Christ can find a cautionary example here. Are we caught up in our own ambitions? In His sacrifice on the cross, Christ has already achieved for us the ultimate accomplishment: complete spiritual freedom. No amount of power, money, or luxury can match that marvelous gift. To seek elsewhere for satisfaction is to live in dismal captivity.

Mighty God, thank You that You overcome evil with good. Let me not be found in any kind of opposition to You or Your will in the world. Deliver me from the captivity of self-centered ambitions. Through Christ, amen.

DEVOTIONS

*C*ome near to God and He will come near to you.

—James 4:8

AUGUST

Gary Allen, Editor

© 2006 STANDARD PUBLISHING, 8121 Hamilton Avenue, Cincinnati, Ohio, 45231, a division of STANDEX INTERNATIONAL Corporation. Topics based on the Home Daily Bible Readings, International Sunday School Lessons. © 2003 by the Committee on the Uniform Series. Printed in the U.S.A. All Scripture quotations, unless otherwise indicated, are taken from the HOLY BIBLE, NEW INTERNATIONAL VERSION®. NIV®. Copyright © 1973, 1978, 1984 by International Bible Society. Used by permission of Zondervan. All rights reserved. Where noted, Scripture quotations are from the following, used with permission of the copyright holders, all rights reserved: *The New King James Version (NKJV),* Copyright © 1982 by Thomas Nelson, Inc. *New American Standard Bible (NASB),* © The Lockman Foundation, 1960, 1962, 1963, 1968, 1971, 1972, 1973, 1975, 1977, 1995.

Count on God's Love

The eyes of the LORD are on all those who fear him, on those whose hope is in his unfailing love (Psalm 33:18).

Scripture: **Psalm 33:12-22**
Song: **"He's in the Midst"**

I paced between rooms, anxiously wondering why my husband, Russ, was so late calling me from Beijing, China, where he was staying on a business trip. Finally the phone rang. "Hi, it's me," Russ said in a hollow voice that told me something was wrong. "I'd meant to call earlier, but I'm sick."

"Sick!" I exclaimed. That was just what I'd feared most about his travel to Asia. "I think I ate something bad today," he groaned.

"What do you . . . " I began, intending to ask him about his symptoms. "Oh, no—I'm dizzy," he interrupted. "I'm sorry, but I can't sit up anymore. Got to go. Call you later."

"Wait!" I pleaded. But I heard a click and then a dial tone. My husband was half a world away, and I had no way of getting to him—but I knew who could. So I prayed for God to help Russ (and He did). Then I went to bed with newfound peace in God's love, a love that never fails.

Father, in my fallen world, where worry can overwhelm me, remind me of Your magnificent power and constant goodness. In Jesus' name, amen.

August 1–5. **Whitney Von Lake Hopler** has served as an editor for several newspapers and periodicals. She lives in Fairfax, Virginia.

Offer What You've Received

If you, O LORD, kept a record of sins, O LORD, who could stand?
(Psalm 130:3).

Scripture: **Psalm 130**
Song: **"Give Thanks to God the Lord"**

The moment Kathy's face appeared, my pulse began to race. About 10 years earlier she had stirred up trouble for me at the college campus newspaper where we'd both worked. A guy to whom she'd been attracted had asked me out instead. She had retaliated by lying to our editor-in-chief about my work in an attempt to get me fired. My job had been saved when the truth came out, but I was livid and managed to avoid her for the rest of college.

Now here Kathy was again—in church, of all places! She approached me and struck up a conversation about the heartache she'd endured over the past decade. Then she apologized for what she did to me in college . . . and asked me to forgive her.

My bitterness evaporated as God reminded me that I had made a few little mistakes of my own over the years! I was no less of a sinner and no more worthy than anyone else of God's marvelous gift of forgiveness through Christ. So I knew I should offer His beloved child Kathy nothing less than what I had so graciously received.

*Praise to You, **Lord of All**, for the gift of forgiveness that comes through Your Son's precious blood! Let me never take this gift for granted or devalue it in any way by refusing to forgive those who may hurt me. This I pray in the name of Him who died for me. Amen.*

Flying Joy

Because of the LORD's great love we are not consumed, for his compassions never fail (Lamentations 3:22).

Scripture: **Lamentations 3:19-24**
Song: **"After the Rain"**

A brownish gray flutter of movement caught my eye as I walked past a neighbor's green lawn. There in the grass was a young robin, struggling in vain to fly. Nearby lay a broken nest that had apparently fallen out of a tree during a fierce thunderstorm the night before.

The robin lifted its head and stared at me with beady eyes that seemed to plead for help. I hesitated as I gazed at the extent of its injuries, but I couldn't deny the sense of hope that pulled me toward it like a magnet. Since God had decided to let the bird survive the terrible storm, I dared to think His compassion in this new day could help it recover.

I called our county's animal control department, and an officer came out to scoop the robin into a cage. "This one has a chance to make it," he said. "We'll try to nurture it back to health." Because God had given me compassion for the robin, it might take flight once again.

And what a sense of joy took flight in me!

Dear God, thank You for the great love You have for everyone and everything in Your creation. Please help me to remember that every person I meet today is equally loved by You. And may I be an instrument of Your love to cause a seeking heart to turn toward You in response. Through the name of Jesus, amen.

Our Only Real Hope

The LORD is good to those whose hope is in him, to the one who seeks him (Lamentations 3:25).

Scripture: **Lamentations 3:25-33**
Song: **"Come Down, O Love Divine"**

From the time he was just a young teen, Willie Williams spent 40 years shuttling in and out of various prisons. Each time he was released, he vowed never to become incarcerated again. But his willpower alone wasn't enough to ensure that he'd emerge victorious from a life of crime.

Nor was it enough to help him break free of his addictions to heroin and alcohol. By the time Williams ended up in a Salvation Army alcohol rehabilitation center (where I interviewed him for a newspaper story), he had exhausted all means of trying to help himself.

He decided to turn to Christ and be baptized.

Then an amazing thing began to happen. Williams found he finally had the power he needed to let go of the anger and addictions that had imprisoned him for so long. He took a productive job that he thoroughly enjoyed and also reunited with several family members. Williams had sought Christ and placed his hope in the right place. The Lord was good to him.

O Lord, all too often I misplace my hope, trusting in my own feeble efforts to engineer my life. Thank You for bringing me to the point of letting go, of knowing that You alone are my only real hope—for this life and the next. In the name of the Father, the Son, and the Holy Spirit, I pray. Amen.

Believe the Upholder

You have seen, O Lord, the wrong done to me. Uphold my cause (Lamentations 3:59).

Scripture: **Lamentations 3:55-59**
Song: **"Held in His Mighty Arms"**

"Hey, look! It's the suitcase girl!" Jen snickered as I walked through our middle school's locker bay. I could feel the heat in my cheeks as they flushed red from embarrassment. Jen had taunted me for several months, targeting my book bag ("It's so big, it looks like a suitcase!"), my glasses ("Hey, four eyes!"), and my quiet nature ("Nobody can hear you! Speak up, baby!").

I had tried both avoiding her and confronting her, but neither approach had stopped her teasing. Finally, one night at home, I whispered a heartfelt prayer that God would change Jen's heart.

Shortly afterward, Jen walked right by me when she saw me in a hallway. I figured she just hadn't seen me, so I cringed the next time I encountered her and our eyes met. I waited for her to say something mean, but she didn't. In fact, she never teased me again.

Had God upheld my cause? I believe it to this day. And I will believe it in the days ahead, too, when justice seems as scarce as common kindness in my world.

O Father, help me remember that no injustice escapes Your notice. Your Son walked the earth and suffered taunting and the questioning of His motives. Uphold me by Your power when it happens to me. Thank You, Lord! In the precious name of Jesus I pray. Amen.

Someone Paid the Price

There is one God and one Mediator between God and men, the Man Christ Jesus, who gave Himself a ransom for all, to be testified in due time (1 Timothy 2:5, 6, *New King James Version*).

Scripture: 1 Timothy 2:1-6
Song: "I Will Sing of My Redeemer"

A workplace acquaintance was having a hard time understanding how Jesus could have paid the price for our sins. But then he related an episode that had just occurred with his new wife. "Things were going fine—until last night," he said. It seems he'd decided to go out with his work crew to celebrate a job well done. He arrived home an hour later than usual. "She just blew up at me," he said.

A little questioning on my part revealed that his wife had previously been married to an alcoholic. Clearly, she feared a repeat experience with her new husband.

"You're paying for that fellow's sins," I said. "He abused her, and now you can't do certain things without aggravating old wounds." I then spoke of how our sins have abused God's law and more than wounded the relationship between us; how Jesus stepped into our place as the perfect Son we could never be; how the Father could lavish His love upon us without violating His justice.

Father, without the mediation of the God-Man, Jesus, what hope would I have of Heaven? Praise You, through my Lord Christ, amen.

August 6–12. **Brad Leach** lives in Loveland, Colorado, and hopes to become a full-time freelance writer some day.

Hidden Dangers

I have kept the ways of the Lord, and have not wickedly departed from my God (Psalm 18:21, *New King James Version*).

Scripture: **Psalm 18:20-24**
Song: **"Rise Up, O Men of God!"**

The company I work for in water-starved Colorado has created a system of canals draining water from the mountains into many reservoirs. The water, as it flows along these concrete chutes, looks inviting to aquatic thrill-seekers. But it contains a hidden danger. The only way water can cross ravines, roads, or rivers is by pipe or tunnel. Either is deadly for someone swimming or riding an inner tube.

Warning signs appear throughout the canal systems. However, occasionally someone ignores the warnings, climbs over the gates, and faces his own demise. Those lucky few who survive usually explain, "I just couldn't imagine such danger existed!"

"The ways of the Lord" (v. 21) in our Scripture today refers to God's laws, and they operate like my company's warning signs. Danger lurks when we ignore them. David was tempted to kill King Saul and make himself king, but he chose to keep God's ways instead. Thus God not only made him king but blessed him with riches and honor.

Father in Heaven, give me the eyes of wisdom that I may read Your words and heed the hidden dangers of straying from Your side. How I long to acquire a taste for righteousness! Work in my heart for just such a purpose. I pray in the name of Jesus, my Savior and Lord. Amen.

It's Where You Finish

"When the righteous turns from his righteousness and commits iniquity, he shall die because of it. But when the wicked turns from his wickedness and does what is lawful and right, he shall live because of it. Yet you say, 'The way of the Lord is not fair'" (Ezekiel 33:18-20, *New King James Version*).

Scripture: Ezekiel 33:12-20
Song: "At Calvary"

Talking about his favorite film series, a friend told me he thought it unfair that at the end of the *Star Wars* saga, Anakin Skywalker was shown happy and restored, after all the evil he had done as Darth Vader. I pointed out that another character, the evil emperor, spends much time initially helping the good guys before his evil nature is revealed. Then he meets a less-than-pleasant end. "Was George Lucas being unfair here, as well?" I asked. My friend decided that "it's where you end up" that counts, not where you start from.

Please don't push this rather dubious analogy too far! However, I do see Ezekiel responding in similar fashion to the charge of God's seeming unfairness. Those who turn and end up doing right shall live; those who start well and then succumb to evil inherit a decidedly sad ending.

May none of us produce a "tearjerker" ending to the story of our days! No matter our situation now, it is never too late to accept the life He still offers.

Gracious and longsuffering Father, *I too harbor a rebellious heart. Work Your will in me, and let me finish in faith. Through Christ, amen.*

It's Not My Fault

"What do you mean when you use this proverb concerning the land of Israel, saying: "'The fathers have eaten sour grapes, and the children's teeth are set on edge'"? (Ezekiel 18:2, *New King James Version*).

Scripture: **Ezekiel 18:1-4**
Song: **"Kind and Merciful God"**

"It's my parents' fault." This is a common twenty-first-century complaint, but here we see the ancient Israelites voicing the same allegation.

Raised during the Depression, my parents constantly reminded me to eat everything you take and clean your plate. Apparently, every spoonful of spinach unconsumed meant another child in India going without (my offer to airmail the leftovers not withstanding).

On the other hand, one surefire attention-getter in my meat-and-potatoes family was to eat stupendous amounts of food. This solicited grins and responses such as, "You must have a hollow leg" or "He's a fine, growing boy." Eating became my reward, and by age 40-something, I was starting to resemble a small, third-world country.

I could blame my parents, right? But honestly, I'm the one who chooses to take every single bite. My confession and repentance, along with God's mercy, will reduce my problem. Blaming Mom and Dad will just set everyone's teeth on edge.

Lord, I know I can't transfer the blame for my poor choices. Help me grow more mature in accountability and responsibility. In Jesus' name, amen.

The Time Is Always Right

"If he has walked in My statutes and kept My judgments faithfully—he is just; he shall surely live!" says the Lord God (Ezekiel 18:9, *New King James Version*).

Scripture: **Ezekiel 18:5-9**
Song: **"Through the Love of God, Our Savior"**

When Ezekiel wrote these words to the Israelites, they faced a future of slavery. They were going to Babylon as a captive people to serve their new masters, and they wondered whether they really deserved this fate. God assured them that if they followed His ways, they would live, no matter what their forefathers had done.

Why? I believe one answer comes through in the words of Dr. Martin Luther King, Jr.: "The *time* is always right to *do* what is right." For Dr. King, the time to turn from racism and hatred was "now." The time to protest injustice was "now." The time for all humans to relate to each other according to character, not skin color, was "now." No excuse was acceptable, no delay in pursuit of righteousness tolerated.

God's statement in Ezekiel's book serves as a call to return to moral ways. Even when our desires often lead us into virtual slavery, it's not too late to turn around. In Ezekiel's day and in ours, the time is always right to walk in God's ways.

Father, without Your Son's gift of true freedom I would have remained enslaved to my own self-centeredness. Yet I pray for Your daily strength to walk close to You in the ways of righteousness. In Christ's name, amen.

Self-Destructing?

"Do I have any pleasure at all that the wicked should die?" **says the Lord God, "and not that he should turn from his ways** **and live?"** (Ezekiel 18:23, *New King James Version*).

Scripture: **Ezekiel 18:19-23**
Song: **"Almost Persuaded"**

Early in the twentieth century, a crime reporter traveled through the South on his way back to New York. When his car broke down, he found himself stranded for two days in a small rural town. Thinking of a possible story, the man decided to visit the local courtrooms.

The morning offered only the usual, small-town misdemeanor infractions of the law. But in the afternoon, a young man came before the judge for sentencing. The journalist sensed the tension in the judge's shaking voice as he pronounced 22 years—the least he could render for the crimes of armed robbery and deadly assault.

Interviewing the judge afterward, the journalist noted the emotion with which sentence was issued and how this man so differed from the jaded, big-city judges he'd known. Then, with eyes moist, the judge confessed that the young man was his son.

Like that judge, our God of infinite, holy character must punish lawbreakers—a thing that surely breaks His heart. As the prophet tells us, there is no pleasure for God in seeing our self-destructiveness unfold before Him.

Holy Lord, turn me from my ways today—the small and large decisions that so often work to bring my downfall. In Jesus' name, amen.

Why Die?

Rid yourselves of all the offenses you have committed, and get a new heart and a new spirit. Why will you die, O house of Israel? (Ezekiel 18:31).

Scripture: **Ezekiel 18:25-32**
Song: **"Breathe on Me, Breath of God"**

Imagine you've bought a fine, solid automobile. You finally feel secure on the roads, convinced you can go anywhere and handle anything. Soon afterward, you hear on the radio a recall notice for your car's year and model. The manufacturer says your car is dangerous, that many have already died. Fear creeps into your mind, and you notice an ominous shimmy in the front wheels. But the radio announcer states the manufacturer will correct the problem—free!

Relaxing, you admit you'll have to get that done some day, and you keep on driving. The highway vibrations get worse, and various parts start coming off, but you press on to greater speeds.

It's foolish to risk death when the fix is without charge. But our unredeemed human natures are those flawed vehicles, destined to maim and kill us. We need a fix and, thanks to Christ, it's free, "in order that the righteous requirements of the law might be fully met in us, who do not live according to the sinful nature but according to the Spirit" (Romans 8:4).

Lord, create in me a new and vibrant heart, one willing to yield every beat to the glory of Christ and His kingdom, in whose name I pray. Amen.

Come as You Are

Draw near to God and He will draw near to you (James 4:8, *New American Standard Bible*).

Scripture: **James 4:6-10**
Song: **"Just as I Am"**

Joy beamed from Chuck's eyes when he shared the story of his conversion to Christianity. He testified to an encounter with Jesus while sitting on his mother's grave-stone in a dark cemetery. That night he gave his life to the Lord. All I could think was, "Is this the real thing?"

Yet he and his wife were off drugs. They toted their Bibles everywhere and told everyone about Jesus. Their rusted-out VW™ bus—with "Jesus Saves" painted on all sides in primary colors—sat in the church parking lot on a regular basis.

I thought back to my own respectable church back-ground and my try-hard-to-be-like-Jesus brand of Christianity. In frustration I cried out one morning, "I *can't* be like Jesus! God, if You are there and want me, I give myself to You." Chuck and I both lacked Bible knowl-edge, but Christ graciously received us when we admitted our need and surrendered ourselves to baptism. No mat-ter what we look like, or what our prayers sound like, He always responds to a heart hungry to know Him.

Dear Father, *thank You for receiving me when I stumbled toward You with confused theology and desperate prayers. In Jesus' name, amen.*

August 13–19. **Sandy Ewing,** mother of 5, grandmother of 13, is a writer and speaker. With her minister husband she's led Christian seminars in several nations.

Rescue Operation

The LORD is compassionate and gracious, slow to anger and abounding in lovingkindness (Psalm 103:8, *New American Standard Bible*).

Scripture: **Psalm 103:8-18**
Song: **"Lo, a Loving Friend Is Waiting"**

I studied the helicopter in the summer sky. In Rocky Mountain National Park, helicopters mean only one thing. "Somebody must be in trouble," I called to my neighbor.

"Park ranger missing," she replied. "Three days now."

The knowledge of someone lost, perhaps injured and helpless, hovered in my mind all day. News broadcasters reported that the young man's friends rushed to join the searchers. When temperatures dropped toward evening, and rain fell, my concern deepened. At daybreak, the helicopter was joined by four others, and the ground crew swelled to 250 people. Five days later, a saddened hiker stumbled upon a broken body at the foot of a cliff.

In the midst of prayers for the ranger, I thought of our own lostness, our own need to be rescued. I recalled that Jesus left His home in Heaven to come to earth and die for our sins. By doing so He restored us to a relationship with His Father. I asked myself: Am I so filled with God's compassion that I will give of myself in some way this day to search out a lost seeker?

Father, open my eyes for opportunities to search and rescue on behalf of those for whom Jesus died. I pray in His precious name. Amen.

Sing Yourself Strong

"Behold, God is my salvation, I will trust and not be afraid; for the LORD God is my strength and song, and He has become my salvation" (Isaiah 12:2, *New American Standard Bible*).

Scripture: **Isaiah 12**
Song: **"I Will Bless the Lord at All Times"**

I glanced at my watch and let out a huge sigh. In 30 minutes, a group of ladies would fill the room and raise their eager faces to me, their Bible study teacher. Waves of worry over a family situation lapped at the shores of my mind. All my faith seemed sucked out to sea. How will I be able to teach today?

I slumped into a chair and flipped open my notebook to the lesson notes for the day, entitled, "Our spiritual blessings in Christ." I read each point aloud and soaked in the promises: love, grace, mercy, supply for every need. Within minutes, thanksgiving and joy began to wash away my dismal outlook. I continued reciting the list, this time in an impromptu song—my own musical creation.

By the time the ladies arrived, I was pounding out my song on the piano—and taught it to them too! "The Happy Song" we named it, with good-natured laughter. My little ditty won't be playing on a radio station near you anytime soon. But the whole episode reminded afresh that God's supply of strength is greater than anything I will face in this life.

Dear Lord, I choose today to declare: You are my strength and song. Fill me today with the joy only You can give. Through my Lord Christ, amen.

Listen Up!

"The LORD Almighty says: 'Turn from your evil ways and your evil practices.' But they would not listen or pay attention to me, declares the LORD" (Zechariah 1:4).

Scripture: **Zechariah 1:1-6**
Song: **"Listen to the Blessed Invitation"**

One of the pleasures we looked forward to after a year teaching English in China was a reunion with our old dog, Woody. After collecting him from the friends who'd cared for him, we headed for our new home eight hundred miles away.

We were happily reunited, but at an overnight stop I made a frightening discovery about our beloved pet. On an early morning walk in a nearby park, I watched Woody head straight for a street choked with rush-hour traffic.

I called, I shouted, and then I screamed. He couldn't hear! With Woody only yards from the street, in desperation I clapped my hands. The sharp sound caught his attention, and he stopped a foot from the curb. He looked back at me, puzzled, but safe. Does he have a hearing problem—or just not *want* to hear?

My hope is that Woody will learn to listen a little better. And that is my desire for my own spiritual growth. "Be still, and know that I am God" says the Lord (Psalm 46:10). Can I sit still for a moment today? Can I stop the constant mental chatter and just listen for Him?

O God, *Your Word reminds me how dangerous it is to ignore You. May I set my heart to listen and obey You today. In Jesus' name, amen.*

God's Fierce Love

"They made their hearts like flint so that they could not hear the law and the words which the Lord of hosts had sent by His Spirit through the former prophets; therefore great wrath came from the Lord of hosts" (Zechariah 7:12, *New American Standard Bible*).

Scripture: **Zechariah 7:8-14**
Song: **"Spirit of the Living God"**

The idea thrilled me. How many times can I run into the middle of the street before the bus passes my house? What a challenge for a 5-year-old! I zoomed out and back. Twice. Three times. One more time?

A hand gripped my arm so hard I winced. My mother's face was a storm of anger. I had to run to keep up with her quick steps as she marched me into the house, sat down on the hall bench, swung me over her lap, and gave me a swat. I was too startled to cry. When she pulled me upright again, I saw tears in her eyes.

"Sandra, whatever were you *thinking?* You could have been killed." She clutched me in a fierce embrace and wept. Years later, when I struggled to understand how a God of love could also demonstrate great wrath against self-destructive sinners, I remembered my mother's tear-stained eyes.

Almighty God and Father, *Thank You that Your love won't let go of me even when I make bad choices. I yield my will afresh to You, asking that You renew a right spirit in me and give me joy and peace in Your service. I pray this prayer in the name of Jesus, my merciful Savior and Lord. Amen.*

Restored

"'They will be My people and I will be their God in truth and righteousness'" (Zechariah 8:8, *New American Standard Bible*).

Scripture: **Zechariah 8:1-8**
Song: **"We've a Story to Tell to the Nations"**

Before my husband accepted a troubled ministry in another state, we knew about the congregational splits, the confused identity, and the dismissal of two previous ministers. But nothing matched the judgment made by a new acquaintance soon after our arrival when he asked, "Well folks, what brings you to this area?" When we told him, his smile disappeared as if we'd flipped a switch. "That church has wrecked many friendships," he said.

Later, I laid our challenge before the Lord in prayer. I felt that, somehow, He would remove the reproach from this assembly of downcast believers, that He would cleanse and lead us on a wholesome path in the future.

Little by little, God worked in our midst. Prayers of commitment followed times of repentance. When we left 14 years later with joy in our hearts, the promise of Zechariah had become a living reality in that place.

The experience left me with a deeper confidence in God and a greater appreciation of His sovereignty in all things—especially in the hearts of His people.

Lord of the church, thank You for caring so diligently for the whole body of Your people, giving it the gifts it needs to function in peace and fruitfulness. Continue to build my community of faith in the graces of love and mutual encouragement, for the sake of Jesus, in whom I pray. Amen.

Transformed Attitudes

"'Let none of you devise evil in your heart against another, and do not love perjury; for all these are what I hate,' declares the LORD" (Zechariah 8:17, *New American Standard Bible*).

Scripture: **Zechariah 8:14-17, 20-23**
Song: **"O to Be Like Thee!"**

"Sandra, don't use the word 'hate'," said Mom. "You may say, 'I dislike' or 'I strongly dislike.' But you may not say 'hate'."

I glared at the untouched, dull-green mound on the china plate in front of me on the dining table. "But I don't strongly dislike spinach," I protested. "I *hate* it." Just the thought of the long, dangly stems trailing down my throat made me gag. Yet my mother's will prevailed, and the word was purged from my vocabulary. I had to gulp down the horrid vegetable.

What a shock, years later, to find the banned *H* word in the Bible! I discovered God doesn't just strongly dislike certain things, He *hates* them—and says so. The list I compiled from my study on the subject included warnings about our attitudes and behaviors toward others.

I decided that if God hates something, maybe I should as well. And whatever God loves, I'd better love too. Seldom could I win an argument with my mother. I figure I can't win one with God either.

Dear Lord, *conform my viewpoints to Yours. May I never be a hateful person, but do help me love what You love and hate what You hate. In the name of Jesus, my Lord and Savior, I pray. Amen.*

With Promise

The LORD redeems his servants; no one will be condemned who takes refuge in him (Psalm 34:22).

Scripture: **Psalm 34:11-22**
Song: **"Redeemed, Restored, Forgiven"**

My parents gave me a new Bible for my 16th birthday. The pages are filled with notes from hometown sermons, National Youth Conference meetings, and Bible college seminars. There are favorite verses highlighted and some letter markings at many verses—*DC* written beside some, and *P* next to others.

You see, I was fascinated when our minister pointed out that every direct command *(DC)* is followed by a promise *(P)*. He challenged us in our Bible reading to note direct commands and then look for their promises.

As a parent, I tend to use this pattern with my children—"Brush your teeth . . . and you won't get cavities." "Do your chores . . . and we'll go to the park." As you read the Scripture selections for this week, I challenge you to look for the *DCs* and their *Ps*. Think about God's reason for giving the command; then claim His promise. In other words, mark up your Bible. It's OK. I promise.

Dear Father in Heaven, *thank You for giving me clear direction in Your holy Word. Help me to see Your plan and cherish Your promises as I read. I pray in Jesus' holy name. Amen.*

August 20–26. **Guyla Greenly** lives with her two children in Casper, Wyoming. She is an avid scrapbooker and addicted to TV decorating shows.

Choose Your Building Materials

If any man builds on this foundation using gold, silver, costly stones, wood, hay or straw, his work will be shown for what it is (1 Corinthians 3:12, 13).

Scripture: **1 Corinthians 3:10-15**
Song: **"The Solid Rock"**

Several years ago we set a manufactured home on a foundation in the middle of an alfalfa field. I live in windy Wyoming, and this house is solid. When the wind blows our gas grill off the deck, I don't hear or feel a thing inside the house—not even the grill crashing into my son's rock garden. My home is built tight and solid, but one strike of the match, and I'd be left with nothing but the foundation once again.

Eight months after moving into the house, I went through a divorce, and my world blazed with pain, down to its foundation. If that foundation had not been Jesus Christ, and a support system of awesome family and friends, I don't know how I would have survived.

And a refining fire it was! With God's leading, I am rebuilding upon the solid-rock foundation of Jesus. As I labor in reconstruction, I'm trying to choose quality building materials—a firm knowledge of God's Word, a daily dependence upon His Spirit, a regular participation in worship and fellowship.

O Father, sustain me through the refining fires! Help me to make wise choices when building upon the foundation of Jesus Christ my Savior. In the name of the Father, the Son, and the Holy Spirit, I pray. Amen.

Who

Judge nothing before the appointed time; wait till the Lord comes. He will bring to light what is hidden in darkness and will expose the motives of men's hearts. At that time each will receive his praise from God (1 Corinthians 4:5).

Scripture: **1 Corinthians 4:1-5**
Song: **"They That Overcome"**

Something about her caught my eye, and I watched her during the speaker's testimony. She sat with arms folded across her chest, chin up, and lips drawn down in a scowl. "There's no way this speaker is getting through to her," I thought. As I watched her armor-like demeanor, I began to pick apart the words of the speaker and mentally list what he was doing wrong in trying to reach this woman.

I later found out the woman had made a decision to follow Christ that night—so much for my ability to interpret body language! This experience taught me a real-life lesson on the old cliché, "You can't judge a book by its cover." I had jumped to a conclusion about this woman's faithfulness. My impulses were critical, while hers were accepting. If God had revealed our inner worlds to that group of women, I would have been humiliated.

It's so easy to become self-righteous, to judge the actions of others without knowing anything about them. It's not so easy to let God be the judge—but I'm trying.

Lord and Judge of all, reveal to me my deepest secrets and private motives. Show me where You would have me change and how You would have me treat others. In the precious name of Jesus I pray. Amen.

Still Another . . .

"'Ever since the time of your forefathers you have turned away from my decrees and have not kept them. Return to me, and I will return to you,' says the Lord Almighty" (Malachi 3:7).

Scripture: **Malachi 2:17–3:7**
Song: **"Ancient of Days"**

I am totally amazed by the patience of God. After centuries of human rebellion, He continues to offer reconciliation with humanity. In the days of Noah, God promised never to destroy humankind with a flood again. He doesn't change, but after 40 years of listening to the Israelites bicker and complain in their wilderness wanderings, I would have sent a few scary thunderstorms, at least! My attitude would be, "Sure, I said I wouldn't destroy you, but I'm God; I can do whatever I want."

Good thing I'm not God, right?

The Lord not only has integrity, He *is* integrity. By His very nature God is all good and pure. He cannot go back on a promise because that wouldn't be consistent with His eternal being and character. I find comfort in that.

We humans are quite fickle, though. Even today, just like those wandering Israelites, I tend to gripe about every little inconvenience. But He doesn't change. He stands steadily by, giving me one more chance . . . then another . . . and another . . .

Lord Almighty, *thank You for being a God of second chances–and more! Help me to appreciate Your gracious love now so I'll be prepared to spend eternity in praise of it. In the name of my Savior, Jesus Christ, amen.*

Excited to Bless

"Bring the whole tithe into the storehouse, that there may be food in my house. Test me in this," says the LORD Almighty, "and see if I will not throw open the floodgates of heaven and pour out so much blessing that you will not have room enough for it" (Malachi 3:10).

Scripture: **Malachi 3:8-12**
Song: **"Give of Your Best to the Master"**

Every Christmas, Dad would choose a special gift for each of my sisters and me, and then hide the packages somewhere in the house. He could hardly stand it while we opened our other presents. "Hurry up!" he'd urge. "Open those presents. I'm hungry." Of course, he didn't really want to eat breakfast; he wanted us to find his hidden gifts. He was as excited to see us hunt for our gifts as we were to find them! He'd give us hints and tell us whether we were "hot" or "cold."

God tells us over and over again in Scripture that if we trust Him and give all of ourselves to Him and His ways, He will bless us. In today's verse He says, in effect, "Try it! Let me prove it to you!" Basically, He's so excited about the many gifts He has in store for us that He's urging us to hurry up. Just as my earthly father was excited to bestow gifts upon me, my heavenly Father wishes to heap His blessings upon all of us who look for Him.

Dear God, thank You for Your many blessings, which are gifts of Your grace. Help me give my tithes and offerings with a cheerful heart, knowing that all I have has come from Your hand. Through Christ I pray. Amen.

Never Wrong to Do Right

"You have said, 'It is futile to serve God. What did we gain by carrying out his requirements and going about like mourners before the LORD Almighty?'" (Malachi 3:14).

Scripture: **Malachi 3:13-18**
Song: **"Search Me and Know Me"**

I followed the formula. I took a vow of purity, prayed for my future spouse, attended Bible college, met him at church, participated in premarital counseling, and had a church wedding.

It didn't work. A giant scarlet *D* is emblazoned across my chest. I did everything I thought I was supposed to do to ensure 'til-death-do-us-part marital success, but I still ended up divorced. What difference did it all make?

At one point in my complaining, a friend said, "It's never wrong to do right." Not exactly the pity-party favor I had in mind! I wanted to feel sorry for myself and blame God. After all, I'd held up my end of the bargain, so why hadn't He? But the Lord spoke to me through those words. *Why* was I doing right anyway? Was it for my own benefit? Or was it to honor a holy God?

It all comes down to either an eternal or temporal perspective, doesn't it? If I'm looking at the temporal, then maybe there really is no point, especially when I sense no personal gain. But if I look at the eternal, then it truly is never wrong—and hardly futile!—to do right.

My God and Father, *today keep my eyes focused on Your kingdom, that I may live to please You above all others. Thank You, in Jesus' name. Amen.*

Joyful Abandon

"For you who revere my name, the sun of righteousness will rise with healing in its wings. And you will go out and leap like calves released from the stall" (Malachi 4:2).

Scripture: **Malachi 4:1-6**
Song: **"You Are My King"**

My life is a series of deadlines—newsletters to print, bills to pay, articles to write. As each due date looms, it weighs heavier upon me. But as I approach a project's completion, I begin to feel a little giddy. Once I finally finish the work, and mark it off my list, I feel like running through a cheesy movie montage. You know the ones—beautiful girl in a gauzy, flowing dress runs down a gentle hill in a slightly out-of-focus meadow. She glides through the wild flowers with her arms upraised on each side, her long, golden curls blowing in the breeze. An overly sentimental song plays while the beautiful girl frolics and dances.

OK, maybe I get a little carried away, but haven't you ever thrown your arms up and spun around in the sunshine—at least once in your lifetime? Do you ever have this feeling bubbling up inside—and you just have to do something with joyful abandon?

That's the joy of the Lord, friend. Let it out; leap in the sunshine of God's goodness. Bring a smile to His face.

God, awaken my heart to Your goodness on this day, whether the sun shines or not. Help me to know without doubt the difference between happiness in my circumstances and joy in Your arms. Through Christ, amen.

From Honor to Glory

You made him a little lower than the heavenly beings and crowned him with honor and glory (Psalm 8:5).

Scripture: **Psalm 8**
Song: **"To God Be the Glory"**

Our antique dining room chair seats needed new rush webbing. We searched in vain for an artisan to do the work. Following a friend's advice, my husband removed the chair seats, and we took them to a man she suggested. As we viewed his workshop, he told his story.

"We lived in upstate New York, and my mother was a member of a co-op of skilled workers," he said. "When she died, two chairs were waiting to be finished. I learned to do this work so her responsibility would be fulfilled."

He replaced the rush in my chairs. Then, years later, I read of his death and wrote a note to his widow. I told her how his dedication had touched me, and how his talent had endured to bring honor to his family.

We are made in the image of God, and, as such, we excel in honor and glory among God's creatures. As creatures, we inherit these enduring qualities. Yet He calls us to greater glory—to honor Him by returning to Him through His Son, Jesus, that we might also know the eternal glory of Heaven.

*I am Your handiwork, **O God.** In every instance of resourcefulness and skill, help me see Your hand at work. Through Christ I pray. Amen.*

August 27–31. **Cos Barnes** is a freelance writer who lives in southern Pines, North Carolina. An avid hand bell-ringer, she has three children, seven grandchildren.

Night and Day

God saw that the light was good, and he separated the light from the darkness (Genesis 1:4).

Scripture: **Genesis 1:1-5**
Song: **"Heavenly Sunshine"**

It's 2:00 AM, and I yearn for daylight. Troubled by woes, I cannot sleep. I keep thinking about my friend, who, after suffering two strokes, is contemplating a move to a nursing facility. And I have recently cried with a college classmate dying of cancer.

As I lie here, all of life's disappointments, failures, and heartaches march by in review: the unfinished manuscript in my filing cabinet, loneliness caused by the distance separating me from my family, concern for those in my neighborhood who are displaced, frightened, homeless. Heavy-hearted, I examine unfulfilled dreams, things left undone, old nagging doubts.

Sleep won't come, so I rise and do menial chores. Attempting to read, I watch the words fly from the page with neither understanding nor entertainment.

Is this what is meant by "the dark night of the soul?" I wonder as I continue tormenting myself, probing the past, questioning the present. Why do these unhealthy thoughts steal through my sleeplessness?

Then I remember age-old wisdom: "It is always darkest before the dawn." The light is on its way.

*Thank You, **God,** for each new day. And thank You so much that You are always good, whether I'm in sunlight or darkness. In Jesus' name, amen.*

What Technique!

God called the expanse "sky." And there was evening and there was morning—the second day (Genesis 1:8).

Scripture: **Genesis 1:6-8**
Song: **"Some Golden Daybreak"**

Genesis reveals the creation of the universe. As the supreme being, God speaks and the design of the world bursts out of nothingness into being. In these verses the expanse or firmament is divided and the sky is made.

I recently viewed the work of a young artist and asked him how he depicted clouds so realistically. He explained his technique: painting the undertones below the clouds with a chopstick.

God also had a technique.

When our children were young, their dad would take them camping overnight in the backyard. Lying on their backs they explored the heavens, repeating after their mentor the names and positions of the constellations. Inevitably, it would rain, and they would scamper into the house in the wee hours. They were wet but exhilarated from this nighttime learning experience.

As the children grew older, they camped out with the Scouts, and deepened their appreciation for the stars and their relationships to the overall pattern of the heavens. They studied the constellations and acknowledged God's handiwork, His most brilliant, incomparable technique.

"For the beauty of the earth," **O God,** *"for the glory of the skies," I give You thanks. In the precious name of Jesus I pray. Amen.*

Winds and Waves Obey

God called the dry ground "land," and the gathered waters he called "seas" (Genesis 1:10).

Scripture: **Genesis 1:9-13**
Song: **"Peace! Be Still!"**

During the autumn of 2005 our country was plagued with hurricanes. We saw the devastation caused by *Katrina, Wilma,* and *Rita,* among others. Large areas were evacuated due to severe flooding, mud slides, and the washing away of entire communities.

Dams and rivers overflowed. Homes, churches, and schools were destroyed. People waited in line for hours to collect jugs of water, ice, and gas. Stores sold out of generators, chain saws, water, and propane fuel. In the midst of this horrendous cataclysm, many wondered: How could God let this happen?

God was in control at creation and He is still in charge of our universe today. Yet He does allow things to occur in our world—at least for a while. This is a time in which He calls all people to repentance and belief in Christ.

The good times and bad can point us to God. In fact, sometimes only the worst of times are able to turn human hearts from their own self-reliance to see and revere the mighty King of the universe. Thankfully, His power to save us knows no limit.

My heavenly Father, teach me to look to You not only in the good times but also when I face the worst crises. You are always there for me! I pray through my deliverer, Jesus, Your Son. Amen.

Dark Park

God made two great lights—the greater light to govern the day and the lesser light to govern the night. He also made the stars (Genesis 1:16).

Scripture: **Genesis 1:14-19**
Song: **"Dark Is the Night"**

In my county, a section has recently been designated Dark Park. By nature it has the clearest, darkest night skies on the Eeastern seaboard between Maine and the Florida keys. Because of its rural location, it attracts astronomers, photographers, scientists, and ordinary star-gazers who love studying the heavens. These gatherings are called star parties, and participants thoroughly enjoy them, sharing their knowledge and findings.

A new form of family fun, star parties were formerly limited to serious astronomy students because telescopes were expensive and required much technical skill to build. Now, however, they are relatively inexpensive; even binoculars are much improved from yesteryears.

Without light pollution, viewers may bask in the celestial wonders of God's heavens. These luminaries are God's way of indicating times and seasons to humankind. And star parties show me that—at least occasionally—we try to use that time wisely.

*Your majesty and Your might, **Dear Father,** I acknowledge. As I go about my routine today, give me pause to look up and recall Your vast creation. Then help me recall the closeness of Your Spirit dwelling within me. In the name of Jesus, Lord and Savior of all, I pray. Amen.*

DEVOTIONS

Gary Allen, Editor

O LORD, our
Lord, how
majestic is your
name in all the
earth!

—Psalm 8:1

SEPTEMBER

Photo © istock

Powerful Reminder

God blessed them and said, "Be fruitful and increase in number and fill the water in the seas, and let the birds increase on the earth" (Genesis 1:22).

Scripture: **Genesis 1:20-23**
Song: **"His Eye Is on the Sparrow"**

"Mom, guess what?" my daughter said when I answered the telephone. Not waiting for a reply, she rushed on, "Today I saw a baby being born."

Sharing my daughter's excitement, I felt goose pimples rising on my arms and legs. My daughter, a third-year nursing student, was learning rapidly.

"It was a perfect baby girl," she continued. "And the parents were so thrilled."

"You have seen God's greatest miracle," I said. "Many people never do. And you assisted in that miracle."

I read more in my daughter's words than the reassurance that she would make a fine nurse; I witnessed the enduring power of God's command to be fruitful on the earth. For at no time are we more aware of the call upon our lives to acknowledge our creaturehood—and to lift thankful hearts to our creator—than at the birth of a child.

Creator of All, thank You for filling the earth with all good things for my enjoyment. Keep me mindful this day of my origin in You and my constant need to depend on Your grace and care. In Jesus' name, amen.

September 1–2. **Cos Barnes,** a freelance writer living in Southern Pines, North Carolina, has three children, seven grandchildren, and is an avid handbell ringer.

What a Heritage!

God made the wild animals according to their kinds, the livestock according to their kinds, and all the creatures that move along the ground according to their kinds. And God saw that it was good (Genesis 1:25).

Scripture: **Genesis: 1:24, 25**
Song: **"Praise God, from Whom All Blessings Flow"**

The first chapter of Genesis has been called a doxology—a hymn of praise to God as creator. In these two verses the repeated phrase "their kinds," is especially meaningful to me these days, as I have been diligently pursuing my genealogy. I recently met a long-lost cousin, and he shared with me some papers written by a kindred ancestor who was a book publisher in seventeenth-century London.

Holding those precious documents, I was overcome with emotion. As I studied the archaic English, the logo of his print business, and saw the pictures of his shop in St. Paul's Square, I gasped, "I feel a connection to this forebearer! All my life I have loved pretty stationery, ink, newsprint—anything to do with the printed word. Now I know why—it's in my blood!"

Similarly, the accounts of Genesis portray an entire family's character by detailing its origins. When we see God in those pages, we see our holy heritage, all that we are meant to be in Him and in His Son.

My Father, You created me to bring You glory in all I do and say. Work in me today a little more of Your matchless character! Through Christ, amen.

Gazing in Love

Lift your eyes and look to the heavens: Who created all these? He who brings out the starry host one by one, and calls them each by name (Isaiah 40:26).

Scripture: **Isaiah 40:25-31**
Song: **"The Wonder of It All"**

As a child I loved stargazing. I lived in a small Oregon town with few streetlights to blur my view of the heavens. My whole family would stretch out on the grass and admire the night's brilliant display.

Dad pointed out the constellations and tried to teach me their names. I only mastered locating the Big Dipper and the Little Dipper. I quickly recognized the North Star being at the end of the Little Dipper's handle, and I later learned that some 88 constellations could be recognized. (Never by me, however.)

Today's Scripture not only tells us that God created the sun, moon, and stars, He also named each one of them. Each is in its place, fulfilling the purpose for which it was designed—bringing light to the world. None are missing.

The God who named the stars also knows us by name. Therefore let us never forget: we are constantly in His loving gaze, through the day and also through the night.

Lord, help me trust Your love and concern for me in a deeper way. Every time I enjoy Your star-spangled sky, let me lift up the eyes of my heart to Your kind gaze. Thank You, in Jesus' name. Amen.

September 3–9. **Pat S. Johnson,** a speaker and freelance writer, served for 20 years as a missionary in the Middle East. She now lives in Temple City, California.

Looking Like God

God created man in his own image . . . male and female he created them (Genesis 1:27).

Scripture: **Genesis 1:26, 27**
Song: **"O to Be Like Thee!"**

While growing up I was perplexed by the idea of being made in God's image. I just didn't look like the illustrations of God in my Sunday school papers! That full-bearded man with the piercing blue eyes and authoritative posture was not me.

Later, of course, I realized that being made in God's image had little to do with my physical attributes. I came to understand my *personhood* as a reflection of God's own nature; I too was a being with intellect, emotions, and will. And my actions were to reflect God's character too. But I would never look like Him.

My initial interpretation of God-like living included never disappointing God in any action or attitude. Therefore, I often felt my self-serving responses to life's irritations and disappointments demonstrated spiritual weakness. As I yearned to develop the attributes of God in my own character, I grew into a transformed understanding of what it means to live as one made in His image. It's about allowing God free reign in my life, to guide and direct me in His ways. Only then can I truly reflect His image to those I meet each day.

Dear Heavenly Father, help me respond to Your Spirit's leading in my life so I can truly mirror You in my world. In Jesus' name, amen.

Every Good Landscape

God saw all that he had made, and it was very good (Genesis 1:31).

Scripture: **Genesis 1:28-31**
Song: **"For the Beauty of the Earth"**

In my 34 years as a missionary, I was blessed to live in different parts of the world. My first assignment was Lebanon—often called the "Switzerland of the Middle East." Its snow-capped mountains, bubbling springs, tide-licked coastline, and fertile gardens reflected creation's beauty in every season.

Our move to Jordan brought a dramatic change to the landscape. Because of the meager yearly rainfall, rolling, rock-strewn hills with little vegetation covered most of the country. The sun's rays reflecting off dust-filled air produced sunsets which were winners on a regular basis. My time in Papua, New Guinea, introduced me to the world of the jungle. There tropical fruits abounded: pineapples, mangoes, bananas, passion fruit, and guavas. It was easy to revel in the land's lush abundance.

In every land where I've lived, I learned to appreciate the beauty of God's earth. When He made this world, He proclaimed it good. We too—if we keep our eyes open to the miracle of life in all its variety—will see the good hand of God in every landscape to which He leads us.

Lord, *I have seen Your world, and it is good. Help me to be a responsible steward and caretaker as I partake of its bounty and enjoy its beauty. In the name of Jesus, my Savior, I pray. Amen.*

Rules or Rest?

God blessed the seventh day and made it holy (Genesis 2:3).

Scripture: Genesis 2:1-3
Song: "Brethren, We Have Met to Worship"

I grew up in a rather strict and conservative religious family. Our Christian lifestyle was controlled by a long list of "don't!" rules. Some of these rules centered on keeping Sunday holy. In my home, for example, we were forbidden to read the Sunday newspaper. It never made sense to me that we could listen to the Sunday news on the radio or watch a news program on television; we just dare not touch that newspaper!

After my husband and I married we developed our own Sunday schedule. It included a Bible study class as well as worship services. We'd sing in the choir, help in the nursery, and bring food for potlucks. (And I must confess, we'd read the Sunday comics in the afternoon.)

When our children were old enough, we began teaching them to give thanks at mealtime and to join in family devotions before bedtime. We also taught them the importance of setting aside Sunday to focus on God. Our family's routine included Sunday school class and morning and evening church services. My point is simple: focusing on worship—going beyond rules—made Sunday holy to us, and still does today.

God, I am thankful that You rested on the seventh day of creation and called us to emulate Your example. May my Sunday activities reflect just that desire—to rest, not just from work but in You. Through Christ, amen.

Let's Go Outside

The heavens declare the glory of God . . . Their voice goes out into all the earth (Psalm 19:1, 4).

Scripture: **Psalm 19:1-6**
Song: **"This Is My Father's World"**

I am the oldest of six children. You'd think it would take a mighty big voice to call all us into supper when we were kids. But Mom's soft, husky tone was designed for polite conversation, not yelling. Nevertheless, she knew exactly how to get our attention—she whistled! It didn't matter whether we were in our own backyard, at the neighbor's house, or at the park, we immediately responded to her one-of-a-kind trill.

Our heavenly Father uses more than words to get our attention. For example, the beauty of the heavens speak for Him, as the psalmist so eloquently proclaims. It's as if a voice from the Lord calls to us, amazing us with a cycle of light and dark, thrilling us in a celestial revelation of His power and glory. God's majesty is declared in the blazing sun by day, the soft light of a changing moon by night, and in the myriad stars lighting up the universe from beyond time.

I've decided to go outside this very night and admire God's handiwork. I want to revel in His marvelous creation, feel His presence and power. Won't you join me?

Father in Heaven, *thank You for Your beautiful creation. Best of all, thank You for letting me hear Your voice through it. In the name of Jesus, Lord and Savior of all, I pray. Amen.*

Reflect His Compassion

The LORD is compassionate and gracious, slow to anger, abounding in love (Psalm 103:8).

Scripture: **Psalm 103:1-14**
Song: **"The Love of God"**

The psalmist tells us that God abounds in love. And because we are to reflect God's image in our world, we also have the great privilege of abounding in love. But how do we do it?

It's easy to love the lovable—those gracious people who say "Please" and "Thank you" and live up to our expectations. It's the *others*, though—the folks who fall into the category of unappreciative or selfish or malicious—that give us our love-challenge. However, choosing whom *to* love and whom *not* to love isn't an option. The very idea of "abounding" precludes that kind of choice.

We are to love whoever comes our way, constantly enlarging our circle of care and concern. That way, our love reaches out to an ever-growing number of people with the kind of compassion and grace we ourselves have received.

Not easy! It requires asking God for a fresh supply of love for each day. Only then do we find the fruit of love ripening and cheering the people in our lives. And what a joyful way to live!

Gracious God, how great is Your goodness to me over the years! Help me reach out to those in need around me as one who, like them, was rescued by Your compassion through no merit of my own. Through Christ, amen.

Crowning of a King

The LORD has established his throne in heaven, and his kingdom rules over all (Psalm 103:19).

Scripture: **Psalm 103:15-22**
Song: **"The Lord Jehovah Reigns"**

It's a big day for a country when it crowns a new king. Pomp and circumstance rule. Parade routes are marked and security measures checked. Streets are swept, tree branches trimmed, and curbs refreshed with new coats of color. It's a public holiday in celebration of the occasion, and leaders from neighboring countries make it a point to attend. At least that's what happened at the 1999 coronation of his majesty, King Abdullah II of the Hashemite Kingdom of Jordan.

I was there, watching the school children excitedly pressing against each other on the curbs, chanting "Long live King Abdullah!" The enthusiastic crowds lining the parade route held bobbing balloons and billowing banners. A formation of fighter planes streaked through the sky above, their roar mingled with the shouts of the crowd. It was a day for the history books.

However, the reign of all earthly kings will end one day. All pomp and glory will pale in the splendor of His Majesty, king of the universe!

*Your reign, **my Heavenly King,** is eternal and all-encompassing. Therefore, let me acknowledge Your undisputed rule within my heart in this quiet moment. In the name of the Father, the Son, and the Holy Spirit, I pray. Amen.*

He's There!

Listen to me, all who hope for deliverance, who seek the Lord! Consider the quarry from which you were mined, the rock from which you were cut! (Isaiah 51:1, *The Living Bible*).

Scripture: **Isaiah 51:1-5**
Song: **"The Rock That Is Higher Than I"**

Northwest of Thermopolis, Wyoming, on State Highway 120, a series of rock formations thrusts out alongside the road. A few miles down that road, these same formations, buried several thousand feet below the surface produce hydrocarbons—one of earth's most important natural resources because of the energy produced when burnt.

We sometimes forget that our Lord is like these rock formations. He can be buried far below the surface of our consciousness, but He also rises to the surface of our lives in our actions and words. He provides the foundation for our production of fruit in His kingdom.

In Isaiah, the Lord reminded the Israelites that they were cut from His quarry and He alone could deliver them. May we too always remember that God is our rock—the rock of all ages—dwelling within us by His Spirit. In every fearful circumstance we can call upon Him for help and deliverance.

Lord, when I'm blinded by the day-to-day problems of my world, open my eyes to Your abiding presence through Your loving Word. I pray through my deliverer, the Lord Jesus Christ. Amen.

September 10–16. **Kristi Stingley**, a retired engineer and lawyer, now dedicates her time to writing Christian novels and inspirational nonfiction books.

Lord of the Stars

He took him outside and said, "Now look toward the heavens, and count the stars, if you are able to count them." And He said to him, "So shall your descendants be" (Genesis 15:5, *New American Standard Bible*).

Scripture: **Genesis 15:1-6**
Song: **"Blessed Assurance"**

When did you last look into the heavens and marvel at the number of stars? I would do this often as a child, but *counting* the stars never entered my mind. Who could count that high?

I imagine God taking Abraham outside on one of those clear, moonless nights that always invite a meditative upward gaze. He pointed to the sky and told His servant to . . . count. I might have said under my breath, "Are you kidding?"

But the Lord delivered on His promise to Abraham, as the apostle Paul confirmed centuries later: "Be sure that it is those who are of faith that are sons of Abraham," (Galatians 3:7, *NASB*). What a vast family God has given this one who believed such an awesome promise as he stood under a cloudless night sky! All through the ages, from his day to ours, Abraham's sons and daughters have been lifting their praise to the Lord of the stars.

Dear Father in Heaven, just as I can't count the stars in the sky, I can't count all the ways You touch and bless my life. Make me ever grateful for Your many blessings and show me Your will in all I will say and do this day. In the name of Jesus, my Lord and Savior, I pray. Amen.

Now We Live in Gratitude

God said to Abraham, "As for Sarai your wife, you shall not call her name Sarai, but Sarah shall be her name" (Genesis 17:15, *New American Standard Bible*).

Scripture: Genesis 17:15-22
Song: "A Child of the King"

Have you ever wished you could be someone different? Would you like to change your name and start over again? Many European immigrants desiring a new life in America change their names, hoping to assimilate into society with more ease.

The Lord provided Abram and his wife with new names but for a different reason. Abram became *Abraham*, and Sarai become *Sarah*, in order to signify their new roles in God's world-saving plan. They would become the father and mother of many nations, and the great, great . . . great grandparents of the One in whom the Lord God would establish His new covenant—Jesus Christ.

We are a part of it all! The Lord gives us new names when we enter the waters of baptism. We're no longer just John or Jane Doe in some no-name family. We are God's adopted sons and daughters, chosen ones, the recipients of eternal life (see Ephesians 1:5). From now on the life of gratitude is the only life for us.

Dear Lord, thank You for making me new in Your name, for giving me a new identity—one that glorifies Your precious name. Keep working in me, transforming me into the likeness of Your Son, Jesus, until I see Him face-to-face. I pray these things in His precious name. Amen.

Bow to Him

[Abraham] said, "My lord, if now I have found favor in your sight, please do not pass your servant by" (Genesis 18:3, *New American Standard Bible*).

Scripture: **Genesis 18:1-8**
Song: **"All Creatures of Our God and King"**

The stewardship ministry team in our congregation recently produced a play titled, *Come to the Castle.* In it, crowds gather to hear the announcement of the king's return. On his journey to the castle, a sty warden ("pig boy" to most) encounters many who shy away from him due to his distinct odor, while others treat him with respect and kindness. In the end it is revealed that the sty warden is the king himself!

In our Scripture today, three men visit Abraham. Unlike those in our stewardship play, Abraham instantly recognizes his king. He bows down at the visitors' feet and asks them not to pass him by but to let him provide for their refreshment.

It makes me consider: What do I do when the Lord calls me? Do I let Him pass by because I just don't recognize Him? Or do I immediately know His voice and bow down in service?

Lord of my life, all glory and praise to Your holy name! Give me an open heart that is ready to hear and receive Your guidance. And when You call, may I, like Abraham, recognize Your presence and answer Your call with all that You have given me—with my time, my abilities, and my money. In the name of Your Son, my Savior, I pray. Amen.

Surpassing Greatness

"Is anything too difficult for the LORD?" (Genesis 18:14, *New American Standard Bible*).

Scripture: **Genesis 18:9-15**
Song: **"He Will Make a Way"**

I have friends whose daughter was in a car accident. At the hospital, after being told their daughter was brain dead, they were asked to donate her organs. What a request! Could you do it?

What is the most difficult thing you have been asked to do? In our Scripture, God tells Abraham and Sarah that at their advanced age they would become parents. They couldn't believe it. Sarah laughed, thinking it sounded ridiculous. But God responded, "Is anything too difficult for the Lord?"

Sometimes we ask ourselves: can God really help with this mess I'm in? As the Lord reminds Abraham and Sarah—and reminds us too—nothing falls beyond the bounds of His abilities. He remains eternally omnipotent and omniscient—all-powerful and all-knowing.

Whatever your struggle today, whether big or small, simple or complex, let the one who can handle anything handle it for you. In so doing, you honor Him, glorify His name, and witness to His surpassing greatness.

Lord, You can do anything; nothing is too large or too small, too simple or complex for Your loving attention. Help me to remember that whatever my struggle, You can help me overcome and be victorious. For Your name's sake, I pray. Amen.

Joy with Me!

Sarah said, "God has made laughter for me; everyone who hears will laugh with me" (Genesis 21:6, *New American Standard Bible*).

Scripture: **Genesis 21:1-8**
Song: **"Down in My Heart"**

I have two sisters. As children, sometimes while playing or joking around, we would break out in uncontrollable laughter. Our dad said, "Who gave you the giggle gas?" This, of course, made us laugh even harder.

Sarah laughed at God when He told her she would bear a child, but it was a somewhat sarcastic laugh. After bearing the promised child, Sarah's laughter turned to a bubbling joyfulness—an infectious kind of laughter like the kind my sisters and I shared.

In fact laughter can be catching. Often people walking in on the end of a joke will start to chuckle, even though they don't know exactly why. Isn't it interesting that God made laughter with such a contagious quality?

He's not our giggle-gas, though. For even when we can't laugh, when joking is clearly inappropriate, when we're immersed in serious pain or heartache, He is the source of a deep-down joy that remains through it all. That joy, of course, goes beyond humor to form a solid basis for all our fellowship and worship.

Lord, help me always remember that You are my source of joy. When I rely on circumstances for happiness, keep me ever mindful that You alone bring true happiness to my life by Your abiding presence. In Jesus' name. Amen.

Step Out in Faith

Abraham trusted God, and when God told him to leave home and go far away to another land which he promised to give him, Abraham obeyed. Away he went, not even knowing where he was going (Hebrews 11:8, *The Living Bible*).

Scripture: **Hebrews 11:8-12**
Song: **"Faith of Our Fathers"**

Have you noticed that faith can lead us to do many things we might not otherwise do?

I ventured over 700 miles away from my hometown in Nebraska to attend college in New Mexico. I believed I would get the education I needed to propel me into a successful and prosperous career as an engineer. My faith wasn't unrequited.

Abraham believed God when He said He would give him a new home, even though Abrham had never seen the place. Abraham also believed God when He said Abraham would be the father of many nations. Through Abraham's obedience, we have an example of how we can demonstrate our faith in the Lord.

Never fear or be ashamed to show your Christian faith because it isn't the popular thing to do. By expressing faith openly, we glorify the Lord (and might just make "faithing it" a little more popular).

Almighty Lord, *make my faith as strong and reliable as Abraham's. Help me never fear or be ashamed to show those around me that I am a Christian and that You are my Savior. And when I hear Your call to go, let my feet be swift to answer! In the precious name of Jesus, I pray. Amen.*

Everybody Else's Fault

Then Sarai said to Abram, "You are responsible for the wrong I am suffering. I put my servant in your arms, and now that she knows she is pregnant, she despises me" (Genesis 16:5).

Scripture: **Genesis 16:1-6**
Song: **"My Tribute"**

Confronted by my manager about a late project, I was ready with excuses. "It was the customers! They didn't know what they wanted and didn't support me. And those people working with me! They didn't do their share, so I had to do both my job and theirs. And, besides, you're always giving me too much to do!" I could go on, but I think you get the general idea. . . .

Notice that everybody else was to blame except me. Even if those other people shared in the blame, I refused to take my share. I was "victimized" by them instead of owning up to my own failings. I was living the old adage, "To err is human; to blame it on others is even more human."

Even though Sarai allowed Hagar to be with Abram, she still blamed him for the problems that followed. There was enough blame for everybody, but she refused to take her share. But then, I thoroughly understand how that could happen.

Dear God, *help me to take responsibility for what I have done instead of blaming others. Through Christ I pray. Amen.*

September 17–23. **Terry Magee** is a writer living in Pennsylvania, where he serves his church while attending school. He is married and has two grown children.

We Are Not Alone

The angel of the LORD **said to her: "You are now with child and you will have a son. You shall call him Ishmael for the L**ORD **has heard of your misery"** (Genesis 16:11).

Scripture: **Genesis 16:7-16**
Song: **"Praise to the Lord, The Almighty"**

The television show *Hee Haw* featured a recurring song that recounted the cast members' dreadful state of life, filled with gloom, despair, and agony. They were poking fun at misery, but it can be easy for any of us to wallow in a woe is me attitude during tough times Especially when we feel that nobody notices or cares—or even that God has turned His back on us.

Yet a common experience of those who seek God with fervent hearts is that they will, at some point, enter what's known as the dark night of the soul. God may indeed feel absent at those times, but our feelings don't give us the true picture. For Christ has promised to be with us always, even when we don't feel Him. And the indwelling Holy Spirit intercedes for us, even when prayerful words won't come to our lips.

All of this to say: Just as the Lord heard Hagar, he constantly beholds us and hears our own hearts. He hears and cares whether we're experiencing joy or misery, gloom or gladness. That we grow to be more like His Son is what matters most to Him.

Dear God, thank You for never abandoning me! Help me enjoy your presence even now. Thank You, in Jesus' name. Amen.

Lasting Inheritance

"Get rid of that slave woman and her son, for that slave woman's son will never share in the inheritance with my son Isaac" (Genesis 21:10).

Scripture: **Genesis 21:9-13**
Song: **"One Pure and Holy Passion"**

Dying childless, the old woman left a sizeable estate. Her surviving family members eagerly awaited the reading of the will, expecting everything to be divided among them.

Not so! Shock preceded anger as they all discovered she'd left everything to one relative. Angry accusations flew, followed by silence, as family members refused to speak to one another. Years later, the rift remains.

Sarai refused Ishmael a share in the inheritance she felt belonged solely to Isaac. She saw that anything given to Ishmael would diminish Isaac's portion.

Many families are permanently broken by money or inheritance struggles. However, we have an inheritance that is limitless in Christ. What we have received from Him can flow out in boundless grace among countless peoples. And since there is more than enough for all, how important that we share it every day of our lives!

Dear God, help me remember today that everything in my earthly life is limited and temporary. Anything I acquire here I will soon leave behind. Therefore, let me live with a view to what is most important: pleasing You in word and deed, living by Your Spirit each moment. Help me do it! I pray this prayer in the name of Jesus, my merciful Savior and Lord. Amen.

Doing Compassion

She went off and sat down nearby, about a bowshot away, for she thought, "I cannot watch the boy die" (Genesis 21:16).

Scripture: **Genesis 21:14-16**
Song: **"Comfort, Comfort Ye My People"**

According to news reports, the family was enjoying a bike ride along a tour road in the Florida Everglades when disaster struck. Their 6-year-old son fell off his bike and landed in an alligator's nest. The mother alligator, reacting to an apparent attack on her offspring, clamped onto the boy. The boy's mother, seeing her son in the alligator's jaws, rushed to his defense, beating the alligator with her bare hands to save her child. Thankfully, everyone survived this rare alligator attack.

Compassion for our young is built into us by God. We show it by risking our lives when they are attacked or by simply being in misery as Hagar was. She felt helpless to stop her son's suffering, yet she did stay nearby to watch over him.

Every parent knows this protective instinct. However, all of us, whether we have children or not, are surrounded by the young, defenseless, or suffering. Hagar knew of no response but to feel compassion. May we ourselves go even further—and *do* compassion.

Dear Father, Your Son always had time to put His compassion into action. Give me the discernment to see those suffering around me. But also help me put my feelings of compassion into action. Help me reach out in the most practical forms of help. In Jesus' name I pray. Amen.

Seeing or Just Looking?

Then God opened her eyes and she saw a well of water (Genesis 21:19).

Scripture: **Genesis 21:17-19**
Song: **"See, Jesus, Thy Disciples See"**

"Where are the car keys?" I asked my wife as I was rushing to leave for an appointment.

"On the dresser," she replied from the next room.

I searched again, including the drawers. "I still can't find them!" I called impatiently. "Are you sure they're here?" She came into the room and, pointing to the dresser, said, "Open your eyes; they're right in front of you!" Just like magic, those keys had appeared on the dresser!

Except that it wasn't magic, was it? I was *looking* without *seeing*.

Of course, it's all too easy to go through life missing the obvious—that God is constantly with us, that people around us long for kind words, that our neighbor might need a little help.

The well didn't magically appear for Hagar; it had been there all along. She just needed God to open her eyes, to show her the source of her survival. What kinds of opportunities and blessings would you like Him to show you this week?

Dear God, thank You for seeing and knowing everything. It is too easy for me to miss what should be obvious. Open my eyes and help me to see everything around me with Your eyes, both opportunities to serve and special blessings from You. In the name of Your Son, I pray. Amen.

Everyday Presence

God was with the boy as he grew up. He lived in the desert (Genesis 21:20).

Scripture: **Genesis 21:20, 21**
Song: **"Lead Us On"**

The golfer had been given a remarkable gift. When his ball was on the green, an imaginary line appeared only to him, a line he could follow to hit his ball in the hole. He was able to use this wonderful gift to join the professional golf tour and fulfill his life's ambition.

I sometimes dream of having some remarkable gift—especially if I could know that it came directly from God's hand.

The Bible speaks of God being with Ishmael as Ishmael grew up, yet it doesn't relate any miraculous examples of God's grace during this time. No doubt God's goodness was unfolding, though, in the mundane, normal activities of his life.

We look for God in miraculous events. But isn't He more commonly present in the ordinary ones? God is just as powerful when working in subtle, almost hidden ways as when He works in dramatic and miraculous ways. In the most ordinary of our daily activities, we can find the Lord of our lives.

Lord of my every moment, *thank You for being with me amid all the routines of my life. Help me enjoy this fellowship with You throughout the day as I learn to pray always. In the name of the Father, the Son, and the Holy Spirit, I pray. Amen.*

Proud Legacy—or Not?

His descendants settled in the area from Havilah to Shur, near the border of Egypt, as you go toward Asshur. And they lived in hostility toward all their brothers (Genesis 25:18).

Scripture: **Genesis 25:12-18**
Song: **"Let Everything That Has Breath"**

I constantly struggled with the heavy traffic and aggressive driving behavior while living in New Jersey. And I often responded by blasting my horn and yelling unkind things at other drivers. I was both surprised and humbled one day when my 2-year-old son, upon hearing a car horn in the distance, yelled "You turkey!"

Children watch us all the time and pick up our behaviors—good and bad. I couldn't pick and choose when my son watched me. I couldn't stop and say, "Don't do what I'm doing, because it's wrong." No, children are like sponges, soaking in everything around them.

Ishamel was born and raised in strife. And he passed that strife on to his children, who lived in hostility with those around them.

We're building a legacy each and every day of our lives. The question is, would it make us proud?

Dear Lord, help me to be aware that I am not alone, that my actions affect and influence those around me. Let me continue to reflect Your love and grace with everyone I know, so that I might build a legacy that brings honor to my family and glory to Your name. Especially keep me mindful of the little ones looking on, learning from me how to be. I pray this prayer in the name of Jesus, the one who died for my sins. Amen.

Can You Loosen Up?

"The LORD . . . will send his angel before you so that you can get a wife for my son from there" (Genesis 24:7).

Scripture: Genesis 24:1-9
Song: "I Will Serve Thee"

When I was a girl, one of my greatest joys was roller-skating. Gliding across the rink made me feel so light and graceful.

But initially learning how to skate had been another matter. My legs were rigid, and my knees were constantly locked tight for fear of falling. I thought that if I could just control my legs and knees, I'd get the hang of it. But then my sister told me to "just let go" and loosen up. When I did, I relaxed—and finally knew the joy of moving across the ice with a free spirit.

Life is like that. We have family or work problems, and our first inclination is to try to seize control of the situation and fix things. We lock our jaws and rigidly "clamp down." Like Abraham's servant, we want to cover all our bases, so we develop a contingency plan.

God's way, though, is to invite us to relax and let Him work out the details. We are simply called to trust and obey Him. When we do that, our walk of faith becomes as graceful as a skater floating across the rink.

Father, I know You are fully capable of guiding me without my constant suggestions. Help me trust You more fully! Through Christ, amen.

September 24–30. **Lisa Konzen** is an administrative assistant for United Way in Janesville, Wisconsin. She also writes health articles for her local newspaper.

All About Attitude

After she had given him a drink, she said, "I'll draw water for your camels too, until they have finished drinking" (Genesis 24:19).

Scripture: **Genesis 24:10-21**
Song: **"The Servant"**

Like most people, I'm not a fan of household chores. But they've become a little easier for me since I learned that I could do them in two different ways. The first way was to view every task as a drudgery; just get them done and move on.

The other way? I found I could offer every mundane chore as an act of service in thanksgiving to God. For instance, as I took up that attitude, washing dishes became more than a cleaning duty. It was now a loving act of caring for the family God had given me.

It's all in the attitude, isn't it? It seems to me that Rebekah invested her chores with meaning too. When Abraham's servant asked her for a sip of water from her jar, she didn't just give it to him. She went beyond what was asked of her and watered the camels too. Her willingness to be kind and generous won the approval of the servant. And her gracious spirit also prepared her for her role as Isaac's wife.

Small things done with love can make wondrous changes in our lives. Just ask Rebekah.

Loving Father, remind me that You care more about the quality of my heart than the length of my good works list. Through Christ I pray. Amen.

Driving Directions

"As for me, the LORD has led me on the journey to the house of my master's relatives" (Genesis 24:27).

Scripture: **Genesis 24:22-27**
Song: **"Follow On"**

When my sister moved into her new home on the other side of town, I had to call her for detailed directions to her house. She told me all the turns to make and even gave me landmarks to observe so I'd be sure of traveling in the right direction.

When we set out on a journey to an unfamiliar destination, it helps to consult a road map. Or do as I did, and call ahead for directions. Without instructions, the journey can be frustrating or even frightening, and we're likely to get lost.

Abraham's servant knew how to find the wife God intended for Isaac. Why? Because he knew he wasn't traveling blindly. God directed him each step of the way, and he was able to find Rebekah without any trouble.

We too have a road map to follow on the Christian journey. God's Word shows us the way, pointing out the turns we must take and the landmarks that will indicate whether we're headed in the right direction. We don't have to go it alone.

Dear Father in Heaven, You have given me the great privilege of knowing You through Your revealed Word. Help me to be faithful in my Bible reading and devotional times, so I'll be able to follow wherever You lead. In the name of Your Son, my Savior, I pray. Amen.

All That Glitters

As soon as he had seen the nose ring, and the bracelets on his sister's arms . . . he went out to the man and found him standing by the camels near the spring. "Come, you who are blessed by the LORD," he said (Genesis 24:30, 31).

Scripture: **Genesis 24:28-32**
Song: **"Little Is Much When God Is in It"**

Movie stars are rich, so they must be doing something right. Correct? Maybe if we could look more like them or buy the products they endorse, we could get in on the blessings they have. Right?

Rebekah's brother Laban also judged by appearances. When he saw the expensive jewelry, he was impressed. If Abraham is rich, he thought, maybe I can get in on that blessing too.

But all that glitters is not always gold. A person's net worth has nothing to do with his or her relationship with God. Although it's true that Abraham was wealthy and that he was a righteous person, his righteousness certainly didn't make God bless him. God blessed him with wealth and righteousness because He chose to do so.

Abraham couldn't earn God's blessings, and neither can we. Affluence isn't necessarily a sign of God's influence in a person's life. In fact, faithful service done in gratitude shines brighter than all the gold in the world.

Giver of all good gifts, I thank You for the greatest gift of all—Your Son Jesus Christ. May I adorn myself with His grace today, the one who loved me enough to die for me. In His name I pray. Amen.

Friend for the Journey

"The LORD, before whom I have walked, will send his angel with you and make your journey a success, so that you can get a wife for my son from my own clan and from my father's family" (Genesis 24:40).

Scripture: **Genesis 24:33-41**
Song: **"Traveling Home"**

My sister is a nervous highway driver, so when she had to travel the 30-mile journey from her home to an appointment with a lawyer, she asked me to accompany her. Somehow, just having me nearby made her calmer, and she actually enjoyed the trip.

What are some of the frightening things you face in life? Isn't it always better to have a friend with you?

A companion may not actually protect us, but having him or her with us calms our fears and helps us face our challenges with greater courage and perhaps even humor.

We can be faithful friends to those around us who face challenges in their walks of faith. Just being there, encouraging and loving them, can help make their journey successful. The same Lord who sent His angel as a companion to Abraham's servant also sends us as messengers to those around us, calling us to convey His peace, hope, and love.

Father, thank You for the people in my life who have held my hand along the way. Help me, in return, to offer my own hand in friendship to fellow travelers on their way home to You. In Christ's holy name I pray. Amen.

Wonderful Counselor

Laban and Bethuel answered, "This is from the Lord; we can say nothing to you one way or the other" (Genesis 24:50).

Scripture: **Genesis 24:42-51**
Song: **"Open My Eyes That I May See"**

Have you ever struggled to discern God's will for you? It would be nice if God would send down a giant neon sign flashing, "Here I am, and here's what I want you to do." But God doesn't usually work that way. So what are we to do?

I find an important clue in today's Scripture passage. Laban and Bethuel listened carefully to what Abraham's servant told them. They had a tough decision to make about Rebekah's future, but they were able to make it easily because they knew God had arranged it all. They knew Abraham's servant was obeying the Lord, and that was enough for them.

When we face our own important decisions, we can be certain that God has given us many faithful counselors to help point the way. Our families, ministers, and other church members will often provide helpful wisdom. But the most important and authoritative guide of all is the Holy Spirit, who speaks to us in Scripture and in our hearts. When we study the Word and listen to His leading, we will know the next step to take.

Lord, I face so many choices every day. Help me find direction in Your Word and by being very attentive to Your still voice within. In the name of the Father, the Son, and the Holy Spirit, I pray. Amen.

Love Through the Generations

The Lord is good and his love endures forever; his faithfulness continues through all generations (Psalm 100:5).

Scripture: **Psalm 100**
Song: **"Great Is Thy Faithfulness"**

My father is 84 years old and quite frail. During his most recent hospitalization, he had some trouble with memory, so the doctors frequently asked him questions like "Where are you now?" and "Who are these people in the room with you?" Often it would be my sisters and I, and then my dad would tell the doctors about his seven children and how proud he was of them. He couldn't remember much else, but he knew his legacy of love lived on in us.

God's love is alive and well in us too. God has always loved, and He always will love. That constancy has not wavered throughout history. From Adam to Abraham, from Moses to David, from the birth of Christ to His future glorious appearing, God's love is eternal.

And just as my dad's love lives on in his children, so too God's love is lived out in the daily lives of His children. Whenever we help our neighbor, we allow God's love to be shared in our generation and in the generations to come.

God of eternity, Your great love causes me to sing Your praises and to offer my whole life as a witness to You. Help me this day to be faithful in serving You as You have always been faithful in loving me. I pray this prayer in the name of Jesus, my Savior and Lord. Amen.

My Prayer Notes

DEVOTIONS

*L*et the hearts
of those who
seek the LORD
rejoice.

—Psalm 105:3

OCTOBER

Photo © Jupiterimages

Gary Allen, Editor

Give Him the Glory

According as it is written, He that glorieth, let him glory in the Lord (1 Corinthians 1:31, *King James Version*).

Scripture: **1 Corinthians 1:26-31**
Song: **"To God Be the Glory"**

On April 29, 1962, President John F. Kennedy made the following comment at a dinner honoring the Nobel Prize winners of the Western Hemisphere: "I think this is the most extraordinary collection of talent, of human knowledge, that has ever been gathered together at the White House—with the possible exception of when Thomas Jefferson dined alone." That witty remark gave perspective to those specially chosen honorees. They were among the world's best and brightest, but the brilliant impact of one man—Jefferson—gave them all a nation that could appreciate and appropriate what they had done.

Paul told the Corinthian believers they'd been specially chosen by the Lord. However, for most of them, at least in the world's eyes, their main distinction was their seeming *lack* of any distinction! But God used the ordinary to do the extraordinary. And, as usual, the Lord deserves all the credit for developing lesser abilities in humble circumstances. When we gather for worship, it is not to congratulate ourselves but to give Christ the glory.

Dear Savior, thank You for Your special calling and using me beyond what was even thought possible. In Jesus' name, amen.

October 1–7. **Richard Robinson** is a minister in Denver, Colorado, and Bible teacher on The Holy Ground Radio Broadcast, aired daily throughout the state.

Guided, Gracious, Grand Life

Laban and Bethuel answered and said, The thing proceedeth from the LORD: we cannot speak unto thee bad or good (Genesis 24:50, *King James Version*).

Scripture: **Genesis 24:50-61**
Song: **"The Guiding Hand"**

The beautiful story of Abraham's servant finding a wife for Isaac presents three striking features: First, we see how this faithful servant was guided by God. As Rebekah's family heard how God precisely answered the servant's prayer, they knew that the events had been issued from the Lord. Like the servant, we should say to all would-be helpers in the drama of God's will, "Hinder me not, seeing the LORD hath prospered my way" (v. 56, *KJV*).

Second, we see how gracious all the parties were in their interactions with each other. Obviously, the right attitude always helps.

Third, notice the grand undertones of this whole story. We sense it from the servant's spontaneous worship, from Rebekah's sweet surrender, even from Laban and Bethuel's reluctant blessing, saying, "Thou art our sister; be thou the mother of thousands of millions" (v. 60, *KJV*). Like them, we all need expanded views of God's will and work. Are we indeed caught up in something bigger than ourselves?

Dear Lord, help me to walk by faith and experience Your guidance, graciously doing Your will in Your grand plan for my life. I pray this prayer in the name of Jesus, my wonderful Savior and Lord. Amen.

A Sigh of Relief

Isaac . . . took Rebekah, and she became his wife; and he loved her: and Isaac was comforted after his mother's death (Genesis 24:67, *King James Version*).

Scripture: **Genesis 24:62-67**
Song: **"O Perfect Love"**

Picture Isaac seeing the camel caravan off in the distance. In anticipation, he went to meet the traveling party. Rebekah saw him walking toward them, inquired of the servant, and was told that it was his master—and her new husband! Upon meeting, Isaac was told the whole amazing story of God's guidance. With appropriate tenderness, Isaac took his new bride into his mother's tent to consummate their marriage.

The void in the patriarch's heart after his mother's death was finally filled by the love and comfort that Rebekah extended to Isaac. Only the right woman matched to the right man could produce this right result—and at just the right time!

God brought Isaac and Rebekah together across a vast space, closing the distance at the appointed time. As Proverbs 18:22 says, "Whoso findeth a wife findeth a good thing, and obtaineth favour of the LORD" *(KJV)*. That kind of favor always ends, as it did for Isaac, with a sweet sigh of relief.

God, thank You for the way You bring others into my life, especially when that special someone is sent to bring comfort. Through Christ, I pray. Amen.

A Shining Moment

Isaac entreated the LORD for his wife . . . and the LORD was entreated of him, and Rebekah his wife conceived (Genesis 25:21, *King James Version*).

Scripture: **Genesis 25:19-23**
Song: **"I Must Tell Jesus"**

Theodore Roosevelt delivered a speech on April 10, 1899, titled "The Strenuous Life" and made this observation: "If we are to be a really great people, we must strive in good faith to play a great part in the world. We cannot avoid meeting great issues. All that we can determine for ourselves is whether we shall meet them well or ill."

These words describe Isaac's situation in today's Scripture. Isaac had now reached a comfortable stage in his life, a peaceful and predictable time. But his wife's barrenness was a growing concern to both of them. This led the easy-going, calm-natured patriarch to "entreat the LORD for his wife" (v. 21, *KJV*). The word "entreat" conveys the idea of pleading, and this prayer was so intense and persuasive that God granted his request. Soon after, the happy couple was expecting.

As Roosevelt pointed out, there is no avoiding "great issues," even in the most secure, well-to-do homes. But we can meet them as Isaac did—by rising to the occasion with our finest prayers. It was Isaac's shining moment.

Father God, in my prayers give me the perseverance and urgency of an Isaac. Let me learn for myself what it means to entreat the Lord with an open and sincere heart. Thank You, in Jesus' name. Amen.

Destiny of Two Boys

The boys grew: and Esau was a cunning hunter, a man of the field; and Jacob was a plain man, dwelling in tents (Genesis 25:27, *King James Version*).

Scripture: **Genesis 25:24-28**
Song: **"Children of the Heavenly Father"**

After Rebekah gave birth to twin boys, the prophecy given earlier began to be fulfilled (see v. 23, *KJV*). Two nations developed, as opposite as the boys themselves. Esau became an avid outdoorsman with a taste for adventure, tending toward the worldly and secular.

Jacob preferred the domestic circle over the great outdoors. He was less active but just as ambitious, using his mind more than his muscle. Jacob also possessed the raw materials of spiritual leadership and became God's chosen patriarch-in-the-making.

These two boys remind all parents that a child's destiny begins . . . in childhood. Several people have been credited with saying, "Give me a child for the first seven years, and you may do what you like with him afterwards." It's true! Young children respond to training—of any kind, from any person, whether good or bad. Thankfully, good parenting still shapes the child who shapes the future. Yet, as Isaac and Rebekah demonstrate, only when parents work together will the future of children be bright.

Dear Lord, may all those with children depend on Your wisdom and grace, remembering that the future of many lives is at stake. In the holy name of Jesus, my Lord and Savior, I pray. Amen.

Birthright at a Bargain

Jacob said, Swear to me this day; and he sware unto him: and he sold his birthright unto Jacob (Genesis 25:33, *King James Version*).

Scripture: **Genesis 25:29-34**
Song: **"Falter Not"**

Compared to the secretive, scheming Jacob, Esau seemed like an open book, freely sharing what was on his mind. When he came in from the field, tired and hungry, Jacob was ready for him. With the delicious aroma of a fresh pot of stew hitting his nostrils, Esau immediately wanted some. Jacob simply said to his brother, "Sell me this day thy birthright" (v. 31, *KJV*).

Esau reacted impulsively with no thought of the consequences and swiftly agreed to the deal. He sold his birthright, ate the stew, and went his way. The Bible puts the whole transaction in its true light: Esau *despised* his birthright, something of precious, inestimable value.

Like Esau, we all have a birthright, those special privileges granted only to children of God. Praying, teaching, counseling, leading, serving, giving—these all tap into our spiritual inheritance. But if we give in to our fleshly appetites, we are prodigal children squandering our birthright. Jacob drove a hard bargain that day, which Esau later regretted. May we never sell our birthright at any price!

Heavenly Father, *keep me from foolish, impulsive, and short-sighted compromises that defraud me of spiritual blessings. I pray, amen.*

He Got What He Wanted

When Esau heard the words of his father, he cried with a great and exceeding bitter cry, and said unto his father, Bless me, even me also, O my father. And he said, Thy brother came with subtility, and hath taken away thy blessing (Genesis 27:34, 35, *King James Version*).

Scripture: **Genesis 27:30-40**
Song: **"Take the World, but Give Me Jesus"**

Intense human emotion drips from this story. Esau finally arrived to receive his father's highest blessing, reserved for the firstborn—only to discover that Jacob had gotten there first! Yes, the schemer had already tricked his father into giving him the birthright. Esau begged his father to bless him anyway, which he did, but not with the great patriarchal blessing.

As it turned out, Esau ended up getting exactly what he wanted. He valued worldly success and material things, so his father blessed him with "the fatness of the earth, and of the dew of heaven from above" (v. 39, *KJV*). God gave him his heart's real desire, but at the awful price of constant striving and a forfeited birthright (v. 40, *KJV*).

It makes me realize that I ought to be very careful what I ask for. I just might get it!

Blessed Father, it is so tempting to choose immediate gratification over the promise of future rewards. But remind me, Lord, that Your promise is sure and unfailing. So cleanse my heart from inordinate affections here on earth, the love of the world and the lusts of the flesh. Instead, let me desire only Your will and glory for as long as I live. In Jesus' name, amen.

Say, Can You Sing?

Sing to him, sing praise to him; tell of all his wonderful acts (Psalm 105:2).

Scripture: **Psalm 105:1-6**
Song: **"O Worship the King"**

Recently, our school district hosted a motivational seminar for a few hundred teachers. At one point our energetic speaker instructed us, "Raise your hand if you can sing." Perhaps 20 hands braved an answer. Amazing! Only that many people regard themselves as singers?

I considered my classroom of 6-year olds. All sing. All paint. All write. In fact, they regard themselves as experts at everything.

How could a singing child mature into an adult incapable of carrying a tune in a bucket? Perhaps mind-set is the answer. Some of us adopt the notion we're inept because we're not the best in the field. However, the Lord never asks us to sing to Him only if we're trained vocalists or if our albums top the charts.

We bless God when we offer melodies from a grateful heart. Today's passage details several of God's attributes worthy of including in a song of worship. We may not be experts in all things, but we've been given so much. A song of gratitude waits to praise Him. Who will sing it?

Lord, *thank You for the goodness You've brought to my life. I want to praise You with heartfelt words, whether spoken or sung. In Jesus' name, amen.*

October 8–14. **Vicki Hodges** teaches first grade and writes from her home in the Colorado Rockies.

Imagination Express

"To you I will give the land of Canaan as the portion you will inherit" (Psalm 105:11).

Scripture: **Psalm 105:7-11**
Song: **"Holy, Holy, Holy"**

A few weeks ago a friend asked, "What is the best thing you can imagine?" A lifetime supply of chocolate, of course! Maybe I should have answered visits with loved ones, or traveling to all the places on *my list,* or always being in sound health. Pause a few moments to explore your own response.

Someone has rightly noted that our most important thoughts are those of God and Heaven. Today's Bible passage overflows with significant descriptions of God. He is: the Lord our God, just, faithful, a promise keeper, and our benefactor. Just as God promised Abraham's descendants the land of Canaan as their inheritance, all followers of Jesus are promised Heaven as an inheritance by their faithful, promising Lord of all.

In his letter to the Ephesians, Paul proclaims that God "is able to do immeasurably more than all we ask or imagine (3:20). That includes taking us to Heaven, of course. Thoughts of Heaven always stretch my mind, but God isn't interested in just confirming my finite thoughts. He continually exceeds my imagination, for Heaven is far better than the best we can envision.

Lord, You are not limited even by my highest thoughts. I am so eager to experience the best You can create. Praise to You in Christ's name! Amen.

Glowing in Grace

Esau held a grudge against Jacob because of the blessing his father had given him. He said to himself, "The days of mourning for my father are near; then I will kill my brother Jacob" (Genesis 27:41).

Scripture: **Genesis 27:41-45**
Song: **"And Can It Be That I Should Gain?"**

Fire needs four ingredients: oxygen, fuel, a heat source, and a chemical reaction. When one of those is missing, flames can't exist. This year at my workplace, some drastic policy changes have produced relational wildfires. Staff tempers grew short, attitudes flared, and production plummeted. And I'm sorry to say, my own bad attitude has contributed to the blaze.

Esau kindled a personal wildfire. Disappointment, anger, and hatred—all natural emotions—fueled his desire to kill his brother. This unchecked seething caused him to become disordered, virtually psychopathic. Twisted thoughts of Jacob's demise consoled Esau, though he could have chosen to enjoy God's goodness instead.

Esau's experience teaches me much. Just as God would have delighted to show grace to Esau, He would also be pleased to shower my life with grace. The climate at work would likely be improved if I would set aside my seemingly justified reactions and choose to let Christ transform my attitudes.

Lord, help me surrender my frustration and anger to You today. By Your example and indwelling Spirit, put out these fires! In Jesus' name, amen.

Never Give a Good Gift

Rebekah said to Isaac, "I'm disgusted with living because of these Hittite women. If Jacob takes a wife from among the women of this land, from Hittite women like these, my life will not be worth living" (Genesis 27:46).

Scripture: **Genesis 27:46–28:5**
Song: **"The Gifts of Love"**

The skillet sizzled with melted butter and fresh fish. I considered the size of this gift. Our friend drove several miles and spent a couple of hours to catch his legal limit of salmon. When he arrived at our house, the fish were cleaned, skinned, filleted, and packaged. He could have handed over a dripping stringer of slimy fish for us to prepare, but he chose to give a *better* gift.

Rebekah was a giver of good gifts. When she learned of Esau's plot to kill Jacob, she insisted her husband send Jacob away. Of course, she diluted the truth by saying she didn't want Jacob marrying a Canaanite. Even though this plan spared Jacob from certain death, Rebekah's means were deceitful. She endowed Jacob with a good gift: the gift of life. However, she could have afforded a better gift: the gift of honesty.

When deciding between a good and better gift, which will we choose? Do we donate the worn-out or the new? Do we prefer the best for ourselves or give it away?

Father, *Thank You for giving Your best gift, Your Son, Jesus, at great sacrifice. My tendency is to give when it's convenient and doesn't cost too much. By Your power, help me to follow Your example. Through Christ, amen.*

Motives and Actions

Esau then realized how displeasing the Canaanite women were to his father Isaac (Genesis 28:8).

Scripture: **Genesis 28:6-9**
Song: **"Fairest Lord Jesus"**

Josh was a boy in one of my elementary classes years ago. He tripped over his untied shoes, had a runny nose and mussed hair. Kids frequently tattled on his abrasive behavior, and he rarely completed class assignments. When his single mom, mired in a custody battle, asked me to write a letter indicating her positive influence on his grades, cleanliness, and behavior, I told her the evidence wouldn't allow me to accommodate the request.

The next day a clean Josh brought me a bouquet of shriveled aspen leaves. The following day he slipped me a purple-crayoned drawing of two stick people holding hands. Now when turning in his homework, he says, "I love you. You're my favorite teacher." (If he'd fork over some chocolate I might cut a deal!)

What motivated Josh to change? Perhaps it was the same thing that urged Esau to shift gears. He realized what it would take to please his parent.

While we likely don't approve of either rationale, both guys made decisions for positive change. Sometimes it takes time for a noble motivation to catch up with our actions. And vice versa.

Lord, *do Your work in my heart, for You know my own actions are often driven by selfishness more than virtue. In Your holy name, I pray. Amen.*

The Best Calling Plan

He was afraid and said, "How awesome is this place! This is none other than the house of God; this is the gate of heaven" (Genesis 28:17).

Scripture: **Genesis 28:10-17**
Song: **"Be Thou My Vision"**

Both our daughters worked abroad during the summer, but geography hardly separated us. While we missed them greatly, phone calls and e-mails helped us stay in touch. We shared news and expressions of love. Though we were physically apart, we remained connected.

When Jacob left home he spent a night in what seemed an arbitrary location. He settled in for the night, sleeping on a rock pillow, dreaming of angels ascending and descending from a stairway bridging earth and Heaven. From above the top step, God spoke to Jacob, establishing His identity and reassuring Jacob that He would be *his* God, as well as being the God of Abraham and Isaac. Imagine Jacob's surprise at finding God in such a random place!

Where do we expect to find God? He is a thought away. Prayer, instant communication between earth and Heaven, is our great privilege. And Jesus, our resident intercessor, bridges both realms as He constantly talks with the Father on our behalf (see Romans 8:34).

Lord, *thank You for Your constant presence. You always listen to me and speak wisdom. Teach me to explore Your mind until I come into agreement with Your heart. Through Christ, my Lord, I pray. Amen.*

Memory Rocks!

Early the next morning Jacob took the stone he had placed under his head and set it up as a pillar and poured oil on top of it (Genesis 28:18).

Scripture: **Genesis 28:18-22**
Song: **"Come, Thou Fount"**

When our family vacations, we generally collect a rock to remind us of the trip, and a section of our front yard is designated for those special souvenirs. We have jade, quartz, petrified wood, copper-streaked stones, a desert rose, agate, rose quartz, lava, sandstone, flint, and a kidney-shaped stone. Each rock holds a special memory, except for the kidney. None of us remembers where we got it.

I think Jacob would have liked our rock garden. After his amazing dream of angels and God's conversation with him, Jacob called that area "God's house" (v. 22). He promptly erected a small memorial from the stone pillow he had used the night before and anointed the top of it with oil. This memory-rock served to commemorate God's promise to bless and multiply Jacob's descendants. It was also a reminder of the vow Jacob made to God.

Any significant encounter with the Lord is cause for celebration, isn't it? Whether we anoint our own memory-rock by journaling, or just by telling family and friends, the remembrance is an important faith-builder.

Heavenly Father, *You are my rock and my salvation. May You always be my best memory, as well! In the precious name of Jesus, I pray. Amen.*

Finally, Breathing!

He will cover you with His pinions, and under His wings you may seek refuge; His faithfulness is a shield and bulwark (Psalm 91:4, *New American Standard Bible*).

Scripture: **Psalm 91**
Song: **"Under His Wings"**

Growing up as a member of a large family that normally rode Greyhound busses for extended trips, I surprised no one when I fell wildly in love with flying at a young age. I equated safety with those huge wings and always looked forward to any flight. However, by the time September 2001 arrived, I'd taken too many business trips to retain my childhood wonder at flying.

About a week after September 11, while flying from the southwest back eastward, I realized I'd unconsciously held my breath ever since the fall of the Twin Towers. Sheepishly, I admitted to a friend my reluctance to board a plane ever again. She advised, "Read Psalm 91. It's one of my favorites."

Reading that psalm flooded me with the image of our powerful God enfolding me within huge, divine, omnipotent wings. I read those blessed, lyric lines, wept . . . and finally exhaled.

O God, forgive me for sometimes losing sight of how grand You are. You are always there with Your loving arms and omnipotent care. All glory to You, in the name of the Father, the Son, and the Holy Spirit. Amen.

October 15–21. **Phillis Harris Brooks** is an experienced devotional writer who enjoys the aspens of Colorado with her husband and son.

If Nothing Else

It came about, when Jacob saw Rachel the daughter of Laban his mother's brother, and the sheep of Laban his mother's brother, that Jacob went up, and rolled the stone from the mouth of the well, and watered the flock of Laban his mother's brother (Genesis 29:10, *New American Standard Bible*).

Scripture: **Genesis 29:1-12**
Song: **"Take Time to Be Holy"**

Imagine a kiss causing death. A news story told of a teenage girl with extreme allergies. One of those allergies involved a reaction to peanut oil. She died after kissing her boyfriend, who had eaten a peanut butter sandwich.

Love requires mindfulness, if nothing else. What does mindfulness look like? In the case of Jacob, it could involve rolling a stone away from a well for his cousin Rachel. Yet, in his case, mindfulness may have taken a backseat to pride. Jacob probably longed to favorably impress his attractive cousin. Perhaps current day mindfulness, for us, might entail investing the necessary time to better appreciate a close friend.

I know that such mindfulness can draw me into closer fellowship with God, as well. If I embrace Him as the lover of my soul, then my soul needs to strive to mirror that which would please my love. And how do I begin to know what would please God? By not being afraid to spend time alone with Him and His Word.

Lord, help me set my mind on You today. Even if I can only spare five minutes, let those moments be genuine and precious. In Jesus' name, amen.

No-Boundary Loving?

Jacob served seven years for Rachel and they seemed to him but a few days because of his love for her (Genesis 29:20, *New American Standard Bible*).

Scripture: Genesis 29:13-20
Song: "Love Lifted Me"

Our family learned a lot about the heaviness of time this previous year. As though under siege, we catapulted from one challenge to another. A favorite aunt died. After 19 years, a brother questioned his marriage. Spring found me recovering from a quadruple bypass surgery, only to have another blockage surface in my leg. And diagnosed with breast cancer early in the year, a younger sister then confronted brain cancer 11 months later.

The disappointments and heartaches of the year reduced time's speed to the slowness of a dance in quicksand. Against such a backdrop, it isn't at all difficult to understand how Jacob's seven year labor of love, heightened by anticipation, would assume the sensation of warp speed for him. Joy and anticipation can color an attitude so that no sacrifice looms too great.

I wonder if it's possible to live for God in the same manner. In this day and age, with its encouragement to set boundaries, that might constitute a pretty scary thought —loving God without any boundaries!

*No matter what the cost, **Lord**, whether health, time, or family, I give my days and years to You. They were never mine anyway; I have always belonged to You. In Christ's holy name, I pray. Amen.*

Entitlements

It came about in the morning that, behold, it was Leah! And he said to Laban, "What is this you have done to me? Was it not for Rachel that I served with you? Why then have you deceived me?" (Genesis 29:25, *New American Standard Bible*).

Scripture: **Genesis 29:21-25a**
Song: **"Have Thine Own Way, Lord"**

How often we've heard the outraged accusation "That's not *fair!*" No matter our age, we all have a keen sense of what constitutes fair play. Don't kick a person when she's down. Share, and share alike.

Many of us appreciate the concept of Camelot, with its Knights of the Round Table to enforce the concept might doesn't make right. Our expectation is that, having agreed to certain terms, the other parties will do the right thing to fulfill their obligations as well.

We really should be grateful, though, that God isn't quite the stickler for rules we sometimes tend to be. God sees each of us believers as His beloved adopted children. He overlooks our tantrums in the midst of adversity, cradles each sobbing child until he's comforted enough to run, play, and . . . throw tantrums again.

Sounds quite a bit like parenting, doesn't it? Yes, we all know how much fairness a good daddy expects to receive.

Father in Heaven, regardless of the experiences I may have had as a child, inspire me to approach You as the loving parent I've desired. I ask this in the name of Your Son, Jesus the Christ. Amen.

Wrong Direction?

But Laban said, "It is not the practice in our place, to marry off the younger before the first-born" (Genesis 29:26, *New American Standard Bible*).

Scripture: **Genesis 29:25b-30**
Song: **"Pure Within"**

One of my coworkers lives for competition. If I'm not careful, I'll occasionally fall into the trap of trying to outshine her. Of course, once I enter into that game, then we fuel each other's egos. The result: the project doesn't turn out quite as well, requires more time, and leaves me with a general sense of dissatisfaction.

I'm pretty sure my disquiet has more to do with my behavior than with the results of my performance. Why? Because I know that I know better. My allowing others to goad me into purely selfish behavior says much more about me than about them.

God deliberately equipped us with consciences to act as moral compasses. Perhaps Laban misplaced his compass! Otherwise, he'd have fulfilled his promise to Jacob, rather than continuing this sad competition for his daughters. In fact, as soon as any of us begin to suspect that we've started in the wrong direction, we can immediately stop and ask God's assistance to regain our ethical bearings.

Lord, You know how quickly I falter, so remind me that when I stumble, You remain at my side to catch me. In the holy name of Jesus, my Lord and Savior, I pray. Amen.

Just Thank Him

She conceived again and bore a son and said, "This time I will praise the LORD." Therefore she named him Judah. Then she stopped bearing (Genesis 29:35, *New American Standard Bible*).

Scripture: **Genesis 29:31-35**
Song: **"Now Thank We All Our God"**

One Christmas when I was 10-years-old, after I'd prayed for a great toy, someone gave me a pair of what had to be the ugliest shoes in the world. Candy-apple red, complete with bone-crushing pointed toes. They looked as though they'd escaped the set of *The Wizard of Oz*. Because of their glitter, passersby found it difficult, if not impossible, to rip their gazes from them.

How I hated those shoes! Yet my mother eventually demanded to know when I intended to write the thank you note for them. I looked at her in astonishment. Why in the world would I thank someone for giving me something so impractical and embarrassing?

Naturally, my mother's outlook differed significantly. "You needed shoes," she said. "And we don't tell God how to answer our prayers. We just thank Him." It took some time before I could take up her outlook as my own. But as Leah must have discovered so long ago, I too have begun to realize that "No" also represents a divine response. Ingratitude only serves to chill my relationship with the one who always answers my prayers.

Giver of every good thing, help me never discard Your greater gifts for the easier way. In the name of Christ, I pray. Amen.

Missing the Alarm?

Then God remembered Rachel, and God gave heed to her and opened her womb (Genesis 30:22, *New American Standard Bible*).

Scripture: **Genesis 30:22-24; 35:16-21**
Song: **"Brighten the Corner Where You Are"**

None of us read the signals my sister's body had sent. Her brow would pucker and she'd admit to one of us, "I don't remember how to get there." We chalked it up to her busy lifestyle or her habit of overextending herself. Thoroughly organized, she made it a point to have her doctor's office conveniently located up the street from where she worked.

One day while at work, she confessed to one of her coworkers, "I don't feel well. I should go to the doctor, but I can't remember where his office is." The alarms had finally transformed into loud warning gongs for our family; she had brain cancer.

There's a sense in which God sends us alarms regularly—those inner longings or feelings of uneasiness—may be God tugging at our sleeves. God's persistence in getting our attention is His way of reminding us that He has not moved but we may have wandered from Him. It is the wandering that leads to our forgetfulness about His constant, abiding presence, no matter our situations.

Light of the world, when I wander from You, my world becomes a darker place. Remind me that Your brightness is ever near, and I need only turn homeward to feel the warmth of Your presence. In Jesus' name, amen.

Why Worry?

"Save me, I pray, from the hand of my brother Esau, for I am afraid he will come and attack me, and also the mothers with their children" (Genesis 32:11).

Scripture: **Genesis 32:3-12**
Song: **"A Prayer for God's Blessing"**

In October of 1942, Eddie Rickenbacker was forced to crash land his B-17 bomber into the Pacific Ocean. He and his crew were out of radio range, so prospects for rescue were dim. After eight days of floating in a small raft, the crew members had run out of rations and were growing hungry. That morning, after their daily devotional time, Rickenbacker leaned his head back and pulled his hat over his eyes. A seagull landed on his head. Rickenbacker caught it, and the crew ate it while using the bird's intestines for bait to catch fish with hooks provided in their survival kits.

A seagull 900 miles from land? Rickenbacker had a simple explanation for their deliverance: "We prayed."

Fearful circumstances often drive us to our knees, don't they? Jacob feared his brother was seeking vengeance, and so we read "Then Jacob prayed" (vv. 9-12).

Any trouble worth worrying about is worth praying about. And once we've prayed about it, why worry?

Dear Lord, strengthen my faith that I might always recognize Your presence in my most fearful times. In Christ's holy name, I pray. Amen.

October 22–28. **Dan Nicksich** is a minister who writes articles and devotionals from his home in Somerset, Pennsylvania.

Time to Reconcile

"You are to say, 'They belong to your servant Jacob. They are a gift sent to my lord Esau, and he is coming behind us'" (Genesis 32:18).

Scripture: **Genesis 32:13-21**
Song: **"Brothers, Joining Hand to Hand"**

I need to get even with my brother. First, he drove a rental truck 500 miles to help pack and move our household goods. Now he hosts family gatherings and opens his swimming pool to us on hot summer days. I really do need to get even with him.

Of course, it wasn't always this way. As a younger brother, I constantly felt I was being abused and harassed by him during our childhood years. Getting even (in a different way) seemed to be a constant, consuming passion. How a little maturity changes such perspectives!

One of the saddest funerals I ever conducted was that of a young man whose brothers and sisters experienced a kind of reunion because of his tragic death. "He'll never know how he got us all together for the first time in years," one sister told me through her tears. How sad it is when we carry such harsh feelings toward others without making an effort to reconcile before death.

Jacob had once outrageously cheated his brother. He'd been a wily deceiver. Now he sought reconciliation. Good for him!

Dear Lord, *if there is someone with whom I have had a falling out, grant me the wisdom and courage to seek reconciliation. In Jesus' name, amen.*

Expecting the Worst?

Esau ran to meet Jacob and embraced him; he threw his arms around his neck and kissed him. And they wept (Genesis 33:4).

Scripture: **Genesis 33:1-4**
Song: **"Count Your Blessings"**

When I entered the hospital room, the elderly couple sat side by side on the bed, holding hands and crying. They had just received good news, no sign of his suspected cancer. They were both in their 80s.

Jacob was expecting the worst. He put his wives and their children in the back of his procession to give them a better chance of escape. His beloved Rachel and favorite son, Joseph, were bringing up the rear—the safest place, should violence erupt.

What joy Jacob must have felt as his brother ran to meet him and overwhelmed him with an affectionate embrace and kiss! Jesus would paint a similar picture in a parable involving reunion between a father and his wayward son (see Luke 15:11-32).

The Bible says that God can bring good from evil (see Genesis 50:20). He has a way of extending His blessings, even when we expect the worst: a clean bill of health despite the gloomy prognosis, peace and love where once bitterness ruled.

Dear Heavenly Father, *sometimes I expect the worst and then experience Your wonderful blessings instead. Help me to trust You always, even when the days seem darkest. I pray in the name of Jesus my Savior. Amen.*

The Other Side of Giving

"Please accept the present that was brought to you, for God has been gracious to me and I have all I need." And because Jacob insisted, Esau accepted it (Genesis 33:11).

Scripture: **Genesis 33:5-11**
Song: **"Give of Your Best to the Master"**

The church wanted to provide Thanksgiving dinners to some of their senior members, and everything was now in place—volunteers to cook meals, others to deliver them. But then they hit a snag. Many of the intended recipients refused the offer; a few even appeared offended.

While the church often teaches on giving, it may be that we also need to instruct our people in the art of receiving. One cannot give what another refuses to receive. A gracious acceptance completes the exercise of gift-giving.

Jacob insisted, Esau accepted. Most people I know are accustomed to being the giver: the caregiver, the gift giver, the willing helper in a time of need. Once the roles are reversed, they struggle to receive. But God says there will be times when those with plenty must supply the needs of others so that, in turn, the roles may be reversed in due season.

Perhaps this is a time of plenty for you, and you are helping provide for others. But are you also willing to be the needful one at times? How else would it be possible ever to experience love, grace, and caring?

*Humble me, **Lord,** that my pride might not hinder the gifts of those who seek only to give of their best to You. Thank You, in Jesus' name. Amen.*

Seeking Favor

"Just let me find favor in the eyes of my lord" (Genesis 33:15).

Scripture: **Genesis 33:12-15**
Song: **"Blest Be the Tie That Binds"**

Ben Franklin once felt that a certain individual seemed to harbor ill feelings toward him, though he could think of no offense or disagreement that had arisen between them. He thought it might have been some perceived, but unintended, slight, or simply a personality clash.

Franklin sent word to the other man, asking whether he could borrow a certain book from his personal library. The book was promptly sent, and thereafter relations between the two were cordial. Franklin's wise approach was to create a situation wherein he was indebted to his potential adversary. He treated the other man as a person of value and worth, and so attained his favor.

Jesus said that even when we are the offended party, we need to take the initiative and seek reconciliation. Of course, this runs contrary to human nature. Shouldn't the offending party bear the burden? But those who simply seek the favor of another will find a way to forgive and move forward.

Esau and Jacob were once again going their separate ways. Once they had departed in anger. Now they departed in peace.

Lord, *may it be that my departure from others would always be in peace. May the regret I feel always be that of the pain of separation and never the pain of unresolved differences. In Jesus' name I pray. Amen.*

Not Really Foolish

There he set up an altar and called it El Elohe Israel (Genesis 33:20).

Scripture: **Genesis 33:16-20**
Song: "Freely, Freely"

I once read a delightful story called "The Foolish Offering." Whenever confronted with an unexpected expense or potential time of financial hardship, this couple would make what they dubbed their foolish offering. They made a special offering, beyond their weekly gift to their church, some mission, or other worthy cause. They gave in faith, anticipating that God would provide for them in their time of need.

I heard of a church once that operated on the same principle. Whenever things were tightest financially, one of their elders was sure to say, "Time to give more to missions."

It's appropriate that Jacob's journey, including his time of reconciliation with his brother, ends in worship. God's actions on our behalf should bring corresponding acts of praise, thanksgiving, and worship. Some are so confident that they respond to God *in anticipation of blessings yet to come.* How fitting that we not forget God once we've actually reaped His favor!

Lord, *I know that You give all good things at just the right time. Help me give praise and thanks to You whenever You have blessed me. But help me also to give in faith beforehand, anticipating Your sure blessings in Christ. In His precious name I pray. Amen.*

Precious Oil!

How good and pleasant it is when brothers live together in unity! (Psalm 133:1).

Scripture: **Psalm 133**
Song: **"Together, Lord, We Come to Thee"**

We purchase perfume by fractions of an ounce. Yet a woman once poured a whole pint of expensive perfume on Jesus, an amount worth more than a year's wages. Some proclaimed this a waste, but Jesus praised her generous act of devotion (see Mark 14:3-9).

It's difficult to relate to the picture of precious oil running down over Aaron's head to the extent that his beard and even the collar of his robes are drenched. Yet the point that comes through is awesome: there are times for a bit of extravagance in our worship of God.

What inspires the outpouring of God's blessings like so much precious oil? Simply this—brothers living together in unity (v. 1). Yet the Bible abounds with brothers who experienced disunity—Cain and Abel, Esau and Jacob, Joseph and his brothers, and the sons of David. You could probably pencil in a few names yourself. You may even know a few examples of brothers or sisters in your own extended family who never seem to reconcile. Thus the precious oil of God's blessing is withheld.

Dear Lord, thank You for the blessings that appear in my world. But wherever there has been injury or disunity, make me an instrument of peace that others would come to know the abundant outpouring of Your blessings. In the name of the Father, the Son, and the Holy Spirit, I pray. Amen.

Child in His Old Age

Israel loved Joseph more than any of his other sons, because he had been born to him in his old age; . . . When his brothers saw that their father loved him more than any of them, they hated him (Genesis 37:3, 4).

Scripture: **Genesis 37:1-4**
Song: **"God Moves in a Mysterious Way"**

After his wife died, Hank remarried to a woman almost 25 years younger than he. When their son, Sam, was born, the 50-year-old father doted on the boy. He bought him lots of toys, played with him in the park after work, and took him fishing on the weekends.

But what about Hank's older children? They became jealous of little Sam. Their dad hadn't bought them lots of fancy toys. Nor had he spent as much time with them.

Joseph's brothers were jealous of him too. Their hatred must have hurt. But both boys, Joseph and Sam, were loved deeply by their fathers. Little Sam, like Joseph, could not know what the future held for him, but he knew he could always depend on the love of his father. In the same way, we are loved by our heavenly Father. We can't know what the future holds, but His unchanging love keeps us secure.

Dear Heavenly Father, *I know You hold the future in Your hands. I ask that You help me expect and accept, as Your plan, those difficult circumstances that come into my life. In Jesus' name, amen.*

October 29–31. **Dell Smith-Klein** shares Bible truths in the form of stories that touch the hearts of hearers. She lives in the Weaver Mountains of Arizona.

Scorned by His Brothers

His brothers were jealous of him, but his father kept the matter in mind (Genesis 37:11).

Scripture: **Genesis 37:5-11**
Song: **"Love Is the Theme"**

Joseph had another dream and felt compelled to share it with his family. His brothers could have begun praising God for revealing something very important to the boy; instead, they succumbed to envy and hatred. And as time went by, they began to scheme against young Joseph.

As I pondered this Bible story, I came up with this scenario: What if someone at church volunteered to be in charge of the children's choir, even though I have always been the choir director? Would I respond with joy that God is working through this person?

In Joseph's case, God was preparing him for leadership long before the need appeared. Joseph didn't know that, nor did his brothers. All they had was Joseph's strange dream about the sun, moon, and stars bowing before him.

It would be hard to figure out the truth if that was all we had to go on—a little brother's dream. After thinking about that children's choir volunteer, I had to ask, "Am I a dreamer like Joseph or a schemer like his brothers?"

Dear God, thank You for guiding me, even when I don't understand the meaning of the difficult events in my life. With all my heart I lean on You and believe that You have my best interest in mind each step of the way. I pray this prayer in the name of Jesus, my Savior and Lord. Amen.

Helped to Glory

A man found him wandering around in the fields and asked him, "What are you looking for?" He replied, "I'm looking for my brothers. Can you tell me where they are grazing their flocks?" (Genesis 37:15, 16).

Scripture: **Genesis 37:12-17**
Song: **"All the Way My Savior Leads Me"**

Stories abound of people who've been helped by an unknown stranger. Some have claimed that the benevolent visitor was an angel, but most of the time the helper is just a good-hearted soul willing to lend a hand in difficult times.

One summer, my husband was driving about 50 miles from home when he saw an older couple parked at the side of the road. He stopped to help and found two very weary 80-year-olds. My husband tried a simple fix on their car, but the couple only drove a few miles before it broke down again. This time, my husband drove all the way home, got the part they needed, and drove back to replace it for them. He wasn't an angel; just a stranger who felt led by God to help.

Joseph knew where his brothers were to be camped, but when he got there, they were gone. A kind stranger directed him to their new location—and to Joseph's rather painful immediate future. But the unfolding of his entire life was in God's hands. And what eventual glory!

Father, I don't know the motives of others, but I know that I can trust You to bring about what is best in my life. I thank You in Jesus' name. Amen.

DEVOTIONS

***M*ay all who seek you rejoice and be glad in you; . . . "Let God be exalted!"**

—Psalm 70:4

NOVEMBER

Photo © istock

Gary Allen, Editor

November 1

Where Will You Serve?

When Reuben heard this, he tried to rescue him from their hands. "Let's not take his life," he said (Genesis 37:21).

Scripture: **Genesis 37:18-24**
Song: **"Servant of God, Well Done!"**

I once had a friend, raised in a minister's home, who sensed from an early age that his gifts for leadership and teaching ought to be used in the church as well. Instead he went into sales.

For years nothing seemed to work out for him in the business world. When he was in his 50s, he realized that he had tried to thwart an essential calling on his life. After a long session on his knees, he signed up for Bible school. Within a few years he became the minister of a church in a small town where he was truly needed.

Joseph's brothers were so consumed with hatred that they didn't take time to think about what they were planning. They saw Joseph coming and let their anger get the best of them.

They couldn't, of course, thwart God's work in Joseph's life. Nor can His plans for us be thwarted as we seek His guidance day by day. Our part is to assess the spiritual gifts we've been given and then put them to use in His kingdom. The Spirit will lead us to just the right place.

Lord, help me to know myself well enough to know where and how I can serve You best. Then lead me there! In Jesus' name, amen.

November 1–4. **Dell Smith-Klein** shares Bible truths in the form of stories that touch the hearts of hearers. She lives in the Weaver Mountains of Arizona.

Painfully, Gloriously Awesome

When the Midianite merchants came by, his brothers pulled Joseph up out of the cistern and sold him for twenty shekels of silver (Genesis 37:28).

Scripture: **Genesis 37:25-28**
Song: **"Where He Leads Me"**

When I was about 8 years old, my cousins shut me in the tack house at my family's ranch. They thought it was pretty funny. There I stood, locked in with dusty saddles, bridles, saddle soap, and curry combs. But surely, my cousins would come back for me soon!

It wasn't funny for me. My heart pounded, and my legs shook as I hollered for them to let me out.

Joseph must have felt like that. I imagine he sat on the musty-smelling floor of that dry well waiting in fear, maybe calling out from time to time. Surely his crazy brothers would come back and lift him out.

I was only locked in the tack house a short time before my teasing cousins pulled the door open, but Joseph's story ended differently. When his brothers finally hauled him out of the pit, he realized their scheme included a business transaction. He watched Midianite merchants count 20 shekels of silver into his brothers' eager palms. What an awesome thing to witness! And even more awesome: though he didn't know at the time, it was all in God's plan.

Lord, *sometimes I feel as if I've landed in a pit of despair. It's not very comfortable there. Help me to a deeper trust today, in Jesus' name. Amen.*

A Father's Grief

All his sons and daughters came to comfort him, but he refused to be comforted. "No," he said, "in mourning will I go down to the grave to my son." So his father wept for him (Genesis 37:35).

Scripture: **Genesis 37:29-36**
Song: **"The Grave Itself a Garden Is"**

In October 2005, the body of a World War II airman was found in a glacier at Kings Canyon National Park. He was apparently part of a crew that crashed in those mountains 63 years earlier. The airman's family knew his plane had gone down, but searchers had never recovered his body. Thus, a family spokesperson said the family's grief had had no ending—until now.

After Joseph's brothers sold him to a traveling band of traders heading toward Egypt, they lied to their father, saying a wild animal had killed his favorite son. Their father's grief was so deep he couldn't be comforted—even when surrounded by all his other children. Never again to look upon, or hold, his child was beyond this father's capacity to bear.

Yet, God's purpose was unfolding. There would come a day in the lives of Joseph's brothers when they would be grateful Joseph hadn't died in that pit. In the meantime, they watched their father mourn the death of a son who was just as alive as you or me.

God, sometimes my grief is so deep! But thanks for walking with me through it. In You I find comfort and peace. In Jesus' name, amen.

Look and See!

You are my help and my deliverer; O L<small>ORD</small>, do not delay (Psalm 70:5).

Scripture: **Psalm 70**
Song: **"Deliverance Will Come"**

Even though his angry brothers tried to destroy Joseph and God's plan, they couldn't do it. And when Reuben tried to rescue Joseph, he couldn't do that either. God had it in control. Every step of the way, from the time of his youth, God's hand was upon Joseph, directing and delivering.

Once when my children were small, we camped in the forest together. At dusk we took a little walk, and I became so interested in showing the children the moss on the rocks and the minnows in the stream that I failed to keep an eye on the setting sun. At dark we were still some distance from our campsite.

It was a moonless night, and we couldn't see the path. My heart pounded as I walked along carrying the 3-year-old and leading the 5-year-old. Then another camper, flashlight in hand, stepped up beside us. He shined his light on our path and walked with us all the way to our campsite. I was so grateful!

Even when we can't recognize God's direction, it's there. He shines His light on our dark pathway and delivers us. When we look, will we truly see?

Lord God, *I praise You as I think how You have, time and time again, led me through dangerous situations. Glory to You, through Christ! Amen.*

One Path to Success

The LORD was with Joseph, so he became a successful man
(Genesis 39:2, *New American Standard Bible*).

Scripture: **Genesis 39:1-6a**
Song: **"Spend One Hour with Jesus"**

Remember the story of King Midas, who requested that everything he touched would become gold? He soon discovered the gift was actually a curse—when his beloved daughter turned to solid gold at his touch! We could say that Joseph had a kind of midas touch. His benefactor was God, and the gift wasn't a curse at all.

The prophet Jeremiah penned the words revealing God's wonderful touch upon His people: He knows His plans for us, plans to prosper us, to give us hope and a future (see Jeremiah 29:11).

God certainly knew what He had planned for Joseph from the beginning. And while it may not have seemed a blessing to be sold by his brothers into slavery—going from the pampered son of a wealthy rancher to a slave doing menial tasks—God had a purpose in it all.

We know the story of Joseph's success and his eventual rulership in Egypt. The thing we must never forget, though, is this: Joseph had nothing to do with his success other than being a willing, obedient servant of God.

Lord, help me see that even in the most difficult circumstances, You have my good in mind. I pray through my deliverer, Jesus. Amen.

November 5–11. **Marjorie Vawter**, of Westminster, Colorado, loves to write and has authored several published devotionals and book reviews.

Plan Ahead!

"How then could I do such a wicked thing and sin against God?" (Genesis 39:9).

Scripture: Genesis 39:6b-10
Song: "Thy Word Have I Hid in My Heart"

As a teacher in a Christian high school, I enjoyed the frequent opportunity to sit under wonderful, godly preaching in our twice-weekly chapel services. Many of the preachers taught our young people the importance of being morally pure. The best piece of advice I heard came from our youth minister: "In order to stand firm in temptation, make the decision to please God *long before* the temptation comes."

Joseph recognized that the temptation he faced would, in reality, lead to a sin against God. God had blessed Joseph with such great stewardship responsibility that Potiphar had no idea what he owned; it was all trusted to Joseph's wise management. The only thing or person Potiphar withheld from Joseph was . . . Mrs. Potiphar! Sadly, Mrs. Potiphar was obsessed with Joseph's good looks.

But isn't all sin ultimately an affront to God? Spurning His wonderful blessings, we choose immediate gratification over long-term peace. But knowing how this grieves God's heart, we can determine far ahead of time our plan of escape.

Father God, help me determine ahead of time to stand firm on the principles of Your Word when I face temptation. In Jesus' name, amen.

Try a Footrace!

He left his garment in her hand and fled (Genesis 39:12, *New American Standard Bible*).

Scripture: **Genesis 39:11-20**
Song: **"Yield Not to Temptation"**

In general the Bible tells us to stand firm and resist our temptations. However in certain sudden, sticky situations, its best just to . . . *run!*

Literally. Like Joseph did.

In the New Testament, Paul encouraged Timothy to flee the lusts of youth and chase after godly virtues, such as righteousness, faith, love, and peace (see 2 Timothy 2:22).

Joseph did just that, leaving his garment in Mrs. Potiphar's hand. He may not have anticipated her anger when she didn't get what she wanted. And he may not have expected to end up in prison. But Joseph did the right thing.

Writer Jerry Bridges, in *The Pursuit of Holiness,* tells us that John's view of holiness (not sinning) was different from his own goal of (not sinning *very much*). It would be like a soldier going into battle with the aim of not getting hit *very much*. If merely this is our aim in life, we can be sure the darts of temptation will hit us over and over again. A good old-fashioned footrace has much better chance of success.

Lord, no matter how hot the battle, keep me close to You in pursuing holiness. When it's time to run, help me do it. Through Christ I pray. Amen.

Waiting for Refining

Two years later, Pharaoh dreamed that he was standing on the bank of the Nile River (Genesis 41:1, *New Living Translation*).

Scripture: **Genesis 41:1-8**
Song: **"How Firm a Foundation"**

Have you noticed how difficult it is to wait on God? Yet God uses those times of waiting to mold and refine us, preparing us to accomplish His plans in our lives. When Habakkuk wondered how long it would be before God fulfilled His promises of deliverance to Israel, God answered: "These things I plan won't happen right away. Slowly, steadily, surely, the time approaches. . . . If it seems slow, wait patiently, for it will surely take place. It will not be delayed" (Habakkuk 2:3, *NLT*).

We don't know much about Joseph's wait in prison other than that he interpreted the dreams for Pharaoh's chief cup-bearer and baker. We don't even know how long his imprisonment lasted. But it was another two years before God was ready to release him and exalt him to the No. 2 position in the land of Egypt.

God used the time well, however: He prepared Joseph for the tasks ahead, even though the waiting must have been hard for the young man. Perhaps Job said it best amid all his patient sufferings: "He knows where I am going. And when he has tested me like gold in a fire, he will pronounce me innocent" (Job 23:10, *NLT*).

Lord, help me each day to wait patiently for you to mold me into a vessel fit for the work You've placed at hand. In Jesus' name, amen.

Can You Focus Like This?

"Now as for the repeating of the dream to Pharaoh twice, it means that the matter is determined by God, and God will quickly bring it about" (Genesis 41:32, *New American Standard Bible*).

Scripture: **Genesis 41:25-36**
Song: **"If You Will Only Let God Guide You"**

What is our usual first reaction when we've been wronged? For me, as soon as I get a chance, I go into defense mode. "This isn't fair! Justice should be done. My rights have been violated."

I'm impressed that Joseph didn't say any of these things when he came before Pharaoh. He didn't talk about being imprisoned on trumped-up charges. He didn't confront the cupbearer for forgetting him those two long years. Instead he focused on Pharaoh's request and kept his eyes on God. Three times in this passage Joseph tells Pharaoh that God sent the dream because God was ready to work in Egypt and the surrounding lands.

Joseph also refused to take credit for his ability to interpret dreams, again pointing his hearers to the sovereign God. Then he followed the dream's interpretation with words of counsel, not realizing God was going to use him to fulfill the plan of action he suggested. If I could keep everything focused on God like that, I know my life would bring greater glory to Him. How is it with you?

Father, Your Son, Jesus, suffered every injustice as my perfect high priest. Let me focus on honoring Him today as I pray in His name. Amen.

Finally, Justice!

Pharaoh said, "Since God has revealed the meaning of the dreams to you, you are the wisest man in the land! I hereby appoint you to direct this project" (Genesis 41:39, 40, *New Living Translation*).

Scripture: **Genesis 41:37-45**
Song: **"God Is So Good"**

Have you ever wondered how Joseph felt when Pharaoh spoke these words? In a single day, Joseph went from being a prisoner to the taking on the second highest position in the land of Egypt—from the chains of imprisonment to the soft raiment and jewels of royalty.

While Joseph's thoughts and words about it aren't recorded, we can know that he recognized God's hand in all of this. Years earlier he'd dreamed about holding this rulership above his family. And Jacob had rebuked him for his pride.

Yet now God fulfilled the dream. After all the years of testing, learning, and waiting, Joseph was ready for the job God had for him. I'm quite sure that God's ultimate justice helped him forget all the cruel injustices done to him. And we can do the same—but with some difficulty. For, as William Penn once said: "Justice is the insurance which we have on our lives and property. Obedience is the premium which we pay for it."

God, You indeed are good! You bring us out of the fire and exalt us above our enemies—in this life or in the next. You work all things together for good to those who love You. For this I praise You, in Christ's name. Amen.

Tested Character

Until the time came to fulfill his word, the LORD tested Joseph's character (Psalm 105:19, *New Living Translation*).

Scripture: **Psalm 105:16-22**
Song: **"Rejoice in the Lord Always"**

The writer of Hebrews tells us that Jesus learned obedience. How? Through suffering (see 5:8). Think of it—the perfect Son of God had to *learn* obedience.

Joseph was a teenager when his brothers sold him into slavery. But even that initial trial resulted in his being an honored servant to Potiphar, captain of Pharaoh's guard. But to truly test his character, God allowed Joseph to be imprisoned on a charge of rape. We're told that he was in fetters that bruised his feet and bound him around his neck. His entire being—body, soul, and spirit—was tested by those chains and the years he was in prison.

Even after the chains were removed, Joseph must have borne the marks of those fetters. Through all of this, Joseph's character was refined. I believe God allowed him the dream of ruling over his parents and brothers to sustain him in his darkest hours. Even Joseph's own testimony to his brothers spoke of understanding that God's way, though hard, is always best: "As far as I am concerned, God turned into good what you meant for evil" (Genesis 50:20, *NLT*).

Lord, help me remember that what seems bad to me, whatever is unfair in my life, whatever chains bind me—these things are opportunities to recall Your presence and draw on Your strength. Through Christ, amen.

Listening, Then Loving

I will listen to what God the Lord will say; he promises peace to his people (Psalm 85:8).

Scripture: **Psalm 85**
Song: **"Lord, Speak to Me"**

I turned off the TV news with a sigh. It was bad news again. Besides another devastating earthquake, I'd watched reports of disturbing crimes committed against innocent children. I couldn't stand to know anymore. I picked up my Bible and began to read. A hundred years ago it took a lot longer for such news to reach us. But in our instant media society, it is hard to avoid contact with the pain of others. How do we deal with all this suffering in the world?

The psalmist helps me here. If I focus on listening to the Lord, I will find personal peace. It is an act of the will to stop and listen to Him.

As we open to His inner peace, we will be strengthened to reach out to others with the first small steps of compassion. We can't save the whole world at once, but we can offer a cup of cold water to the one suffering next door. That is my prayer this day—that I will listen to the Lord and then reach out with the power of His peace.

Lord, I thank You that You desire to speak to me—even more than I want to listen. Help me to hear Your voice in the many ways You communicate with me every day. Then move me into loving service in Jesus' name. Amen.

November 12–18. **Janet Bair** is a freelance writer and a children's librarian. She lives in Ansonia, Connecticut, with her husband and two daughters.

Remember Me?

Although Joseph recognized his brothers, they did not recognize him (Genesis 42:8).

Scripture: **Genesis 42:1-20**
Song: **"Face to Face with Christ, My Savior"**

Has anyone ever come up to you and exclaimed, "Hi, remember me? I almost didn't recognize you." And as he or she talks on and on . . . you are still wondering who, exactly, *is* this person?

Sometimes we recognize that sudden stranger, and sometimes, like Joseph's brothers, we don't. The person's looks may have changed significantly over the years. Simply growing up changes peoples faces.

Joseph was 17 years old when his brothers sold him into slavery, and about 25 years had passed before they met again. Pharaoh had given him robes of fine linen and put a gold chain about his neck. At age 42, Joseph not only looked different but he was in a totally unexpected place when his brothers saw him again.

While we may have the same problem of recognizing people we knew long ago, there is one person we should always be able to recognize—Jesus. Someday when we see Him face-to-face in Heaven, we will know Him by His love for us. We will recognize His character. We will see the marks on His hands and feet. We will remember all He has done for us, and we will be eternally thankful.

Lord, as I learn more about You every day, help me to learn more of You in this wonderful relationship. In Your precious name I pray. Amen.

Don't Delay!

As it is, if we had not delayed, we could have gone and returned twice (Genesis 43:10).

Scripture: **Genesis 43:1-15**
Song: **"The Savior Is Waiting"**

Carol frowned as she looked at her long To Do list. She couldn't put off doing those chores any longer—the phone calls to make, a costume to alter, grocery shopping to do, and a huge yard of leaves to rake before it rained.

Procrastination! We're all guilty at times.

Joseph's brothers delayed going back to Egypt after their first visit during the famine. Even though Simeon was waiting in prison, they ate all of the grain before they went back. Judah finally reminded his father that they could have already gone—and come back twice—in the time it was taking Jacob to make a decision!

Sometimes I too hesitate to get moving. When the Lord prompts me to do something, it's usually pretty clear. God's still, small voice may nudge me to go and talk to a lonely neighbor or give some money to a struggling college student I know. It may be a small or a big thing. It may not make sense at the time. But the Lord has His own purposes and plans. And I long to be a part of the solution rather than a cause of delay.

Lord God in Heaven, help me with my procrastinating tendencies. I know that if I follow Your leading, the plans You have for Your kingdom will be accomplished in my small part of the world. Thank You for using me today. In the name of the Father, the Son, and the Holy Spirit, amen.

Don't Finish This

Deeply moved at the sight of his brother, Joseph hurried out and looked for a place to weep. He went into his private room and wept there (Genesis 43:30).

Scripture: **Genesis 43:16-34**
Song: **"Father, Make Us Loving"**

Have you ever been to a large family reunion with relatives you haven't seen in a long time? At such times, we wonder why we waited so long to get together.

Sometimes you want to cry for joy at seeing everyone again. The great Joseph wept when he saw his beloved brother Benjamin. In spite of the fact that his brothers had sold him into slavery, he was overcome with emotion upon seeing his family reunited again. Now Joseph was a tough man, ruling over thousands in Egypt, but he had a tender heart for his family.

God calls all of His people to have caring, reconciling hearts. As Hebrews 12:14 tells us: "Make every effort to live in peace with all men." Family reunions offer us the opportunity to resolve conflicts as we reconnect. God gives us these special times of great food and conversation to catch up on news but also to show how we can pray for one another and build one another up. As humorist Don Marquis once quipped: "I would rather start a family than finish one."

Lord, *thank You for the families and friends that You have placed with me. Help me to be a good listener and to see their true needs, praying for them with discernment. In Your name I pray. Amen.*

Another Test

Put my cup, the silver one, in the mouth of the youngest one's sack, along with the silver for his grain (Genesis 44:2).

Scripture: **Genesis 44:1-13**
Song: **"Wonderful Grace of Jesus"**

In a sermon one Sunday, Chrissy heard the story of how Joseph forgave his brothers. The closing prayer included an invitation to forgive any family member who had caused hurt. Later that day, Chrissy's forgiveness capability was tested. Another family member yelled and berated her at a party. Surprisingly, Chrissy was able to keep quiet and walk away. Later she realized the power of God had been at work in her life. For it is incredibly difficult to forgive while the sting of hurt or embarrassment still simmers in our hearts.

There are many tests in the Christian life, though most aren't as elaborate or as planned as Joseph's. When he had his own silver cup put in Benjamin's sack, he wanted to see whether his brothers really had changed. Would they abandon Benjamin as they had heartlessly left Joseph himself so long ago?

God will test our faithfulness too. But not for the purpose of failing us. Rather He will confirm and strengthen our faith through each trial. As Job proclaimed: "When he has tested me, I will come forth as gold" (Job 23:10).

Lord, let forgiveness always be on my heart and lips. And thank You for growing me toward maturity, even through the tough times. In the holy name of Jesus, my Lord and Savior, I pray. Amen.

Launched Back to Joy

Judah replied. "What can we say? How can we prove our innocence? God has uncovered your servants' guilt" (Genesis 44:16).

Scripture: **Genesis 44:14-34**
Song: **"My Sins Are Blotted Out, I Know!"**

"Did you finish your dinner?" Mom would ask as she was busy cleaning up. *Well* . . . I used to sneak those hated lima beans to our cat under the table. And my little brother would hide his unwanted food in a napkin and then throw it out. Funny how, so many years later, I can remember doing a little thing like that. I am sure I told my mother "Oh yes, I ate it all."

Secret sins stick with us, big or small.

Joseph's brothers had a secret sin that loomed large before them. When they met Joseph again 25 years later, and things weren't going well for them, their consciences quickly prodded them. They felt uncovered, soul-naked in their guilt.

Unconfessed sin can plague us like that. And it's a good thing it does! Then we can take it as a gracious call to open our hearts to God, to let Him know the hurts, the desires, the alienation that drove us to some sad form of self-destructiveness. There, at His feet, we obtain sweet mercy—and the courage to launch into life again with joy.

Heavenly Father, how I wish to serve You in all purity and perfection! But when I fail, help me run to You with unguarded heart to receive Your forgiveness. I pray through my deliverer, Jesus. Amen.

A Reconciliation Model

It was not you who sent me here, but God. He made me father to Pharaoh, lord of his entire household and ruler of all Egypt (Genesis 45:8).

Scripture: **Genesis 45:1-15**
Song: **"Others, Lord"**

Cindy sat down with her preschool class and began to color with the children. As soon as she started coloring her picture, two of the kids began watching her intently. They used the same colors she used and copied her picture—even down to the blue and green stripes she added on the boy's shirt.

Cindy was stunned to see how quickly they wanted to emulate her every move. She thought, "What else do the children copy?" She was humbled to find herself such a powerful public role model!

Children model adults as if it were second nature; they do need patterns to follow as they grow up. Joseph's forgiveness of his brothers—and their final reconciliation—is a good family model for any of us to copy. No matter how serious the offense, family members can work towards reconciliation. And it will benefit all concerned. As someone once put it: "When chickens quit quarrelling over their food they often find there is enough for all of them."

Lord, *thank You for Joseph's model of reconciliation. In my family where there are hurts, help us to take them to the cross where all is forgiven. In the name of the Father, the Son, and the Holy Spirit, I pray. Amen.*

Big Promises

"Never mind about your belongings, because the best of all Egypt will be yours" (Genesis 45:20).

Scripture: **Genesis 45:16-20**
Song: **"Standing on the Promises"**

God makes great big promises. Read the New Testament and see: We are promised fire that burns hot. We are promised wind that blows strong and light like that of a city set on a hill. God adds to those promises the startling radiance of a marriage banquet.

Pharaoh promised Joseph's family land in Egypt. It was a promise that eased an old past and pointed to a new future; a promise they could trust, invest their lives in, and look forward to. It was a promise they knew would come true. But Pharaoh promised even more: the most excellent land in Egypt.

God's promises are true and they are tremendous. Read the New Testament. It is the fatted calf and the best robe. It is abundant grace and unspeakable joy. It is a pearl of great price and a great, big box full of treasure. God's promises are true. They are also excessive, extravagant, and exceedingly abundant.

Dear God, *thank You for wrapping Your strong arms around me, pouring out Your great love into my life, and lifting me up to the highest mountain of gift and blessing. Thank You for wide doors through which to pass and large rooms in which to stand. In the name of Christ, I pray. Amen.*

November 19–25. **Phillip H. Barnhart**, writer of 14 books, retired in 2002 after 45 years in ministry. He lives on Perdido Bay, Florida, with his wife, Sharon.

Our God Speaks

God spoke to Israel in a vision at night and said, "Jacob! Jacob!" (Genesis 46:2).

Scripture: **Genesis 46:1-4**
Song: **"Speak to My Soul"**

It is no problem for God to speak to us. We are made in God's image, so God communicating with us is not unlike us communicating with one another. As God spoke to Jacob on his way to Egypt for a family reunion, He also speaks to us in all sorts of circumstances.

Besides the obvious—Bible meditation and prayer—we hear from God in the when and where and what of how things go in life. A road taken here, a page turned there, and we look back to see God's voiceprint all over our decisions and choices.

God is keen on self-revelation, isn't He? He likes to make himself known to us. It gives Him joy to plop down in our lives in ways we are foolish to deny. I've noticed that He occasionally likes to send a friend my way with a word for me that could have only come from Him. He likes to stir up a favorite emotion and speak to me from the wind that blows in the heart of my feelings. The point is, no venue is out of bounds for the voice of God.

My Father in Heaven, You are knowable to me. Every day, any place, I can hear from You. I am glad You aren't secretive about yourself! Of all the things You reveal, the most important are the incomparable aspects of Your character. And since You never quit speaking, may I never stop listening. In the name of Your Son, my Savior, I pray. Amen.

What a Hug!

Joseph got in his chariot and went to meet his father. When they met, Joseph hugged his father around the neck and cried for a long time (Genesis 46:29, *Contemporary English Version*).

Scripture: **Genesis 46:28-34**
Song: **"God Be with You Till We Meet Again"**

Joey was 13-months-old when his estranged father kidnapped him and took him to a faraway state to live. Years later as Joey visited an Internet chat room, a couple became curious about him. Joey's story sounded like another they'd heard. The couple contacted the police and, not long afterward, the FBI showed up on Joey's doorstep to tell him his mother had been searching for him for the past 14 years. Just before Christmas of that year, Joey and his mother were joyfully reunited.

In our Bible passage, Jacob is on his way to Egypt to be reunited with his son Joseph. It is a glorious journey as every step he puts down on the road leaves a footprint of joyful anticipation. He can't wait to see his boy again. Upon approaching Joseph, he throws his arms wide open, runs with abandon toward his son, and puts a hug on Joseph that will not let go. There is shouting, crying, dancing. There is the immeasurable joy of reunion.

I like to imagine how it will be when we, His long lost brothers and sisters, finally see Jesus face-to-face. What will that hug be like?

Dear God, *no matter how far I roam, I will come home to You. Thank You for Your ready arms of welcome. In Jesus' name, amen.*

Family Time

Joseph also provided his father and his brothers and all his father's household with food, according to the number of their children (Genesis 47:12).

Scripture: **Genesis 47:7-12**
Song: **"The Family of God"**

Little Mikey asked his mother, "Where was I born?" The answer came, "In Michigan." Another question had queued up behind the first one. "Where was sister born?" So Mom replied, "She was born in Wisconsin."

Little Mikey was not through. "How about you and Daddy?" Mikey's mother accommodated her son. "I was born in Georgia, and your dad was born in Oregon." Mikey thought about all of that information for a minute and then said, "Isn't it great we could all get together?"

After years of separation, Joseph gets together with his father and brothers. They are reunited and Joseph takes advantage of the reunion to give his family everything they need. His generosity celebrates his love for each and all of them. It is family time in Egypt, and like the best of family time everywhere, love communicates and joy dominates. No matter what the future holds, it's OK because the caring family is together. Each member rests in a haven of safety and security. Everyone knows this is where they belong, and these are the people they can count on. There's no time like family time.

Thank You, **Dear Father,** *for giving me a place in Your family. In this family, I am Yours and You are mine. Through Christ the Lord, amen.*

Going Home

"When I rest with my fathers, carry me out of Egypt and bury me where they are buried" (Genesis 47:30).

Scripture: **Genesis 47:27-31**
Song: **"On Jordan's Stormy Banks I Stand"**

I have decided what I want engraved on my tombstone. Put my name, year of birth and death, and then put, "To Be Continued."

When I die I will pass across the threshold of death into the storehouse of life forever. My sequence begun in the heart of God continues in the presence of God. I pray for the kingdom to come and I come to the kingdom.

When Jacob dies he wants to go home, to end up in his homeland, not in a foreign land. Joseph promises his father he will go home, just as God promises us that we will go home.

Yes, we will go home where the light never fails because the sun never sets. We will go home where the little chords we hear on earth become full-scale symphonies of beauty and majesty. We will go home where our speculations and intimations become absolute certainties. Heaven is the destination, the completion of a journey, the fulfillment of a promise. Heaven is home.

O Lord, You are God of earth and Heaven. You are God of beginnings, endings, and continuings. You are God of yesterday, today, and tomorrow. You are the God who comes and never leaves. You are God who always finishes Your sentences with the exclamation point of forever! In the holy name of Jesus, my Lord and Savior, I pray. Amen.

Bountiful Blessings

Jacob told him that in the future the people of Israel would ask God's blessings on one another by saying, "I pray for God to bless you as much as he blessed Ephraim and Manasseh" (Genesis 48:20, *Contemporary English Version*).

Scripture: **Genesis 48:8-21**
Song: **"There Shall Be Showers of Blessing"**

Every time someone tells me I'm lucky about something, I say, "Not lucky—*blessed.*" I consider any so-called good fortune to originate in the heart of God's love for me. All the goodness of my life has its source in God's grace, and that grace shows up in full benevolent apparel at the beginning of each day. Each day that I wake up is a beautiful day, and I am blessed in it.

Jacob blessed Ephraim and Manasseh in such a way that people talked about it for generations. Similarly, God blesses me with the gift of life that opens my mouth in celebration and praise. That gift of good life takes many shapes, has many embodiments, and soaks itself into me everywhere.

There have been many times in my life when I have been pretty much blessed off my rocker! Times when I drink out of my saucer because my cup has overflowed. Times when I sit at God's table and am filled with God's blessings—but still He says to me, "Here, have another one."

Dear God, *each and every blessing You pour out to me in grace and love, I give back to You in thanksgiving and praise. In Jesus' name, amen.*

Tell It All

I will exalt you, my God the King; I will praise your name for ever and ever (Psalm 145:1).

Scripture: **Psalm 145:1-13a**
Song: **"Praise Him! Praise Him!"**

I cannot offer enough praises to God. I get paper and pencil to itemize the blessings for which I praise Him, but I run out of paper and my pencil wears down to a tiny nub. The most prevalent position for my arms and hands on any given day is a vertical one. They are lifted up, as my heart is elevated in appreciation for what God does and who God is. I am forever a psalmist, raising my praise to God.

Yes, the hard times come too. But let us be faithful in our adoration—not spasmodic and intermittent, but steady and consistent—showing up every day to praise God who gives us what we have and makes us who we are. Why not be exuberant in our adoration!

I've begun to see there is no better use of my vocal chords than utilizing them to express my thankfulness to God. Therefore, I want to be prolific in my adoration, go on a rampage of praise every now and then, and mention everything great and small that comes to mind. Yes, in the next few moments, I'm going to tell it all to God.

Dear God, I am far more concerned about what You do for me than I am about what I can do for You. I realize how You bless me. I see how You guide me. I know how You make me more able than I am. How I thank You, in the name of Jesus, my Savior and Lord. Amen.

Compliment Him

Say to God, "How awesome are your deeds! So great is your power that your enemies cringe before you" (Psalm 66:3).

Scripture: **Psalm 66:1-4**
Song: **"Praise the Lord, for He Is Good"**

"See, I told you. Things never work out for me." Linda used those words often, to the extent that they gradually became an overused phrase, a cliché that her friends tuned out. Soon people quit listening altogether. Sadly, they no longer heard Linda's cries for help.

Linda had experienced many disappointments. Because of this, she focused on her problems, undesirable circumstances, and past failures—most of them not her fault. Yet her perceptions often made bad situations even worse.

Then one day Linda met a Christian woman named Sandy. Sandy listened past the clichés and heard the cry of Linda's heart. Sandy suggested that Linda change the way she prayed. Instead of complaining to God, compliment Him. Her outlook on life changed dramatically. It didn't take long for her friends to notice the improvement.

God is a patient listener. He hears us when we talk about our problems, bemoan our circumstances, or complain about all the evil in the world. Even so, God surely enjoys our praises too!

Dear Lord, I am so thankful that You listen to my hurts and concerns. Help me to lift up my praises this day as well. Through Christ, amen.

November 26–30. Charles E. Harrel has been a minister for more than 30 years. He currently directs His Place Outreach in Portland, Oregon.

All That He Commanded

Both of them were upright in the sight of God, observing all the Lord's commandments and regulations blamelessly (Luke 1:6).

Scripture: **Luke 1:5-7**
Song: **"Go Forth at Christ's Command"**

As a 10-year-old, I visited my Uncle Mel and Aunt Millie one summer. Since Mel was a preacher, I knew that meant going to church. Not exactly my idea of a vacation, rating only slightly higher than going to the dentist. On Sunday morning, I put on my coat and tie. "Why are you wearing that stuff?" my uncle asked. "You better change into some blue jeans and grab a cowboy hat—you might need them later." Now he had my attention.

My aunt and uncle were a dedicated couple who obeyed God in all things. They sponsored a youth outreach with riding horses on Sunday afternoons. They also hosted a carnival on the church grounds every summer. Some members thought they were foolish; others left the church. The complaining stopped, however, when revival spread to the surrounding churches and nearby cities.

Following God and living uprightly has benefits. Elizabeth and Zechariah conceived a child of promise. For Mel and Millie, God granted what they wanted most: salvation for their young nephew and revival for their city.

Precious Lord, teach me to live my life in obedience to Your will. Even when Your ways seem unconventional to some, may I always follow the path You have marked out for me. In Jesus' name I pray. Amen.

Your Prayers Are Heard

**The angel said to him: "Do not be afraid, Zechariah; your
prayer has been heard. Your wife Elizabeth will bear you a
son, and you are to give him the name John"** (Luke 1:13).

Scripture: **Luke 1:8-13**
Song: **"The God of Salvation Hears"**

Laura wanted another child. She and her husband were
happy with their two girls; still, she dreamed of having
one more. God heard the cry of her heart. Although she
was nearing the age when most women stop having children, she felt she had God's assurance to proceed. It even
seemed that God gave her a name—a boy's name.

When she told her husband, Charles, he was less
than sympathetic. "Are you sure? How do you know
God wants us to have another child? What about hospital costs?" Charles had many concerns. However,
when Laura mentioned that God had given her a name,
he settled down and listened. She explained that God
wanted this baby to have a special heritage and a name
that pointed back to the Redeemer. With fears alleviated,
they put their faith and love to work. Nine months later,
little Christopher came into the world.

Sometimes it seems as if God forgets us, even ignores our
prayers. But that is never the case. He listens to our every
word. Even our thoughts are known to Him. Zechariah's
prayers reached Heaven, and so do ours.

*Dear God, teach me to trust You in all things. Whenever doubts arise,
remind me that You always hear my prayers. In Jesus' name, amen.*

Forerunners Still Needed

He will go on before the Lord, in the spirit and power of Elijah, to turn the hearts of the fathers to their children and the disobedient to the wisdom of the righteous—to make ready a people prepared for the Lord (Luke 1:17).

Scripture: **Luke 1:14-17**
Song: **"I'll Go Where You Want Me to Go"**

Johann Gutenberg designed a printing press with replaceable wooden or metal letters. His press furthered the gospel message by printing Gutenberg Bibles, the first books published in volume. In 1803, Lewis and Clark led an expedition across a newly acquired land, most of it unexplored; their efforts paved the way for a great westward expansion in America. The Wright brothers and their Wright Flyer became the first heavier-than-air machine to achieve controlled flight with a pilot aboard; their design opened wide the doors to modern aviation.

All these people, and countless others like them, were forerunners. They blazed new trails or repaired old ones, setting the stage for those who followed them. And thus was John the Baptist. His messages turned the hearts of many people back to God and prepared them for the arrival of Jesus the very Son of God.

God still uses forerunners today. They preach a common message: Get ready; Jesus is coming back.

God and Father of My Lord Jesus Christ, I may not have the notoriety as others, but I can still reach out to my neighbors and befriend them. Help me do it with all graciousness for Your glory. In Jesus' name, amen.

Age Doesn't Matter

Zechariah asked the angel, "How can I be sure of this? I am an old man and my wife is well along in years" (Luke 1:18).

Scripture: **Luke 1:18-23**
Song: **"After the Mist and Shadow"**

I never knew her first name. Everyone at church simply called her Lady J. Her husband had passed away years before, and her grown children lived out of town, wrapped up in their own lives. Although Lady J stayed busy, loneliness filled her days. What she missed most was being a mother.

One Sunday after church, the minister asked asked her to teach a class for young married couples. With his offer came the opportunity to be a "mother" again! God used Lady J in the senior years of her life. She wasn't given just one child to raise like Zechariah and Elizabeth; she was given many. Her nurturing and parental guidance inspired the class to serve Christ. In fact, most of her students became ministers, including me.

Zechariah thought he was too old for a blessing, but age doesn't determine our eligibility. The call of God doesn't depend on age either. The Lord can fill the barren places in our lives with a wave of His hand. If He wants to bless you, just believe and never ask why.

Lord God, Your promises are sure words that never fail. They do not weaken with age, nor do they expire with time. Throughout the ages, Your promises have blessed so many—eternal testimony to Your awesome lovingkindness. Thank You, in the precious name of Jesus. Amen.

My Prayer Notes

DEVOTIONS

*P*raise be to God, who has not rejected my prayer.

—Psalm 66:20

DECEMBER

Photo © istock

Gary Allen, Editor

Pondering God's Purpose

After this his wife Elizabeth became pregnant and for five months remained in seclusion (Luke 1:24).

Scripture: **Luke 1:24, 25**
Song: **"Alone with God"**

I needed a break—or at least a short sabbatical. Maybe our church building project had affected me more than I realized. Although I enjoyed being a minister, my heart was somewhere else these days. My interests were changing. After decades of ministry, did God have other plans for me? Why would God ask me to start writing now?

I needed time to mull things over. I remembered that the apostle Paul sought solitude after his conversion experience on the Damascus Road. He allowed time for God's message to saturate his heart (see Galatians 1:16-18). Moses spent time on Mount Sinai. Elijah rested by a brook. Jesus himself sought out the quietness of the wilderness. In seclusion, they all communed with the Father. Similarly, Elizabeth remained by herself to reflect on the favor of God.

We today also need time alone with God. Thankfully, He draws us to "isolated places" in our lives that we might simply wait on Him. In the quiet, we can ponder His goodness and learn more of His purposes.

Draw me away, **O Lord,** *to that secret place of prayer. Help me listen closely for Your still, small voice. In Christ Jesus, I pray. Amen.*

December 1, 2. **Charles E. Harrel** has been a minister for more than 30 years. He currently directs His Place Outreach in Portland, Oregon.

Just Tell It

Come and listen, all you who fear God; let me tell you what he has done for me (Psalm 66:16).

Scripture: **Psalm 66:16-20**
Song: **"I Love to Tell the Story"**

The gold-plated fish hook on the man's shirt collar grabbed my attention. It reminded me of my dad; he often pinned his favorite fishing fly or lure on his hat. After I'd snuck several glances, the man walked over and introduced himself. Our conversation soon turned to fishing.

I discovered this gold hook was John's favorite one; he had caught more fish with it than any other. He told me that he once hooked a 200-pounder with it!

John always kept his favorite hook handy in case he saw a fish. In fact, he said, he had one on the line now (and he started to tug on his collar as if a fish were nibbling). That's when I realized John had been fishing for me. With his hook set, John told me the story of his own experience of being caught—by the greatest fisherman of all.

Our witness matters. People may dismiss our doctrine, or disagree with our beliefs, but they cannot deny what God has done in our lives. If we'll just tell them how God has graciously reached into our hearts, we can let Him take care of the rest.

Father, I know we all have different stories. Some have experienced Your healing, others a wonderful answer to prayer. But all of us have known Your unconditional favor through Christ's work of atonement. Help me to tell of Your great goodness in my life. In Jesus' name, amen.

Trusting for Each Step

Blessed is the man who makes the LORD his trust, who does not look to the proud, to those who turn aside to false gods (Psalm 40:4).

Scripture: **Psalm 40:1-5**
Song: **"I Could Not Do Without Thee"**

As I read Psalm 40 for my morning devotions, the fourth verse really seemed to stand out. I realized how often I am tempted to trust in people or things more than the Lord. Why? For one thing, we're constantly bombarded by media messages calling us to find our security elsewhere—with all kinds of appealing false gods.

And those gods come in many forms, don't they? Yet science and technology can't solve all of our problems. And mere possessions won't deliver a solid and settled joy. Even modern medicine—a great boon to civilization—can subtly pull us away from ultimate trust in God for our well-being. As educator Harold W. Dodds once said: "The way to be safe is never to be secure. . . . Each one of us requires the spur of insecurity to force us to do our best." Perhaps that is why God calls us to walk by faith and not by sight, one step at a time.

Dear Lord, I live in a world filled with so much that is questionable—or downright evil. Help me resist the allure of finite pleasures and trust You, instead, for every good thing. In the holy name of Jesus, my Lord and Savior, I pray. Amen.

December 3–9. **Gerry Kershner** writes from his home in Lancaster County, Pennsylvania. In addition to devotionals, he writes poetry and magazine articles.

Troubled by Good News?

Mary was greatly troubled at his words and wondered what kind of greeting this might be (Luke 1:29).

Scripture: **Luke 1:26-29**
Song: **"Joy to the World"**

Mary later exhibited tremendous joy and faith concerning this miraculous event. But why was she initially so troubled at Gabriel's words, wondering "what kind of greeting this might be"? This sudden introduction was a great surprise, of course—even a bit shocking. And no doubt Mary needed time to adjust to her new role.

We too may initially react to good news with a troubled spirit. In a wonderful 1983 film about redemption, *Tender Mercies,* the main character (played by Robert Duvall) is baptized and changed forever. But he later says to the lady who brought him into the church: "I prayed last night to know: *Why? . . .* I don't know why I wandered to this part of Texas, and you took me in, pitied me, and helped me to straighten out. . . . Why did that happen? You see, I don't trust happiness. I never did and never will."

We may not be able to explain (or fully trust) the sudden goodness of God in our lives, for sometimes that grace enters in almost shocking ways. We are right to be troubled—at least for awhile—until our consternation turns to unspeakable joy.

Dear Father, *during this season when we celebrate the birth of Your Son, I am overwhelmed with Your sudden entrance into this world. Help me to accept Your many good gifts with joy. In Jesus' name, amen.*

Let the Kingdom Show Through!

He will reign over the house of Jacob forever; his kingdom will never end (Luke 1:33).

Scripture: **Luke 1:30-33**
Song: **"There's a Song in the Air"**

Like many other Christians, I'm distressed by the crass commercialism and secular activities associated with Christmas in our culture. Every year we seem to experience less of the true meaning of Christ's incarnation.

As I read Luke 1:33 I wonder what the angel Gabriel means when he says that Jesus' kingdom will never end. Then I'm reminded that (at least for now) Jesus' realm is not a political, earthly kingdom. He refused political rule during His time on earth. No, Jesus reigns forever in the hearts of His followers, a kingdom that will never end.

As followers of Jesus we can share His love, His joy, and His peace with others during the Christmas season and throughout the year. We can do this no matter how others celebrate. In this way we can be a part of maintaining Jesus' kingdom and even helping spread it in our neighborhoods and throughout the world. As Jesus himself said, "The kingdom of God is within you" (Luke 17:21). But will we let His reign in our hearts be visible in the most practical and loving forms of outreach?

Lord, help me to keep my eyes, mind, and heart on You, continually reminding me that Your Kingdom is within me. And do move me to share Your love, Your joy, and Your peace with others during this Christmas season. In the name of Jesus, who came as Lord and Savior of all, I pray. Amen.

Back to Basics

The holy one to be born will be called the Son of God (Luke 1:35).

Scripture: **Luke 1:34, 35**
Song: **"Silent Night"**

For many of us, the Christmas season is harried and hurried. We have gifts to make or buy, boxes to wrap, cards to address and send, parties to plan, food to buy and prepare, and church activities to fit into our busy schedules. Most of these activities are good, but I'm thinking of "going back to the basics."

I'm starting with the basic question, "What is Christmas all about?" In today's verse the angel tells Mary that the child to be born will be called the Son of God. In that brief announcement we can see that Christmas is really the most important event in the history of the world. God came to the world as a flesh-and-blood human being!

In light of this amazing truth, all of our Christmas activities take on new meaning. The gifts, cards, food, parties, and church activities now all become our part of celebrating the radical entrance of the Son of God. What a birthday this is—calling us to slow down, to contemplate its miraculous unfolding, to make room for many silent nights of praise.

Dear Father in Heaven, I come to You during this harried and hurried season, asking You to help me get back to the basics. Keep me focused on the great miracle of Your Son coming in person to love Your world. And help me love Him with all my heart in return. In His name, I pray. Amen.

Mary, the Lord's Servant

"I am the Lord's servant," Mary answered. "May it be to me as you have said" (Luke 1:38).

Scripture: Luke 1:36-38
Song: "Mary, Did You Know?"

Rereading the wonderful story of Christmas in the first chapter of Luke's gospel, I am struck by Mary's humble acceptance of the angel's dramatic announcement that she is to be pregnant. And her child was to be called the Son of the Most High!

After all this fanfare, she simply answers, "I am the Lord's servant. May it be to me as you have said" (1:38). Yes, she may have been a bit confused, or troubled, but she apparently did not need to know all of the minor details and long-term implications, as I usually do. God said it, and that was enough. Such child-like faith is a lesson I often need to relearn.

I think any of us can learn much from Mary. We don't normally receive angelic visitations, but we do often experience God moving in ways we do not understand. And this is where we can remember Mary's example. Rather than trying to understand the big picture all at once, we can simply take the next step with God.

Dear Lord and Master, thank You so much for Mary and the many other biblical role models You've given me, that I may lead a life pleasing to You. I too am Your servant. So help me live with simple, child-like faith in Your good will and guidance in my life. In the name of the Father, the Son, and the Holy Spirit, I pray. Amen.

Elizabeth's Joy and Faith

As soon as the sound of your greeting reached my ears, the baby in my womb leaped for joy (Luke 1:44).

Scripture: **Luke 1:39-45**
Song: **"My Faith Looks Up to Thee"**

We can hardly imagine the joy that Elizabeth felt when Mary visited her. She who had been childless during her normal child-bearing years was now pregnant. She must have been overjoyed when she immediately recognized that her relative, Mary, was also pregnant in a miraculous way. Elizabeth's joy in the autumn of her life must have been especially sweet.

Yet through all those childless years, Elizabeth kept her strong faith in God. She was upright in the sight of God. She observed all of the commandments and regulations blamelessly. Later, she believed that the One who made the promise would keep the promise. Simply put, she kept the faith.

Many of us have dreams that remain unfulfilled, causing us, at times, to doubt God's goodwill toward us. Yet, like Elizabeth, we need to keep the faith, because our faith is more important than our dreams. As writer Henry Thoreau once said: "The smallest seed of faith is better than the largest fruit of happiness."

Dear Lord, strengthen my faith. Help me to remain true and faithful even when I have no visible evidence, like Elizabeth during her childless years. Help me to keep the faith so I may also experience joy as Elizabeth did. In Jesus' name I pray. Amen.

Mary's Song of Praise

My soul glorifies the Lord and my spirit rejoices in God my Savior (Luke 1:46, 47).

Scripture: **Luke 1:46-56**
Song: **"How Majestic Is Your Name"**

I am humbled by Mary's song of praise in these ten verses, traditionally called the *Magnificat*. After a spontaneous outburst of praise for her personal blessing, she continues to praise God for His mercy, power, and goodness in the past as well as the present.

I must confess that far too often I do not praise God and give Him the glory for the small, and sometimes even the larger, blessings in my life. Oh yes, I pray on a daily basis like many other Christians. But my prayer requests often far outnumber my praise items. Obviously, Mary had many personal prayer needs at this time, but none of them are included in this short song of praise.

Study of this song has convinced me to make a deliberate, personal effort to include more and more praise in my prayer life. In fact, I hope it will become a spontaneous and constant part of my relationship with God. After all, prayer is primarily an opening of hearts up to God, just as Mary did. Sometimes it is simply a wordless adoration or a period of silent listening for Him. But couldn't many of us use a little boost to our prayer lives by adding small songs of praise to our daily devotional times?

Dear Lord, *You are so good! Help me to praise you spontaneously and sincerely this day. In Your holy name I pray. Amen.*

Messengers

See, I will send my messenger, who will prepare the way before me (Malachi 3:1).

Scripture: **Malachi 3:1-4**
Song: **"If Jesus Goes With Me"**

When I feel unimportant, I recall the words I once heard a minister preach: "You may be the only Bible some people will ever read." John the Baptist must have understood this thoroughly. He was the messenger God chose to prepare the way for Jesus' arrival.

On the face of it, John was unimpressive. He lived in the wilderness, ate bugs, and wore strange clothes. Yet people flocked to hear the message of repentance he preached. They came, not because John was attractive, but because he was a faithful messenger, telling the people what God wanted them to know.

We may never know the impact we have on the people we encounter, day in and day out. A kindness done to a stranger, a hug given a stressed-out coworker, or time spent with a little child may seem like simple, unnoticeable acts. But to God, they are a witness to the world of Christ's love. When we allow God to use us as messengers of the gospel, we may even amaze ourselves.

Lord, I feel so unworthy of the calling to be a messenger of Your good news. Help me be faithful, in word and deed—and be on the lookout for those in any kind of need. In the name of Christ I pray. Amen.

December 10–16. **Lisa Konzen** works for United Way in Janesville, Wisconsin. She also writes health articles for seniors in her local newspaper, *The Janesville Gazette*.

Standing Up

But his mother spoke up and said, "No! He is to be called John" (Luke 1:60).

Scripture: **Luke 1:57-61**
Song: **"Stand Up, Stand Up for Jesus"**

I used to be quite a pushover. If my food was served cold at a restaurant, I'd meekly eat it instead of sending it back. If I wasn't satisfied with something I bought, I'd stash it away in my closet instead of returning it to the store for a refund.

But not anymore. What made the difference? The day I realized that some things are worth standing up for. My father was in the hospital, and because he had many health problems, full and complete information about his status wasn't always communicated very well. I had to approach doctors and nurses rather assertively for the answers I needed.

It taught me a valuable lesson: Sometimes, you just have to be tough. Not unkind, and certainly not violent. But tough. It all depends on what you're standing up for. I imagine Elizabeth trembled a little when her relatives challenged her decision to name her son John. But she knew that was what God wanted her to do. So, despite being a woman in a society that did not highly value a woman's opinion, Elizabeth stood up for God.

Holy God, too often I've been timid when I should have been bold. Yet You are the source of all my courage. Fill me with Your presence to the extent that I have no room left for fear. In the name of Jesus, amen.

Tongue Un-Tied

Immediately his mouth was opened and his tongue was loosed, and he began to speak, praising God (Luke 1:64).

Scripture: **Luke 1:62-66**
Song: **"Praise the Savior"**

Have you ever been tongue-tied when trying to talk about your faith? You know you should say something, but it's so difficult. Maybe you're going through a rough time, and bearing witness for God seems to require more faith than you feel you have.

Zechariah knew about being tongue-tied. When the angel Gabriel told him his elderly, barren wife Elizabeth would bear a son, he asked for proof. His lack of trust was met with a stern promise from Gabriel that Zechariah would not be able to speak until the child was born. And sure enough, Zechariah was mute until the day he said, "His name is John" (1:63).

I think we can learn a lesson from Zechariah. His lack of trust in God led him to mute ineffectiveness. Similarly, when our faith falters, we may find it difficult to speak about the good news of the gospel. But the same Holy Spirit who loosened Zechariah's tongue and restored his faith can do the same for us. Our simple willingness to be used by Him is the first movement toward a full-bodied trust that won't falter.

Word of God, *speak through me. My tongue is dry, and my heart is empty without You. But when You dwell in me, rivers of blessings pour forth from my lips as I sing Your praises! In the name of Jesus, amen.*

Without Fear

He has raised up a horn of salvation . . . to rescue us from the hand of our enemies, and to enable us to serve him without fear (Luke 1:69, 74).

Scripture: **Luke 1:67-75**
Song: **"All Your Anxiety"**

You've probably heard of the fight-or-flight response. It's the wonderful system God designed in our bodies that helps us react to dangerous situations. When we're in crisis, the hormone adrenaline is released. For example, a grizzly bear challenges us in the woods. We can either try to tackle him to the ground or . . . run away. Fast!

We rarely face grizzlies in modern living today. Yet, our bodies react the same way when we feel under pressure day after day, or experience even a minor conflict with a coworker or spouse. Adrenaline still shoots into our hearts; we react with fear—and fight or flee.

Problem is, when the crisis passes, many of us can't seem to turn off the response! Chronic fear can contribute to the development of generalized anxiety, depression, and a host of physical maladies, including heart disease. Our hectic lives have turned what was once a blessing from God into a curse.

But it doesn't have to be that way. In Christ, we are set free. We'll still face stress, but as we cast our cares upon our Savior, we can let go and let God rescue us.

Dear God, it's so easy to become afraid these days. But You asked me to cast my cares upon You, so that's what I'm going to do. Through Christ, amen.

Knowing the Word

To give his people the knowledge of salvation through the forgiveness of their sins (Luke 1:77).

Scripture: **Luke 1:76-80**
Song: **"More About Jesus"**

The minister of my church is a strong believer in Bible study, and with good reason. Because he is so faithful in teaching the truth of God's Word, we know the history and mystery of our faith. History, because he painstakingly presents the narrative of the Scripture, exploring the time lines and themes.

But he goes way beyond that, teaching us the mystery of the grace of our Savior, Jesus Christ, and the way His life, death, and resurrection free us to serve Him joyfully.

And serve Him we do. From hunger walks to "Christmas in July" fund raisers for the local food pantry, our church practices what our minister preaches. New ministries inside and outside of the church are continually springing up. But if all this sounds like bragging, that's because it is. Not about our members, or even about our minister. We're just responding to the gift of salvation freely given that we learn about as we study Scripture. All the praise, glory, and honor go to Jesus, the Word of Life who writes His gospel across the lives of His people. For without Him, we can do nothing.

O Lord, help me to rededicate myself to studying the Scripture each day. I want to be knowledgeable so I can share the treasures of Your truth with every open-hearted person I meet. In Jesus' name, amen.

Pedigree or Mutt?

Do not begin to say to yourselves, "We have Abraham as our father." For I tell you that out of these stones God can raise up children for Abraham (Luke 3:8).

Scripture: Luke 3:7-14
Song: "A Child of the King"

All my life we've had dogs. I remember Bagel, so named because we were told she was a beagle, only to learn later that she was a Pit Bull mix. Peggy, a black Labrador retriever, who was so smart and loving. And Princess Su Linn, a Lhasa Apso who was the only pure-bred dog our family ever had.

Pedigreed or mutt, it really doesn't matter. What matters with dogs is not who their parents were, but the love given by their owners. A dog won't snub us because his sire was a best in show. Dogs stand on their own four paws, protecting and loving us because they're part of our family.

We can learn a lot from our pooch pals. It doesn't matter what our name is, where we're from, or how much money sits in our bank account. What matters in the church is that we're all part of God's family. It has nothing to do with any effort on our part. God adopted us and calls us to love each other as brothers and sisters in Christ.

Heavenly Father, *thank You for adopting me into Your family as a precious child. Help me to remember the pure grace that made it possible—and therefore to love unconditionally all my siblings in the faith. I pray this prayer in the name of Jesus, my merciful Savior and Lord. Amen.*

Proud to Be Humble

John answered them all, "I baptize you with water. But one more powerful than I will come, the thongs of whose sandals I am not worthy to untie" (Luke 3:16).

Scripture: **Luke 3:15-20**
Song: **"The Unveiled Christ"**

Have you ever heard someone complain about having to play second fiddle? Perhaps it was an employee whose co-worker was just promoted. "I hate playing second fiddle to him," the disgruntled worker might grumble. Playing second fiddle means you are not the one in charge, not the one getting all the attention.

But have you ever wondered what the phrase literally means? An orchestra has sections and subsections. Within the strings are violins, in subsets of first and second violins (violins being the dressed-up name for fiddles). The role of the second violins is to support the work of the first violins, enhancing them with glorious harmony.

John the Baptist wasn't ashamed to play second fiddle to Jesus. He knew he had a job to do, and he wasn't in it for the limelight. For him, playing second fiddle was right because he knew Jesus was the Savior whose sacrifice would save him and the world. Perhaps next time we're asked to serve in the shadows, we'll remember the prophet in the wilderness who was proud to be humble.

Dear God and Father, may my thoughts, words, and actions take the spotlight off me and glorify You. Let me bring harmony to Your kingdom. Through Your precious Son, Jesus Christ, I pray. Amen.

Making It a List

Sing to the LORD a new song. . . . Splendor and majesty are before him; strength and glory are in his sanctuary (Psalm 96:1, 6).

Scripture: **Psalm 96:1-6**
Song: **"Glorious Is Thy Name"**

I'm a year-round list-maker. Lists keep me focused—especially at Christmas time. Let's see, what do I need to do in order to be ready? Cards, decorations, gifts, parties, programs . . . and on it goes.

I do something similar when I study God's Word. If I come to a passage that includes a list of God's attributes or commands, I love to list them in my journal. Then I might use a Bible dictionary to jot some definitions next to each item. Even the subtle differences I find between quite similar words give me much food for thought. The next step is to consider how to apply what I've learned.

A particular favorite this time of year is the list of names in Isaiah 9:6: Wonderful Counselor, Mighty God, Everlasting Father, Prince of Peace. Even today's passage lends itself to such a word study with phrases like: praise His name, proclaim His salvation, declare His glory, splendor and majesty, strength and glory. What do each of these mean to you?

Lord, Your Word is so rich. May I pause at even familiar words and find in them a new song to sing Your praise. Through Christ my Lord, amen.

December 17–23. **Susan Miholer,** a grandmother and special education assistant, owns Picky, Picky Ink, her editorial service in Salem, Oregon.

The Trinity of the Slide

Give him the name Jesus, because he will save his people from their sins (Matthew 1:21).

Scripture: **Matthew 1:18b-21**
Song: **"The Name of Jesus"**

"Grandma, come get me!" Four-year-old Nicholas was at the top of the slide at a fast-food restaurant, too scared to come down. I assumed some uncomfortable positions as I crawled through the not-quite-adult-sized tunnels to get to him, and then I rode down the slide with him. Not my most dignified grandmotherly moment! He, on the other hand, thought it was great fun. I kept envisioning the newspaper headline: "Grandmother Stuck—Fire Department Summoned."

I didn't feel very god-like that day; in fact, I was glad there were few witnesses to my actions and attitude. But later I saw the whole episode as a picture of what God did for us. As the Father, He saw our need of a Savior. As the Son, He assumed the uncomfortable positions of the Incarnation to rescue me. And as the Holy Spirit, He rides with me through the twists and turns of this slide-ride we call life.

Jesus. There's just something about that name—something that tells us so much about God that we can never comprehend it all.

Heavenly Father, when I consider how You reached down through Your Son, I'm humbled that You included me in Your great plan of salvation. Thank You for the sacrifice of the Incarnation! In Jesus' name, amen.

A New Chapter

So Joseph also went . . . to Bethlehem. . . . He went there to register with Mary (Luke 2:4, 5).

Scripture: **Luke 2:1-5**
Song: **"O Little Town of Bethlehem"**

During the last few weeks of my pregnancies, waddling anywhere was a challenge. Travel for any reason other than essential errands and appointments was pretty much out of the question.

Mary probably wasn't eager to travel from Nazareth to Bethlehem in her condition. But regardless of the discomforts involved, she was no doubt relieved to be getting away from the whispers and judgmental stares in her old neighborhood. She was probably both exhilarated and frightened about her new role as mother too—a new chapter in her life. Bethlehem might well provide a clean slate for her and Joseph.

When God ushers in a new chapter in our lives, we often experience the same emotional mix—the exhilaration, yet the questions about what is happening and why things are unfolding the way they are. And, like Mary, we can face the challenge with a similar response: "May it be to me as you have said" (Luke 1:38).

Facing a life-change in this season of your life? Look to God as He leads you into a new chapter.

*Thank You, **God,** that You have gone before me into the unknown of my life. Allow me to trust You for the grace, strength, and wisdom to face today's challenges. In the name of Jesus, my Savior, I pray. Amen.*

No Room in the Family?

There was no room for them in the inn (Luke 2:7).

Scripture: **Luke 2:6, 7**
Song: **"No Room in the Inn"**

At the birth of my first grandchild, we grandparents practically elbowed each other out of the way to be first in the room to see our new baby boy. But Scripture is strangely silent about Mary and Joseph's families. I would think that several members of Joseph's family would have been in Bethlehem. Didn't they have to go there to register as well? If this was Joseph's ancestral home, I'd expect there may have been relatives in Bethlehem with whom they could have stayed. But they seemed so alone in that place.

I know Scripture doesn't give us all the details, but I'm wondering if Mary's circumstances had ostracized Joseph and Mary so much that even close family members wouldn't extend hospitality to them—or at least some loving concern. That would take the phrase "no room for them in the inn" (2:7) to another level, wouldn't it? Not only was there no room in the inn, there may have been no room in the family circle.

Yet Jesus' earthly parents model for me the response I should have when I feel cut off from others. Follow God anyway.

Father, I sometimes feel there's no room for me in certain situations because I've chosen to follow You along the narrow way. At those times, may I rest assured that You are always with me. Through Christ, amen.

Creative Announcement

Today in the town of David a Savior has been born to you; he is Christ the Lord (Luke 2:11).

Scripture: **Luke 2:8-14**
Song: **"Angels We Have Heard on High"**

People have gotten creative with birth announcements lately, as the computer provides all kinds of new ways to announce a baby's entrance into the world. Families design entire websites to share the news. I've even seen custom-printed wrappers that slip over a regular chocolate bar. The front of the label (and its color) let people know the baby's vital statistics. And the parents' names replace the standard ingredients label.

But the most creative of all birth announcements occurred on a hillside over 2,000 years ago as a bunch of ordinary (and probably scruffy) shepherds settled their sheep and themselves for the night. As they adjusted their cloaks to ward off the evening chill, and breathed that last relaxed sigh of impending sleep, an angel amid the glory of the Lord delivered awesome good news. And then the sky seemed to explode as the heavenly host underscored the grand message.

No other birth in history has been announced in such magnificent style. Nor has any other birth in history had the same eternal consequences. No wonder the angels praised God!

Eternal God, *may I, like the angels, praise You and say, Glory to God in the highest! In the name of the incarnate Christ I pray. Amen.*

Different Reactions

Mary treasured up all these things and pondered them in her heart (Luke 2:19).

Scripture: **Luke 2:15-20**
Song: **"O Come, Let Us Adore Him"**

Different people react differently to good news. Some clap, some cry, some dance, and some just stand there looking surprised. I've done all four—and sometimes two or three at the same time.

Recovering from the spectacle of God's glory and the good news of Christ's birth, the shepherds couldn't get to Bethlehem fast enough. Having seen the baby, their exuberance bubbled over as they told everyone of the angel's announcement and what they had seen. People were astonished. Even without e-mail, the news traveled quickly. But Mary, precious Mary, the one who had known for months whose child this was, quietly pondered what was happening, filing away memories of her Son.

Emotions run high at Christmas time. Like the shepherds, we may push and shove to get there first. We may be so excited about the good news of Christmas that we sing the familiar carols with new enthusiasm, astonished by the discovery of new facets in the familiar story. But like Mary, I also want to carve out times of quiet reflection upon who Jesus really is—my Lord and my God.

Dear Father, the birth of Your Son changed the course of history. May I understand a piece of the Christmas story in a new way this year. Keep my focus on who Christ is and why He came. In His name I pray. Amen.

Who's the Author?

Ascribe to the LORD the glory due his name; bring an offering and come into his courts (Psalm 96:8).

Scripture: **Psalm 96:7-13**
Song: **"Creation's Lord, We Give Thee Thanks"**

We don't use the word "ascribe" very often anymore. The dictionary says it suggests an "inferring or conjecturing of cause, quality, or authorship." If you're a Shakespeare scholar or an expert on Picasso, you know what to look for in a specific play or work of art to indicate its creator. Sometimes, though, even the experts don't agree as to whom a particular work ought to be ascribed.

But there is no disagreement in today's passage about who is responsible for, who is the author of, all the beauty in nature. Every aspect of the natural world—the seas, the hills, the forests, even the living beings—point us toward their creator. And that same author is the author of our salvation, the baby whose birth we celebrate at this time of year.

Born in obscurity, He is the author of this world and everything in it. And if anything good and admirable blossoms within our hearts . . . He is the author of all of those virtues too. For our heart is the place He has chosen to make His dwelling place. Ascribe glory to Him!

My Father in Heaven, Your Son came to the earth to be the author of my salvation. Thank You, from the bottom of my heart. I want to worship You in the same spontaneous way Your creation does, pointing others to You. In the name of the Father, the Son, and the Holy Spirit, I pray. Amen.

The First Christmas Gift-giver

That you may bring my salvation to the ends of the earth (Isaiah 49:6).

Scripture: **Isaiah 49:5, 6**
Song: **"It Came Upon the Midnight Clear"**

Our familiar white-bearded Santa harks back to a third-century bishop born in Turkey. Renowned for his humility and generosity, Nicholas became the patron saint of many nations, causes, and groups, including sailors and children. A body of legend grew around his person, including the idea that he dressed in red and gave gifts at Christmas time.

Poet Clement Moore leaned on such legends as he wrote the whimsical, "A Visit from St. Nicholas" in 1832 to amuse his children. But the reindeer-powered Christmas Eve trip around the world was Moore's unique idea. His poem gained immediate fame and imposed a curious persona on humble Nicholas that would have amazed him.

We need not fuss about the folklore from many lands that colors our Christmas celebrations. But tree lights, holly, and mistletoe must not overshadow the manger, where the true Gift-giver was born. He offers His gift to the ends of the earth, not once a year, but every day—and throughout all generations to every tribe and tongue.

Thank You, **Lord,** *for offering Your gift of eternal life to all, whether they have been naughty or nice. All praise to You, in Christ's name. Amen.*

December 24–30. **Lloyd Mattson** is a retired minister and author of Christian camping books. He and his wife, Elsie, live in Duluth, Minnesota.

Poor Joseph and Mary!

Joseph and Mary took him to Jerusalem to present him to the Lord . . . and to offer a sacrifice in keeping with what is said in the Law of the Lord" (Luke 2:22, 24).

Scripture: **Luke 2:21-24**
Song: **"Thou Didst Leave Thy Throne"**

Joseph and Mary came to the temple with birds, the sacrifice of the poor. Similarly, throughout His ministry, Jesus depended on others for food and shelter. Yet we seldom think of Jesus or His family as poor. After all, poverty is relative; our poorest seem rich beyond imagining to earth's millions who are starving.

While Jesus placed no premium on poverty, He spoke often about greed. That's why Christmas appeals move us to give to the needy, and we rightly feel good about doing so. The Magi, too, presented gifts, but we can't know the worth of those gifts until we know what they had left.

What do we have left? Our benevolent giving marks us as among earth's most generous people, yet America has little cause for pride. Consider what we keep! The American dream wears a dollar sign, and a good Christmas usually means retailers sold more than they did the year before.

The point is, giving isn't really giving until it costs us something. And at Christmas time we can remember: We celebrate the birth of a man who owned nothing.

Heavenly Father, that I might embrace Your presence in me to the fullest, please help me loosen my grip on everything else. In Jesus' name, amen.

A Devout Nobody

Now there was a man in Jerusalem, called Simeon, who was righteous and devout. He was waiting for the consolation of Israel, and the Holy Spirit was upon him (Luke 2:25).

Scripture: **Luke 2:25, 26**
Song: **"Spirit of Faith, Come Down"**

A remarkable man, Simeon. He held no office or honors, yet the Holy Spirit was upon him. How could that be? Pentecost was at least three years away. Was not that the day the Holy Spirit came?

We tend to arrange God's affairs according to our limited understandings, keeping Him safely within the boundaries of our doctrinal preferences. We ought not do that, for the sovereign God works where, when, and among whom He chooses, and that truth abides today.

Simeon came to the temple at just the right time. As far as he knew, it was an ordinary day. Many people, priests, Levites, scribes, and teachers of the law bustled about. Did any of them long for Messiah's coming? But Simeon had a God-ward heart, and the Holy Spirit had given him a remarkable promise.

That day Simeon's longing was fulfilled. And the least of Jesus' followers can draw comfort from Simeon, a devout nobody who longed to see the Christ.

Dear Father above, *grant me holy desires this day. And thank You for Your gift of the Holy Spirit, who fulfills the desires of my heart. I pray this prayer in the name of Jesus, my merciful Savior and Lord. Amen.*

Take Him to Your Heart

When the parents brought in the child Jesus to do for him what the custom of the Law required, Simeon took him in his arms and praised God (Luke 2:27, 28).

Scripture: **Luke 2:27, 28**
Song: **"Into My Heart"**

I once read a little anecdote about a shabby lad who rushed into a department store on Christmas Eve, just before the store's closing. Out of breath, he pled, "Could we borrow your Jesus? Ours got busted." That line was irresistible, and I later wrote a story about a clumsy young man who knocked over a Christmas tree and shattered the porcelain pieces of a nativity scene. The story's theme: We all need our own special relationship with Jesus

Simeon experienced this when Mary came to the temple bearing a precious, six-weeks-old bundle. The baby's humanity and deity wasn't the issue, nor was His transcendent holiness. Moving beyond theology, Simeon simply took the mystery of Incarnation into his arms. For those moments, he had his very own Jesus.

We can take Jesus to our heads and acknowledge His historic reality. That is well and good—and quite necessary. We can assign Him the highest place of transcendence in our doctrines and worship. But day by day, do we keep Him at the center of our lives? Simeon, a simple, devout man, took Jesus to heart—and praised God.

Father in Heaven, grant me each day a continuing sense of Your presence in my life, through the indwelling Christ. In His name I pray. Amen.

Marvelous Pronouncement

The child's father and mother marveled at what was said about him (Luke 2:33).

Scripture: **Luke 2:29-33**
Song: **"My Savior First of All"**

A quiet, elderly woman came to our small church. Though she had had no formal Bible training, she eventually became our favorite Sunday school teacher. One day my wife asked where she had gained such heart-warming, intriguing insights. The woman replied, "Elsie, it takes a lifetime to know the Scriptures." She might have added, "It takes a lifetime—and beyond—to know Jesus."

Joseph and Mary marveled at Simeon's song, and little wonder. They were ordinary folks; how could those things be?

Joseph had taken Mary to be his wife at great risk. Who would believe her story? She had endured birth pangs and held the newborn to her breast in a stable. She had not yet digested the angel Gabriel's mysterious words or the song of her cousin Elizabeth. Now could the new parents not marvel at Simeon's prophetic pronouncement?

We, too, will marvel as we grow in the grace and knowledge of our Lord. There is much, much more to Jesus than our quaint renditions of the Christmas story. It will take a lifetime and more to learn it all.

*Thank You, **Lord,** for the privilege of knowing You. As I open my heart to You daily in prayer, lead me into an ever deeper knowledge of Your presence and purpose in my life. In the name of my precious Savior, I pray. Amen.*

Couldn't Lie to Her

(And a sword will pierce through your own soul also), that thoughts out of many hearts may be revealed (Luke 2:35, *Revised Standard Version*).

Scripture: **Luke 2:34, 35**
Song: **"Grace and Truth Shall Mark the Way"**

I could not bring myself to lie to Mother. I lied easily to my sister, and I could stretch a point with my father, but I could not lie to Mother. A quiet, small woman, Mother seemed able to read my thoughts. I believed that because I knew her character. I could depend on her, and I couldn't imagine her telling a lie. I fully believed lying to her was useless; she would know the truth.

We were not an overtly religious household, and few Christian artifacts hung on our walls. We attended church faithfully, though, and rarely missed a mealtime prayer. The Bible was prominent, faith in Christ was genuine, and Mother was warm and affirming. She embodied what I imagined Jesus to be.

An early memory finds me snuggling close to Mother's breast in an heirloom rocking chair. As we rocked, "Jesus Loves Me" resonated from her. Mother loved me, she loved Jesus, and so did I, even at age three. Yes, even then I understood that nothing was hidden from Mother, nor from God.

Lord, we are all the products of what we've been taught by people we trust. Thank You for my own teachers. May I be trustworthy, so that those who follow me will be following You. Through Christ I pray. Amen.

A Touch from the Old

She was very old . . . . She never left the temple but worshiped night and day (Luke 2:36, 37).

Scripture: **Luke 2:36-38**
Song: **"Beyond the Sunset"**

August was old and dying. I was his young, green minister. He told me one day he had seen Jesus. It seems the Lord was standing in the meadow just beyond a small stream on his old country farm, beckoning. "I will go home soon," August said.

I smiled at the old man's odd vision and prepared to read a psalm. A thin, pale hand slipped over the page. "Read from your heart, my brother." That I couldn't do, and so he led me, verse by verse, through the beloved passage, his words tinged with the gentle accent of his homeland. Within a few days, August died.

Cherish your godly elders! They are wiser and closer to Heaven than younger people can be. Come to think of it, those who have eternal life can never grow old. They will change dwelling places, but they can never age. I think often of August. I'm glad Jesus came to him when he was very old, so he could touch the heart of a young, green minister.

*Thank You, **Lord,** for elderly friends. Throughout the new year, nudge me to spend more time with them, so they can minister to me in their special way. And help me to never look down on those who are close to seeing You, face to face. I pray this prayer in the name of Jesus my Savior. Amen.*

December 31

Praise from Deep Within

Praise the Lord from the earth, you great sea creatures and all ocean depths (Psalm 148:7).

Scripture: **Psalm 148:7-14**
Song: **"All Creatures of Our God and King"**

Beneath the ocean's depths exists an amazing world of God's creation that most of us will never see. Yet even nature unseen functions as a testimony to God and offers its praise to the one who sees it, created it, and maintains it. The depths of the earth's oceans, and the creatures contained within, cause us to marvel. So many small creatures, such as jellyfish, sand dollars, starfish, and sea horses. So many grand creatures, such as manatees, dolphins, sharks, and whales. So many shapes and sizes and colors of marine life grace the seas. Even in a fallen world, God's creation is breathtaking.

Like the creatures of the sea, we too praise the one who intricately designed and assembled us, He who maintains us and sustains us. We worship Him who knows us and loves us despite our sin.

The unseen in us? He sees our deepest hurts and cares. And like the rest of creation, we too praise God, especially when we live according to our ultimate purpose on earth: to become more and more like His Son, Jesus.

Sovereign God of all Creation, *I worship You. And as I live each day on earth, may my life reflect Your greatness. In Jesus' name, amen.*

December 31. **Brian J. Waldrop** is a freelance writer and professional copy editor. Originally from Champaign, Illinois, Brian now resides in Mt. Healthy, Ohio.